Wildlife Tourism and Conservation

Wildlife Tourism and Conservation

Ramakanth Rajput

RANDOM

RANDOM PUBLICATIONS

NEW DELHI (INDIA)

Wildlife Tourism and Conservation

ISBN 978-93-5111-881-7

Published in 2016 in India by

RANDOM PUBLICATIONS

4376-A/4B, Gali Murari Lal, Ansari Road
New Delhi-110 002
Phone : +9111-43580356, 011-23289044, 011-43142548
e-mail: sales@randompublications.com,
info@randompublications.com, randomexports@gmail.com

Type Setting by : Friends Media, Delhi-110089
Printed at : Sanat Printers

Preface

Tourism is travel for recreation, leisure, religious, family or business purposes, usually for a limited duration. Tourism is commonly associated with international travel, but may also refer to travel to another place within the same country. The World Tourism Organization defines tourists as people "traveling to and staying in places outside their usual environment for not more than one consecutive year for leisure, business and other purposes".

Tourism has become a popular global leisure activity. Tourism can be domestic or international, and international tourism has both incoming and outgoing implications on a country's balance of payments. Today, tourism is a major source of income for many countries, and affects the economy of both the source and host countries, in some cases being of vital importance.Wildlife tourism can be an eco and animal friendly tourism, usually showing animals in their natural habitat. Wildlife tourism, in its simplest sense, is watching wild animals in their natural habitat. Wildlife tourism is an important part of the tourism industries in many countries including many African and South American countries, Australia, India, Canada, Indonesia, Bangladesh, Malaysia, Sri Lanka and Maldives among many. It has experienced a dramatic and rapid growth in recent years worldwide and is closely aligned to eco-tourism and sustainable-tourism. Wildlife tourism is also a multimillion-dollar industry offering customized tour packages and safaris.

Wildlife tourism has been heralded as a way to secure sustainable economic benefits while supporting wildlife conservation and local communities. But how well is it achieving this, and what needs to be done to secure this vision? This book explores the impacts of wildlife tourism. We define and classify wildlife tourism, provide a framework for its planning and management and explain why wildlife tourism is important.

– Author

Contents

1

Wildlife Conservation

THE CURRENT STATE OF RHINO IN ASSAM AND THREATS IN THE 21ST CENTURY

Assam, India, is one of the last remaining strongholds of the Indian rhino, an animal that is dependent on conservation because of threats from poaching and destruction of habitat. Field research was carried out in Assam to ascertain the current state of the rhino and to evaluate various threats. This paper highlights the latest status of rhino in Assam after the census of 1999, and the intense fieldwork carried out between January 1998 and September 2000. Poaching and floods are both named as major problems that greatly hamper conservation. The rhino population in Pabitora Wildlife Sanctuary had increased from 54 in 1987 to 74 in 1999; in Kaziranga National Park it increased from 1164 in 1993 to 1552 in 1999. However, in Orang National Park, the rhino population decreased from 97 in 1991 to only 46 in 1999, mainly because of unabated poaching. In the anti-poaching operation in Pabitora since November 1997, large numbers of poachers were arrested and arms and ammunition were recovered.

Kaziranga witnessed the lowest poaching in 1999 with only 4 rhino killed by poachers, down from 8 in 1998. Anti-poaching staff of Kaziranga arrested 18 rhino poachers in 1999, a marked increase from 2 in 1998. To ensure the future of the rhino in Assam, forest anti-poaching staff need further government support. Habitat conservation and protection need to be given priority. Forest officials, the various collaborating NGOs and local people need to work together to conserve the rhino in the 21st century. The state of Assam in India has successfully set aside areas for conserving and protecting the great Indian one-horned rhino, *Rhinoceros unicornis,* in its distribution range. Rhino numbers have increased from about 20 at the beginning of this century to 1700 animals in 2000. This success has been achieved through the dedicated efforts of the governments of Assam and India, supported by the local people. Vigne and Martin, in updating information on the state of the rhino in Assam in 1997, put the number at 1406. This paper highlights the latest status of rhino in Assam, especially after the census of 1999, examines current threats to rhino from poaching, and looks at other factors. The paper also details statistics on the rhino population and poaching of rhinos from January 1998 to September 2000 in various protected areas of Assam. The study analyses the rhino census data of 1999 and details the intense fieldwork carried out between January 1998 and September 2000.

RHINO STATUS IN PABITORA WILDLIFE SANCTUARY

Although it is commonly believed that rhinos came to Pabitora only during the 1970s, history reveals that they have been present there and in the Mayong area since 1925. According to the local people, during the tenure of King Rohan Singha, a rhino calf was brought to the palace as a pet; however, after a few months it died from diarrhoea. Past records also show that 3 rhinos were found dead, at Raja Mayong, Sildubi and Barhampur. The villagers handed over the rhino horns to the Nagaon police. According to the census conducted in March 1999 in the Pabitora Wildlife Sanctuary, there are 43 adult rhinos, which is 58.11% of the total rhino population; 12 subadults, 16.22%; and 19 calves, 25.68%.

The 24 adult male rhinos make up 30.43% of the population, the 31 females 41.89%, and calves the balance. The male-to-female ratio stands at 1:1.29. Only 8 rhinos were found in 1971 when the government of Assam declared Pabitora a forest reserve. In a span of about 28 years, the rhino population in Pabitora increased from 8 to 74. However, poaching remains the major threat to these rhinos. Poachers have used various methods to kill rhinos; those used since 1987 are summarized in table 2. From 1987 to March 2000, poachers killed 45 rhinos—22 males and 23 females, 21 inside the sanctuary and 24 outside it. Talukdar discussed factors affecting the status and conservation of rhinos in Pabitora.

It has been monitored that 25 to 30 rhinos strayed out of the sanctuary during winter from November until March and raided crops of the adjacent villages. To solve this problem, the government of Assam expanded the area of Pabitora from 16 km2 to 38.84 km2 in 1999 to provide the rhinos with more grazing area. The success of the present range officer in Pabitora, who joined the sanctuary in 1997 to control poaching and whose work has been recognized and lauded is summarized in table 3. Flood is another major problem that greatly hampers rhino conservation. During the flood of 1998, two rhino calves died in Pabitora. Flooding also increases silt deposition in the existing wetlands, making water scarce for the rhinos. This may have caused the rhinos to stray out of the sanctuary during winter, exposing themselves to danger from poachers. Livestock grazing inside the sanctuary is another cause of concern for Pabitora. According to the Forest Department of Assam, more than 50% of the grasslands have degenerated because livestock have overgrazed it. To solve this problem, the Pabitora range officer has constructed a pound—a temporary enclosure where the livestock are confined to prevent them from grazing in the sanctuary. Now livestock owners are fined if their animals are found inside the sanctuary. During patrol, the forest guards herd the livestock that they find inside the sanctuary into the pound.

RHINO STATUS IN ORANG NATIONAL PARK

The status of rhino in Orang has been of great concern of late because of the increased number of incidents of poaching. As a result of the conservation efforts made since Orang was declared a wildlife sanctuary in 1985, its rhino population increased from 65 in 1985 to 97 in 1991. However, Vigne and Martin showed that the number of poaching incidents increased during 1994 to 1997, when poachers killed 36 rhinos. The current study shows that from January 1998 to September 2000, 25 more rhinos were killed by poachers in Orang, resulting in only 46 rhinos counted during the 1999 rhino census there.

The local NGOs and officials from the forest department considered the seriousness of the situation and proposed that the Assam government upgrade the Orang Wildlife Sanctuary to a national park. In April 1999, the government finally declared Orang a national park. A number of NGOs, mainly Aaranyak, supported by the David Shepherd Conservation Foundation, have donated 18 walkie-talkies and 10 solar panels to Orang to enhance the anti-poaching efforts of the forest staff. The Rhino Foundation, supported by the US Fish and Wildlife Service, has donated two base stations for wireless communication and more walkie-talkies, thus strengthening the wireless network system to a great extent. A Gypsy 4-wheel-drive vehicle was donated to Orang by Care for the Wild, a local NGO, and Aaranyak and the David Shepherd Conservation Foundation donated a locally made metal speed boat to improve the mobility of the forest staff and allow them to carry out their duties effectively.

The improved wireless network in Orang has led to fewer rhinos being poached—from 12 in 1998 to 7 in 1999 and 6 in 2000 by the end of September. The forest guards of Orang killed a poacher in an encounter in 1999. Local NGOs in Assam like the Rhino Foundation, Aaranyak and Early Birds fully supported Orang during those years of heavy poaching, helping staff to bring the situation under control. Aaranyak organized two legal awareness camps for range officers, forest guards and officials, which the divisional forest officer also attended. An advocate of the Gauhati High Court who was also the Aaranyak legal consultant conducted the orientation camps. The participants learned various aspects of existing law and law enforcement to protect endangered species. The Rhino Foundation repaired the boat used in the anti-poaching efforts, and Early Birds held vaccination camps for the domestic cattle in the villages bordering the park to stop the transmission of the deadly anthrax from domestic cattle to wild rhinos.

The Early Birds' plan of creating an immune belt to stop the spread of anthrax is aimed to have a long-term effect in reducing rhino death from the disease in the national park. Most deaths that are termed natural are caused by anthrax or related diseases. Although flood is one of the major disasters in Kaziranga National Park and the Pabitora Wildlife Sanctuary, its impact on Orang National Park is negligible. Not a single rhino in Orang has been killed by flood. Although some areas of Orang are flooded, the higher northern terrace remains dry, and rhinos migrate to these areas when floodwaters are high. Protection measures need to be improved to further strengthen the anti-poaching network and reduce rhino poaching in Orang. The NGOs continue to improve their support.

RHINO STATUS IN KAZIRANGA NATIONAL PARK

The Kaziranga National Park (KNP) is one of the most successful stories of conservation of *Rhinoceros unicornis* in the world. From a population of a mere dozen rhinos in 1908, when the Kaziranga was declared a forest reserve, the population has grown to 1500 over 90 years of conservation. The rhino census conducted in Kaziranga in April 1999 recorded a population of 1552 compared with 1164 in 1993. The population figures by block that were recorded during the 1999 census are summarized in table 4. The park is situated on the floodplains of the river Brahmaputra. The terrain is flat, with a gentle slope running down from east to west.

The soil is rich in alluvial deposit that the annual floods lay down. Park location on the floodplain eases the task of demarcating blocks for the rhino census. The census used the direct visual total count method. It was conducted over two days, 8 and 9 April 1999, because it was not possible to cover the entire area in a single day. The park was divided into eight major blocks, as listed in table 4. These blocks were further divided into compartments: the Baguri block into 12 compartments, the Bhawani, Charighoria, Haldibari, Kaziranga, Panbari, Tamulipathar blocks into 5 each, and the Boralimora block into 3, totaling 45 compartments in the eight blocks within the 429.3 km2 of KNP.

Eight more areas were included in the census: the first addition to KNP, Burapahar, with an area of 43.70 km2; the second addition, Sildubi, 47 km2; the third addition, Panbari, 0.69 km2; the fourth addition, Kanchanjuri, 0.89 km2; the fifth addition, 1.15 km2; the sixth addition, the shore areas of Brahmaputra, 376.05 km2; the Panbari Reserved Forest, 5.08 km2; and the Moriahola area in the northern part of KNP, 5.00 km2. The census of 25 compartments was completed on the first day, 8 April; it included the first, second, third, fourth and fifth additions to KNP and the Panbari Reserved Forest. The remaining 20 compartments, the sixth addition and the Moriahola area were covered on the second day, 9 April. River Diffalu, which bisects the national park roughly into half, was taken as the dividing line for each day's count.

The rhinos south of the river, including those in the addition areas, were counted on the day 1, and those north of the river were counted on day 2. Since the river is deep, with well-defined high banks, the chance of rhino crossing it on any one day was considered almost negligible. The tall grass in KNP is burned every year as a management practice. In 1999, to assure a clear view for sighting the rhino, the grassland was burned before the April census was taken. After completing the pilot field survey, the Forest Department prepared a map of each compartment showing such features as the wetlands, channels, roads and patrolling paths. The starting point and the end point for the census in each compartment were clearly shown to avoid any confusion the enumerators might have in identifying their respective areas of census.

Each enumeration party consisted of one enumerator in charge of the party; one assistant enumerator, usually from the media or an NGO; one guide, usually a forester or a forest guard with thorough knowledge of the area; and a mahut with an elephant.

The park has four rangers. The rhino population as recorded in the 1999 rhino census operation is shown in table 5. Rhinos in KNP die from natural causes or poaching. The natural deaths come from floods, predation, old age or disease. Death by poaching comes from gunshot, pit poaching, electrocution or poisoning. The total death of rhinos in KNP in six years, between January 1993 and December 1998, stands at 462; 335 animals died of natural causes and 127 died from poaching. That means an average of 56 rhinos died a natural death each year during the six-year period of 1993 to 1996 and 21 died from poaching.

Thus the average net annual mortality from 1993 until 1998 is 4.11% from natural death and 1.55% from poaching. From January 1998 to September 2000, poachers killed 16 rhinos but a fairly large number of poachers have been arrested or killed and firearms and ammunition seized. In 1999, poachers killed only 4 rhinos, which is an all-time low for the history of Kaziranga since it became a national park in 1974.

Flood is another threat to the rhino population, especially the calves. In the devastating flood of 1998 about 39 rhinos were drowned in KNP, of which 18 were adult, 5 subadult and 16 calves. In the 1988 flood also, 38 rhinos were drowned of which 9 were adult, 10 subadult and 19 calves. Some of the KNP rhinos were found migrating to the adjoining hills of Karbi- Anglong through certain paths, but most of the rhinos remained inside the park.

They were found taking shelter on the high land within the park in the flood of 1998. After the flood of 1998; the Forest Department and the Indian Army constructed more highlands to reduce the loss of wildlife, particularly the rhinos, because of high floods. It is hoped that in future floods the newly constructed highlands will offer some relief to the wildlife.

THREATS TO RHINO IN ASSAM IN THE 21ST CENTURY

Conserving and protecting rhino in the 21st century in Assam will depend on continued relentless efforts by the forest staff to save the rhinos from poachers. Poaching will remain a major threat to the rhino population. Therefore, anti-poaching efforts have to be improved and maintained. Receiving information in advance on the movement of poachers and wildlife smugglers is extremely crucial in apprehending illegal wildlife traders and disrupting their activities. It is therefore imperative that clandestine channels of information are developed and a collection system is maintained to assist anti-poaching staff. In addition to the hazards caused by rhino poachers, natural floods and diseases, the state of Assam is likely to experience a further increase in human population.

Weakly protected rhino sanctuaries would easily fall prey to encroachers, especially around the Brahmaputra Valley. Unless the government of Assam expands its rhino sanctuaries in the next two years, the increased human population pressure will threaten the future of the rhino living in the few existing pockets like Kaziranga, Orang, Pabitora and Manas. The six additions to KNP cover an area of 430 km2. Some were handed over to KNP last year, but the government has not yet handed over the sixth addition, which covers an area of around 376 km2. The expanded area to Pabitora Sanctuary also urgently needs to be handed over to provide more habitat for the increasing population of rhinos in Pabitora. It will also reduce the incidence of rhinos straying out of the sanctuary because habitat and food are in short supply.

A number of water bodies in the rhino-bearing areas in Assam have shrunk in size and depth because of the siltation brought about by flooding. It is therefore imperative that these water bodies be desilted to maintain the wetland habitats for the rhinos. The future of the rhino will depend not only on ecological and natural factors but also on sociopolitical factors. The need is urgent to enhance the existing intelligence network and to initiate social welfare for the fringe villages with the aim of controlling village population explosion. If zero population growth could be achieved in the villages at the fringes of the rhino-bearing protected areas, the conflict between villagers and rhinos would be reduced. The Forest Department and the NGOs need to work together to achieve this uphill task. Hence challenges before us are many, and only coordinated efforts will help us achieve our task of rhino conservation during the 21st century. Working in isolation will create more problems than solutions. With dedicated efforts, the Forest Department, which has nearly a hundred year of experience in rhino conservation, and with support from the NGOs and local people, the challenging task of conserving rhinos in Assam for next hundred years seems not a distant cry. Periodic evaluation of the successes and the failures of rhino conservation in various parts of Assam by the Forest Department and the NGOs will certainly make action at the appropriate time more possible.

STATUS AND CONSERVATION OF GOLDEN LANGUR IN CHAKRASHILA WILDLIFE SANCTUARY

The golden langur is endemic to a limited area of western Assam in India and a neighboring part of Bhutan. The distribution of this endangered species lies north of the Brahmaputra River, bounded on the east by Manas River, and on the west by the Sankosh River. The range in south-central Bhutan is between the Sankosh River and a high mountain ridge in the west, and Manas River, Mangde Chu and the high mountain ridge west of Chamkhar Chu in the east. There have been a number of studies that have examined the distributional limits and the population status of the species in India and Bhutan. Srivastava *et al.* estimated a population of 1,500 in India. There are reports on population dynamics of the species from different forest frag-ments.

The golden langur occurs in three protected areas in Bhutan: the Jigme Singye Wangchuk National Park, Royal Manas National Park and the Phibsoo National Wildlife Sanctuary. In India, the golden langur receives the highest legal protection as a Schedule-I species in the Indian Wildlife Protection Act (1972), yet nearly all of the areas where it is still found lie outside the protected area network. Chakrashila Wildlife Sanctuary in the districts of Kokrajhar and Dhubri is the only protected habitat for golden langur in the country. Datta it was who first reported the occurrence of golden langur in Chakrashila Wildlife Sanctuary, and a few studies on the ecology and behavior of the species have already been conducted there. Chetry *et al.* also carried out an education and awareness program for the conservation of the golden langur in the vicinity of the sanctuary. There was no system-atic attempt, however, to examine the population status of the species in the sanctuary even after 11 years of its declaration as a protected area specifically for the golden langur.

Rapid loss of habitat and habitat fragmentation are the major threats for the golden langur in India. Chetry reported substantial anthropogenic pressure in and around Chakrashila and, with this in mind, we decided to carry out a study to assess the status of the golden langur population in this protected habitat. Here we provide an estimate of the size (number of individuals and groups, and average group size) and composition of the golden langur population in the Chakrashila Wildlife Sanctuary.

METHODS

Chakrashila Wildlife Sanctuary

Chakrashila Wildlife Sanctuary is in the districts of Kokrajhar and Dhubri in Assam. The sanctuary, in the southernmost part of the range of the species, is the only protected area for the golden langur in India. The hilly terrain is covered with dense forest which is mostly semi-evergreen and moist deciduous, with patches of grassland and scattered bushes. The forest type falls in the category 3C/C.1.a(ii) following Champion and Seth. The communities living around the sanctuary belong to various ethnic groups, including Bodo, Rabha, Garo, Rajbanshi, Nepali and Muslims.

Survey

The survey was carried out from December 2006 to January 2007, and data were collected using both direct and indirect methods. A modification of the line transect method was used, depending upon the habitat and the forest condition. Twelve transects totaling 120 km were set up in a stratified random manner to cover all representative areas of the wildlife sanc-tuary. Three people walked the existing forest trails (and occasionally off the trails), covering an average of 10 km per day. Transects were initiated at 06:00 and terminated in the evening. The observers walked slowly through the transect pausing regularly, at least every 500 m. On sighting the golden langur, the global positioning system (GPS) co-ordinates, altitude, group structure and, when possible, age, sex and number of individuals were recorded.

At 500-m intervals and at each location where golden langur were encountered, the observers estimated the tree height, canopy cover, ground cover, dominant tree species, and shrub and herb species in a 10-m radius. Observers also took notes *ad libitum* on any evidence for, and degree of, grazing and logging in the study area.

We recorded indirect evidence for the presence of pri-mates, such as grunts, branch shaking, and sounds associated with locomotion and feeding. All such indications were used to trace the animals and we stopped for about 10 minutes to collect the details. Secondary information was also gath-ered by talking with the local people in the vicinity of the sanctuary.

RESULTS

Population of golden langurs

In all, direct sightings during the survey resulted in an estimate 474 individuals in 64 groups. The average group size ranged from 3 to 15 individuals, with a mean of 7.40. These 64 troops were recorded from both peripheral and core areas of the sanctuary. Groups were located at altitudes of 34 m to 417 m above sea level. Table 1 gives the loca-tions of the golden langur troops in the Chakrashila Wildlife Sanctuary.

Population structure and group composition

We counted the numbers of all troops and individuals we saw, and also analyzed the age–sex composition of the groups. Of the 474 individuals, 236 were adults, 159 were juveniles and the rest were infants. Thus, 49.78% were adults, 33.54% were juveniles and 16.66% were infants. The demographic records further revealed that the adult sex ratio was 1:1.53. Of the 64 groups, most were single male/multi-female, while 19 groups had two-male/multi-female social structures. Only two all male groups were seen during the survey period. The population density in the sanc-tuary was estimated at 65.83/km^2.

Sympatric primates and other mammals

Two other primates were recorded in the Chakrashila Wildlife Sanctuary: rhesus macaque and slow loris. Other mammal species include tiger, leopard, clouded leopard, wild pig, barking deer, sambar, and pangolin.

Threats

Dogs kill the langurs particularly in the fringe areas of the sanctuary. We recorded seven incidences during one year of golden langurs being killed by dogs in the nearby villages; of these, two of the victims were adult females and five were juveniles. General forms of exploi-tation and disturbance of the forest were also found to be a threat to the langurs in the sanctuary. They included illegal logging, the collection of firewood and non-timber forest products, and grazing. Although not evaluated systematically, interviews and qualitative observations during the study indi-cated that the golden langurs were not hunted.

DISCUSSION

Our results indicate that the Chakrashila Wildlife Sanc-tuary is an important stronghold for the endangered golden langur in the western-southernmost part of its range in India. The Chakrashila population is one of the largest in the coun-try, and the current age structure indicates that it is a healthy and growing population. The population density is high when compared to other localities and the single-male/multi-female group which is predominant in Chakrashila is the most stable social system for golden langur. Ghosh also counted 501 individuals in 66 groups in Chakrashila Wildlife Sanctuary and its adjacent areas.

An important measure for its conservation in the sanc-tuary will be to stop the ongoing illegal felling of trees and the encroachment. The golden langurs in the forest at Nay-akgaon were evidently part of a single population with those in Chakrashila but the connection has been lost. The current high density of golden langur in the sanctuary may result from lack of oppor-tunities for dispersal, a threat over the mid-term. In this context, we recommend that efforts should be made to restore the lost continuity between the sanctuary and other isolated forest pockets, planting natu-ral corridors using bamboo species along with other preferred food plant species of golden langur.

Bamboo is recommended not only because it grows fast, but golden langurs also eat the stem cortex of growing bamboo shoots and it provides the thick canopy which the langur uses to hide from predators. There are a number of native bamboos which are intricately associated with the traditional life styles of local people, so local communities can benefit not only from being involved in planting the corridor, but also in promoting the availability of non-timber products of interest to them.

The absence of hunting pressure is positive and probably one of the reasons that the area still has a high density of the species, despite habitat degradation and other human pres-sures. The concentration of langurs mostly in the periphery of the sanctuary however, may be an indication of potentially high predator pressure in the core area. All the incidences of killing of golden langur by domestic dogs recorded during the study need special attention. Chetry *et al*. also identified dogs as a threat to the golden langur. Illegal fell-ing still continues in the area, with a significant ongoing loss of canopy cover as a result. Overall the conservation of the golden langur in and around the Chakrashila Wildlife Sanctu-ary requires a landscape approach. An integrated management program of forest fragments taking golden langur as a flag-ship species will also ensure the conservation of other wildlife in this part of Assam.

HOOLOCK GIBBON CONSERVATION

As a megadiverse country India supports a rich floral and faunal diversity, including 25 primate species. Only two of these are apes: the western hoolock gibbon and the eastern hoolock gibbon. Their distribution is restricted to the seven states of northeast India, including Assam, Arunachal Pradesh, Meghalaya, Manipur, Tripura, Nagaland and Mizoram. Even in this region their distribution is further limited to the southern bank of the Dibang-Brahmaputra Rivers system. The occurrence of the eastern hoolock gibbon in India was confirmed only recently and is restricted to specific localities in Arunachal Pradesh and a small forest pocket in Assam. The estimated abundance of the western hoolock gibbon in India is up to 7,000 individuals, whereas for eastern hoolock gibbon it is unto 3,000 individuals. The western hoolock is recorded as Endangered, and the eastern hoolock gibbon as Vulnerable in the IUCN Red List. Primate species in India, including the hoolock gibbons, are declining in number throughout their distribution ranges. Northeast India, with the highest primate diversity, has also experienced a rapid decrease in biodiversity over recent years. Habitat destruction in various forms and hunting are the major threats for the primates in the region. As a result, all the primate species of the region, especially the hoolock gibbon, need targeted attention to improve their conservation status.

PRE INDO-U.S. PRIMATE PROJECT PHASE

Gibbon conservation efforts before the Indo- U.S. Primate Project were sporadic and mainly confined to inventorial and distributional studies. In addition, two short studies on behaviour and ecology of hoolock gibbon were conducted in Assam and in the Garo Hills, Meghalaya. These pioneer studies are also of significance for hoolock gibbon conservation.

INDO-U.S. PRIMATE PROJECT PHASE

The launch of the Indo-U.S. Primate Project led to an increase in primate conservation efforts in India. During the project, systematic primate surveys were conducted in various parts of India, especially in the regions with the highest primate diversity (i.e. northeast and south India). The project was also successful in creating a new generation of primate field biologists. Long-term ecological and behavioural studies on some of the least studied primate species in the country were initiated, and the project also laid the foundation for a more diversified approach to hoolock gibbon conservation. Some of this period's major achievements in hoolock gibbon conservation are described below.

Capacity building

The project was instrumental in generating a group of trained field primatologists. A group of young students were trained to undertake qualitative research on the primates of the region including the hoolock gibbon. This group contributed greatly to primate conservation in general and hoolock gibbons in particular, and their contribution continues after the closing of the project.

Generation of baseline information

For the first time, extensive and systematic surveys for hoolock gibbons were conducted by a trained team from the Indo-U.S. Primate Project. These surveys generated baseline information and the first comprehensive overview of the status, distribution and demography of the hoolock gibbon. During this period, the first long-term study on the behavioural ecology of the hoolock gibbon was initiated. Population monitoring of hoolock gibbon in Borajan (Borajan-Podumani-Bherjan Wildlife Sanctuary) documented the severe detrimental impact of canopy cover loss on the hoolock gibbon. This was one of the major achievements of the project.

Declaration of Gibbon Wildlife Sanctuary

The information generated for the hoolock gibbon by this project played a pivotal role in the declaration of the Gibbon Wildlife Sanctuary. The Hoollongapar Reserve Forest in the Jorhat District of Assam was identified as an Eden of primates, supporting hoolock gibbons and six other primate species, and is home to a further 34 mammal species. This finding acted as a catalyst in the government's decision to upgrade Hoollongapar Reserve Forest to a sanctuary in 1997. The area was renamed the Gibbon Wildlife Sanctuary. It is the only protected habitat in India to be named after a primate species and the first protected area in the country where the hoolock gibbon is the target species for conservation. The Gibbon Wildlife Sanctuary is located south of the Brahmaputra River system in the district of Jorhat, Assam. It is an isolated forest pocket of 21 km2, which sustains a substantial population of hoolock gibbons.

POST INDO-U.S. PRIMATE PROJECT PHASE

Based on the foundation laid by the Indo-U.S. Primate Project phase, action-based gibbon conservation activities were initiated throughout the distributional region and particularly in Assam. A number of individuals, institutions and organizations contributed to hoolock gibbon conservation in the first decade of the new millennium. These included Gauhati University, Gibbon Conservation Centre, India (GCC), Aaranyak, Primate Research Centre, Northeast (PRC), School of Desert Science (SDS), Centre for Education and Environment (CEE), Ashoka Trust for Research, Environment and Ecology, WII, Zoo Outreach Organization (ZOO), Wildlife Areas Development and Welfare Trust, the Assam Forest Department, and the Arunachal Pradesh Forest Department. The impact of forest fragmentation on the hoolock gibbon in Assam was first documented by Kakati. Various papers were published on research related to hoolock conservation, the education and awareness programme, and the capacity building programme. In general, hoolock conservation efforts reached a new dimension in this period. Some of the major achievements are described below.

Establishment of Gibbon Conservation Centre

In 2004 the Forest Department provided a building of 86 m2 as a permanent conservation and research base for work in the Gibbon Wildlife Sanctuary and in northeast India. The building was named the Gibbon Conservation Centre (GCC). The centre is suitably furnished and equipped to conduct various field-based training programmes. The Gibbon Conservation Centre is run by a trust in collaboration with the Assam Forest Department and Aaranyak.

Hoolock gibbon conservation programmes in the Gibbon Wildlife Sanctuary

With support from the U.S. Fish and Wildlife Service and in collaboration with the Assam Forest Department, the Gibbon Conservation Centre organized two gibbon conservation programmes consecutively in the Gibbon Wildlife Sanctuary, a prime habitat of the western hoolock gibbon in Assam. The sanctuary is surrounded by human habitations. Fragmentation of the habitat by a railway line through the reserve and anthropogenic pressures in the form of cattle grazing, and collection of fuel wood and non-timber forest products are the major threats for gibbons and other wildlife in the sanctuary. From the beginning, the hoolock gibbon conservation programmes in the sanctuary were designed as a multi-dimensional approach addressing conservation activities including research, education and awareness, training and capacity building, plantation and habitat improvement, socio-economic development, and community involvement.

These activities were carried out and evaluated in phases in order to improve long-term conservation of the endangered ape species. The programmes produced a trained group of foresters, students, teachers, researchers and NGO workers to carry the message of gibbon conservation to a greater circle. Two popular books on hoolock gibbons were published: "Aamar Holou" and "Hoolock: The ape of India". They provided basic information on hoolock taxonomy, distribution, ecology, and ethology, and proved to be instrumental in disseminating information on the gibbon. In addition, the education and awareness part of the programmes reached 33,425 students from primary to college level. During the programmes, local people received alternative income-generation training in mushroom cultivation, honeybee keeping, and duck husbandry.

Moreover, 29 self-help groups were formed for economic improvement for fringe communities. To reduce the pressure on the forest, improved *chullah* and bio-gas plants were distributed among families selected through socio-economic studies. In addition, handlooms and ducks were also distributed among the self-help groups for income generation. Training, monitoring and legal orientation programmes were carried out for the Forest Department staff in the sanctuary to boost their capacity. The multi-dimensional initiatives of the hoolock gibbon conservation programmes produced very good results in the Gibbon Wildlife Sanctuary. There was reduction in fuel wood pressure. The resulting changes were observed both in the gibbons as well as in the habitat. 64 gibbons in 17 groups were counted during a census in 2004. The population increased to 106 gibbons in 26 groups and five solitary males in 2009. Population sizes of elephant and the other six primate species in the sanctuary also increased. Canopy cover increased by 3.45%, and degraded forest decreased by 4.08%. It should be noted, however, that the apparent population increase may result not only in intensive conservation and management efforts, but also in improved survey methods.

Development of a conservation action plan for the western hoolock gibbon

Das *et al.* (2005) developed an action plan for hoolock gibbon conservation in Assam for the first time. This was a major breakthrough for hoolock gibbon conservation during the post Indo-U.S. Primate Project phase.

Discovery of the eastern hoolock gibbon in India

In 2006, the occurrence of eastern hoolock gibbons in India was first reported from Lohit District of Arunachal Pradesh. Subsequently this species was also reported from Lower Dibang Valley District of Arunachal Pradesh and in the Sadiya area of Assam. These discoveries opened up new perspectives on gibbon conservation in India.

Capacity building

This phase was successful in improving awareness towards the conservation of hoolock gibbon and their habitat among the common masses beyond the scientific community to a great extent. The Gibbon Conservation Centre alone has reached 33,425 students through its education and awareness program. Forest Department staff, who were previously more concerned with charismatic wildlife such as tiger, rhino and elephant, have now developed a sense of responsibility for the conservation of the gibbon. The two books on the hoolock gibbon, which were developed as education materials, have been successful in increasing awareness among people from different backgrounds with Assam and other northeastern states towards the conservation of hoolock gibbon.

Gibbon Conservation Centre took another noble step by providing two-week hoolock gibbon conservation training to the Forest Department field staff of Assam. Along with Gibbon Conservation Centre, Aaranyak and Primate Conservation Centre, Northeast, Wildlife Areas Development & Welfare Trust, the Zoo Outreach Organization also contributed towards the conservation of hoolock gibbon especially in capacity building through education and awareness to the educators in the 2007. ZOO for the first time conducted a Population and Habitat Viability Assessment for western hoolock gibbons. In 2010, the Centre for Environment Education, Northeast also launched an education and awareness program for gibbon conservation.

SUGGESTIONS FOR FUTURE ACTIVITIES

Despite the conservation efforts of the various, mainly non-governmental, organizations, the hoolock gibbon is not out of danger. Large-scale habitat destruction continues throughout the entire distribution range of the species in India. The Government of India has yet to consider seriously the conservation issues affecting the hoolock gibbon and other primate species. Even today, India does not have a nationallevel agenda for the country's only ape species. We are hopeful that an increasing number of in-depth studies and appropriate government policies will eventually enable us to conserve the hoolock gibbon in India. In order to make this possible, we propose to focus on the following conservation activities for the hoolock gibbon in India:

- Initiate multi-dimensional conservation approaches, as practised in the Gibbon Wildlife Sanctuary, in other hoolock gibbon areas in India.
- Further research in the following topics:
  - Re-assessment of hoolock gibbon status
  - Ecological study of the eastern hoolock gibbon

  - Long-term study on population dynamics
  - Habitat quality assessment
  - Habitat mapping (GIS)
  - Genetic study
  - Parasitological study
- Education and awareness:
  - Initiate education and awareness for different target groups in gibbon habitat, especially in the protected areas
  - Launch formal education programmes with effective modules in schools, colleges and universities
  - Initiate informal education and awareness programmes in the villages of the fringe areas of gibbon habitat
- Gibbon conservation training for Forest Department staff, teachers, students, NGO staff, and researchers
- Advocacy:
  - Lobbying for the inclusion of gibbons in the academic syllabus of schools, colleges, and universities
  - Lobbying for the government of India to launch a "Project Gibbon" in line with existing tiger and elephant projects

HUMAN–ELEPHANT CONFLICTS IN NORTHEAST

Northeastern (NE) India is comprised of several states, including Arunachal Pradesh, Assam, Manipur, Meghalaya, Mizoram, Nagaland, Tripura, Sikkim, and the northern parts of West Bengal. This region covers approximately 274,680 km2 and represents a global biodiversity "hotspot". The region is dominated by the Eastern Himalaya Mountains, the Meghalaya Plateau, hill ranges, the plains of the Brahmaputra and the Barak rivers, and the Manipur valley. NE India contains diverse habitat including grassland, wetland, swamps, tropical evergreen and deciduous forest, subtropical and temperate forests, and alpine tundra.

The region has the highest diversity of mammals and birds in India, many of which are threatened. Human population increases and development have reduced and fragmented wildlife habitat. Settlement, cultivation, and developmental activities have dramatically encroached on natural habitat, resulting in severe conflicts between humans and wildlife (especially elephants, *Elephas maximus*).

Between 1980 and 2003, more than 1,150 humans and 370 elephants have died as a result of human–elephant conflicts in NE India. Unlike parts of Africa, however, there is little documentation of case studies in this part of India. Brief overviews on Sumatra and Karnataka, southern India are found in Santiapillai and Widodo. This article presents several case studies from NE India to illustrate the diverse nature of human–elephant conflicts. In addition, it discusses the strengths and weaknesses of possible strategies for mitigating these conflicts.

METHODS

Data for this article were obtained from field studies aimed at a broader survey of wildlife in general in different areas of NE India. These studies examined the presence, distribution, and status of different species of wildlife, especially elephants. The fieldwork also recorded conflicts between humans and elephants. Effort was made to interview the villagers, forest staff, and hunters/ poachers that had experienced conflicts with elephants.

RESULTS

The tiger, leopard, snow leopard, jackal, dhole/wild dog, wildcats, civets, and mongoose were often in conflict with humans throughout NE India, as these species kill livestock and poultry. Much of the habitat and prey of these species has been lost as a result of human population growth and development. Humans hunt several of these species for their pelts and bones. Rhinoceros, wild buffalo, hog deer, wild pig, rhesus macaque, and birds such as the purple moorhen also cause damage to cultivations and gardens. Many species of wildlife are affected by the impact of human development on their traditional habitat and food sources. Conflicts between humans and elephants in NE India, however, are more serious and have become a major conservation issue. NE India is home to more than 10,000 wild elephants, around 25% of the world's elephant population. With the decrease in forest cover due to human population growth and development, the conflict increases daily; more than half of the elephants' habitat has been lost since 1950.

Crop raiding by elephants is a common occurrence throughout the region. During the paddy season, for example, many elephants travel to the plains of Assam and remain at the edge of the forest for a few weeks. Among the *jhumiyas* and the individuals living in the hilly areas, human–elephant conflicts occur when the elephants raid their crops, which are scattered over a large area of fields interspersed with forests. Depredation in human settlements is another major area of human–elephant conflict. Most of these conflicts, however, occur in small forest pockets, encroachments in elephant habitat, and on elephant migration routes.

CASE STUDIES

Sonitpur, Assam

The Kameng area in Arunachal Pradesh and Sonitpur in Assam support a large elephant population that varies between 900 and 1200 animals. Inside Sonitpur in Assam, approximately 500 to 800 elephants occur at different times of the year. During the paddy season, the elephants travel down from the Himalayan foothills in Arunachal Pradesh. In the early 1990s, these elephants sometimes damaged property and raided crops. A few human deaths occurred as a result of these human–elephant conflicts, but elephants were usually unharmed.

Politically motivated developments by the mid 1990s, however, heightened the level of encroachment. By 2002, at least 50% of the prime elephant habitat in the region was lost and human–elephant conflicts became commonplace. Human deaths from elephants increased in 1993, and 2002 and in retaliation, over 30 elephants were poisoned from 2001 to 2002 in Sonitpur and adjacent areas. Human awareness, motivations, and compensation for human injury and death intensified and an "Elephant Reserve" was developed. One of the only possible solutions to mitigate this conflict is to restore elephant habitat to pre-1990 conditions.

Cachar, Assam

In the 1950s, around 100 elephants lived in the foothills of Barail range in Cachar, Assam and in the Jaintia Hills in Meghalaya. By the early 1980s, however, this herd of elephants was reduced to 25–30, as they were separated from Jaintia Hills due to habitat fragmentation and other human-related disturbances. In 1993, only 18 elephants were counted and by 1997, only 4 remained. Since 1998, no elephants have been seen in this region. Elephants became extirpated from the area. From 1991 to 1997, these elephants killed 41 humans. The elephants had wandered aimlessly for about a decade due to the encroachment and destruction of habitat within their range, fears of poachers, and government sponsored shootings of "rogue" elephants.

Nambor-Garampani, Assam

Nambor-Garampani forest in Assam is well known for its elephants. Like most areas in NE India, the habitat has suffered from human encroachment and deforestation. A busy national highway passes through the forest. In the early 1990s, some elephants became a serious and regular hazard, displaying noticeable behavioral changes as they searched vehicles for food. This area became a popular tourist attraction in 1991–92. Some of the elephants were poached, but little poaching is currently reported. The bulk of the remaining habitat in this forest has been protected as wildlife sanctuaries and the diversion of the highway will help to improve the situation and mitigate human–elephant conflicts in this area.

Other Case Studies

Garo Hills, Meghalaya is a major habitat of elephants (over 1,800 in 1993 and 1,200 in 2002). In this area, increased *jhum,* coal mining, logging, and poaching significantly disturbed elephants. Over 200 elephants descended on the Assam's Goalpara district where none were recorded during the census of 1993 (small numbers used to be seen seasonally). Approximately 100 elephants currently live in the scattered forest blocks and damage surrounding houses and property.

From 1990 to 1992, there were no human deaths as a result of conflicts with elephants, but a few people have been killed every year since 1993. There is no apparent solution in sight. In Mizoram, Nagaland, and in the hilly areas of Manipur, human–elephant conflict has had a different history. The elephants have almost always been persecuted for their flesh, which is a local delicacy. Currently, 10–12 elephants are found in Mizoram and in the hills of Manipur, most are occasional/seasonal visitors. Elephants have vanished from most parts of Nagaland, but some are found in a few pockets where the area is contiguous with Assam.

CONSERVATION ISSUES

Habitat Loss and Fragmentation

One of the major instigators of human–wildlife conflict is competition for space. Destruction of forests through logging, encroachment, slash-and-burn shifting cultivation, and monoculture tree plantations are major threats to the survival of the elephant. The forest cover in NE India is disappearing at an alarming rate. For example, more than 1000 km2 of forest were destroyed annually in the 1970s and 1980s. Forest cover had declined from 51% in 1980–1982 to 24% in 1995 in Manipur (a closed forest has canopy cover of >40%). During the same period, the forest cover in Meghalaya declined from 33% to 18%, and from 43% to 17% in Tripura. Encroachment into forested areas is a major problem.

In the 1970s and 1980s, for example, almost the entire population of elephants and other wildlife had disappeared from the 900 km2 rain forest tract comprising Nambor south, Diphu, and Rengma in Golaghat district because of border problems with Nagaland and subsequent logging, poaching, and encroachment. In the hilly areas throughout NE India, shifting cultivation is an important contributor to forest destruction. For example, in a small state such as Manipur, this practice currently covers more that 1,800 km2 or 8.2% of the total area. Even in the hilly areas of Assam, the area currently under shifting cultivation is more than 2,600 km2. The destruction of the forests is reducing and fragmenting habitat.

Poaching

Many species (including elephants, rhinoceros, and tigers) are killed for international trade of their body parts. Although poaching is not a direct source of conflict, injured elephants and other animals often retaliate by killing humans and damaging their property.

Developmental Activities

Developmental projects invite conflict between humans and wildlife. Human development destroys and fragments wildlife habitat, blocks migration routes, facilitates encroachment, and encourages poaching. For example, bamboo harvesting for paper mills (Jagiroad, Panchgram, and Jogighopa in Assam; Tuli in Nagaland), oil mining/exploration, and opencast coal mining have disturbed and destroyed wildlife habitat, as well as caused pollution. The workers, many of whom are poachers, have encroached on adjacent forestlands.

New settlements have been developed due to other subsidiary activities. Construction of roads, railways, and other infrastructure projects destroy and fragment natural habitat, and allow encroachment, logging, and poaching to occur. Planned hydroelectric projects along the Siang, Lohit, Dibang, Subansiri, and Barak rivers will flood considerable forest habitat. The elephants will have less space to live and may loose many migratory routes; conflicts have the potential to increase.

DISCUSSION

For human–wildlife conflicts in NE India, especially with elephants, the blame should be placed entirely on humans. Elephants were domesticated for a long period of time and many people worshipped them as "Lord Ganesha." However, people were not concerned when the elephant became extirpated in southern Assam's Cachar district.

The worst case of human–elephant conflict ever recorded was in the northern area of Darrang (now in Udalguri district, Assam) in October 1992 when 4,000 villagers belonging to 900 families fled their villages and took shelter in relief camps set up by the government. A recent study in Assam found that an area between Karbi Anglong and Kaziranga National Park lost a third of its annual production of paddy to elephants. This area is located near an elephant migration route. Humans have died from conflicts with elephants in NE India.

In just one week in August 1993, elephants near Burhachapori and Laokhowa wildlife sanctuaries in Assam killed more than 50 people. A lone "rogue" bull caused more than half of these deaths. From 1980 to 2003, as many as 1,010 people in Assam and more than 1,150 people across NE India have died from human–elephant conflicts. In 1997 alone, 68 people died from conflicts with elephants in Assam. Elephants have also died as a result of human–elephant conflicts.

More than 370 elephants were killed or poached in NE India between 1980 and 2003, many of which were killed in retaliation by villagers. Individuals and families affected by human–elephant conflicts are usually paid compensation by government agencies, but the lack of adequate funding, delays in processing, and the tendency among many villagers to submit false claims complicate the problem.

In 1992–93, as many as 3,856 persons were paid compensation for human–elephant conflicts in Meghalaya. Beating tins, shouting, brandishing fires, and bursting firecrackers are the most common methods used for warding off elephants. However, these do not work in many places. Capturing and relocating live elephants was also considered as a measure to mitigate depredation.

For example, 1,298 elephants were captured in Meghalaya from 1960 to 1981 and 12 elephants were captured in Assam from 1994 to 1995. Capturing these elephants has likely decreased depredation. Construction of electric fencing has failed to eliminate conflicts in Hollongapar despite its initial success. When the fencing was erected, the elephants innovated an intelligent method of breaking fencing posts by holding the top of the wooden posts by their trunk and breaking at the middle by gently pushing their foot, thus avoiding the live wires.

Digging trenches is expensive and difficult to maintain in areas such as NE India where heavy rainfall is common. Elephants are protected under the Schedule I of the Indian Wildlife Protection Act (1972), which is the highest level of protection accorded to any species in the country. The elephant is also listed as an "endangered" species by the IUCN (2002). However, it is often difficult to enforce regulations in remote areas because of the delayed information, inaccessibility, and problems of insurgency.

Only about 25% of the elephant habitat is located within protected areas in NE India. Therefore, there is high potential for human–elephant conflict in a large amount of terrain. The ultimate cause of the destruction of the elephants' habitat in NE India is the rapid growth of the human population in this region. Unless the growth rate of human population is controlled, a lasting solution to human–elephant conflicts may not be possible. The human population in India is doubling every 30 years.

RECOMMENDATIONS

The following recommendations are offered for mitigating human–elephant conflict in NE India. First, new protected areas need to be created. With only about 25% of the habitat of elephants within protected areas, there is an urgent need to create more protected areas. Although declaring an area as "protected" is not enough, it does offer a vital legal step toward conservation and reducing conflicts. Second, wherever possible, the existing protected areas should also be enlarged and fragmentation of protected areas should be discouraged. Third, elephant migration corridors should be legally protected.

Corridors used regularly by the elephants should be given legal protection. This is important because it is highly unlikely that all of the corridors will be combined into national parks or sanctuaries. Legal status should be granted in the form of a wildlife sanctuary where the corridors transect forestland. Problems arise, however, when corridors transect tea plantations, shifting cultivations, and human villages. Humans and elephants are mainly in direct conflict in villages. Conflict is less of a problem in other corridor areas because elephants usually migrate at night. It is recommended that provisions for "protected elephant movement corridors" be amended to the Indian Wildlife Protection Act.

At tea estates and areas of shifting cultivation, the land should continue to be managed by the private owners, but the amendment would ensure that land-use changes do not occur in the corridors. At other places, the government can acquire strips of land under the Land Acquisition Acts and pay suitable compensation. Fourth, poaching wildlife for trade and meat consumption should be strictly monitored. Anti-poaching staff need to be better trained and equipped, and penalties for poaching should be more severe. In addition, all unlicensed arms should be confiscated.

Fifth, shifting cultivation needs to be controlled/regulated. Although it is unlikely that this practice will completely stop, as it is a deeply ingrained lifestyle and culture, measures should be taken to control it, especially near prime wildlife habitat and migration routes. Sixth, encroachment should be strictly monitored.

New encroachments should be discouraged or banned, especially in the reserve forestlands. Recent encroachments such as those within elephant habitat (e.g., Nambor and Balipara forests in Assam) should be evicted and restored. Seventh, there should be a ban on commercial forestry/logging in NE India.

Given the poor remaining tree cover in several parts of NE India, commercial forestry/logging in the remaining natural patches of forest should be discouraged. Uncontrolled cutting of the grasslands should also be strictly monitored and controlled. Finally, all areas currently designated as protected require consistent and adequate protection through effective patrolling and enforcement. Other measures include:

- Conservation education with active involvement of local and international nongovernmental organizations;
- Strategies for reducing depredation;
- Expeditious payment for loss of human life and damage to property;
- Reduced dependency of fringe villagers on the forest lands;
- Increased empirical research on the ecology, behavior, and movement of wildlife, especially elephants; and
- An extensive review and rectification of some of the human development in NE India. These suggestions could potentially mitigate human–elephant conflicts in NE India.

CHECKLIST OF TURTLE FAUNA SO FAR RECORDED FROM NORTHEAST INDIA

The northeastern region of India covering an area of 2, 62,179 km2 (7.6% total area of the country) is a biologically highly diverse area and one of the most important biodiversity hot spots of the world. The region is at the conjunction of the Himalaya and Indo-Burma biodiversity hotspots. It is regarded as one of the major centre of turtle diversity. However, the region has been poorly explored scientifically with regard to surveys, conservation and monitoring of turtle fauna.

The turtle and tortoise diversity of northeast India is the highest in the country and 23 of 29 species are found in this region. However, the lack of recent field information has created a gap in conservation and management of turtle species in the region. The present paper reports a checklist of turtles and tortoises from the northeastern states which are recorded in the field work during the last four years.

MATERIALS AND METHODS

Field surveys were carried out by the Centre for Wildlife Research and Conservation Action, Department of Zoology, Gauhati University, Assam during January 2005-December 2008 using three different methods including interviews of peoples using photo sheets of turtles, trappings using nets with the help of fishermen and visual encounter surveys (VES). Fishermen, traders, collectors and field workers of respective states were interviewed to learn about their distribution, habitat and extent of exploitation. Literature searches also carried out for the detailed information. During the survey, both living specimens and any signs of their presence including dead specimens were noted. For identification of the species, Das (1995) was followed. The following measurements were taken using the dial vernier callipers: straight line carapace length, plastron length. Subsequently the live specimens were released in their habitat.

OBSERVATIONS

The recorded chelonians were photographed and the sex of the specimens were attempted to identify though it is difficult morphologically. However, the bigger sizes of the soft-shell turtle were female in *_ilssonia nigricans, _ilssonia hurum, Chitra indica, Batagur kachuga, Pangshura sylhetensis.* It has been observed that generally the females are being caught and killed due to their size and the small sized males are released into the water, thereby sex ratio imbalance has appeared as major threat. Moreover, the hunting of the animals and destruction of eggs are the major threats for this little known aquatic creature.

RECOMMENDATION

Lack of recent field information has created a gap in conservation activities and status evaluation of almost all turtle species. Immediate adoption of conservation measures is essential for the conservation of endangered turtle genetic resource available in this region. As a part of the conservation of genetic diversity, the following studies are proposed:

- Survey of the different turtle species,
- Reproductive cycle of endangered species,
- Study on allozyme variation and molecular phylogeny to analyze the polymorphism and evolutionary history,
- Breeding in captivity, and
- Generate awareness against killing and need of conservation through community participation.

WRAPPING UP

Habitat loss and over exploitation for meat is considered persistent threat to chelonians of the region. Gupta and Guha (2002) reported tradition and conservation of turtle in NE India. Gupta (2000) reported certain areas rich in freshwater chelonian diversity of Northeastern India including Assam. Out of 23 species found in northeast India, 6 species namely *Pangshura sylhetensis*, *Pyxidea mouhotii*, *Nilssonia nigricans*, *Chitra indicia*, *Manouria emys* and *Indotestudo elongata* are listed by IUCN (2007) as most endangered species of Asia. The soft-shell turtle *Chitra indica* needs special attention as it is on the new list of the 25 most endangered turtle species of the world. As a part of the conservation of turtle diversity, we emphasize on some important research and conservation initiatives.

LOSING THREATENED AND RARE WILDLIFE TO HUNTING IN ZIRO VALLEY, ARUNACHAL PRADESH

ARUNACHAL PRADESH is the largest state in the northeastern region of India and forms 2.5% of the total geographical area of the country, 15.76% of the Indian Himalayan region and 43.62% of the biological hotspot of Eastern Himalaya. The state is inhabited by 26 major tribes and 110 sub-tribes. The vast majority of the indigenous inhabitants of the region are meat-eaters and many in the community are hunters. In spite of having 61.5% forest cover and being acclaimed as part of a biodiversity hotspot a protected area in Arunachal Pradesh was found to be 'empty'. A recent study found that hunting was reported in 23 out of the 28 states and 7 Union Territories of India. Among the 350 mammal species, 114 are reported to be hunted in India. Researchers have emphasized the existing knowledge gaps pertaining to wildlife hunting, their impacts and the sustainability in the northeastern states and Arunachal Pradesh in particular.

In certain tracts in India like those inhabited by the Bishnois there is a rich tradition of protecting wildlife and its habitats. However, this tradition is not prevalent in the northeastern states, where the indigenous communities have the tradition of obtaining meat from wild animals. In Arunachal Pradesh, hunting is a widespread cultural practice that has probably led to low wildlife abundance.

This study reports on the hunting of 134 wild animals comprising mammals, birds and reptiles. A study on wildlife hunting in East Kameng, Lohit and Anjaw districts of Arunachal Pradesh, reported a total of 33 mammal species being hunted, with 57% of these being endangered, threatened or vulnerable. A study in West Kameng and Tawang districts of Arunachal Pradesh revealed that 26 mammal species were hunted locally.

Another study in Nagaland and Arunachal Pradesh reported about the hunting of 43 species of mammalian fauna. Studies on wildlife hunting in India and the North East region are particularly in infancy stage. Currently, we have documentation of only hunted species, hunting practices, etc. The exact impact of wildlife hunting and sustainability of these hunting practices have to be studied scientifically. In this background, we conducted a study to document wildlife hunting by the indigenous Apatani people in the Ziro valley, Lower Subansiri district, Arunachal Pradesh.

This study was part of the DST-sponsored dhole project in Arunachal Pradesh. The Lower Subansiri district is located in the central western part of Arunachal Pradesh and lies between 26°55¢–28°21¢N and 92°40¢–94°21¢E. The Ziro valley is inhabited by the Apatani tribe whose unique land-use pattern, resource management and culture of conservation have made them a globally significant community. The valley has 35 villages, with a population of 24,650 and a density of 23 people per sq. km. The terrain is undulating, ranging from 1830 to 2900 m. The villages surveyed include Hija, Hong, Hari, Kalung, Nenchailya and Tajang.

The survey was carried out twice between March and April 2011 and 2012. Interviews were conducted using a semi-structured questionnaire. Eighty-five households were randomly selected for interviews from each village. Village heads and hunters also were interviewed.

Encounter rate of skin was calculated as the number of individual animal skins/total number of households surveyed. Among the 85 households surveyed, 54.11% reported hunting for subsistence, 25% for commercial trade, 10% for medicinal purposes and 4.7% reported hunting for pleasure. The major species hunted are mostly those protected by law. The orange-bellied Himalayan squirrel is specifically hunted for medicinal purposes and social ceremonies. About 55.3% respondents used guns, 35.3% used traditional traps and guns, and only 9.4% used traditional methods such as noose traps, glue traps, bow and arrow.

The youngest hunter was reported to be 8 years old and to have hunted birds for consumption. Maximum hunting was observed in the age group between 30 and 40 years (47%), followed by 30% in the age group between 20 and 30 years. Hunting was generally performed twice a year in winter and summer seasons, with an average eight hunters per group.

Trophies and skins of birds, orange-bellied squirrel, Malayan giant squirrel, barking deer and sambar were frequently encountered during our survey. The results of the survey revealed the hunting pressure on several rare and threatened mammalian species. Faunal depletion in tropical forests will have myriad consequences and a devastating effect on the forest ecosystem. The factors attributed to hunting include physical, geographical, biological, social, cultural, religious and economic.

Several positive impacts of wild meat harvesting and consumption to human health have been documented. Animal sourced food are generally known to be rich in energy, protein and micronutrients that have greater bioavailability than vegetable resources. Hunting and bush meat trade though ignored largely, play a vital role in the economy of numerous tropical forested countries. In a study conducted at Madagascar, a group of 77 children under 12 years of age were examined.

On the contrary, severe negative impacts due to hunting have also been documented. Mass extinction of large-bodied animals due to hunting practices especially threatens the Southeast Asian region. The impact due to hunting on mammalian fauna is comparatively lesser in other tropical forests in Africa and the Amazon. The extirpation of mammalian fauna by hunting can lead to serious impact on the forest structure and dynamics.

Though wildlife is immensely valuable to humans, the impact of hunting causes several changes in the biological communities. As a result, there is loss of pollinators, seed predators, seed dispersers and predators, which finally results in an empty forest syndrome. Though hunting of wildlife is mostly done for subsistence in this region, access to the markets drives the hunters beyond their subsistence needs for additional income and this needs to be curtailed by enforcing strict protection to the wildlife. Social taboos traditionally provide a safeguard against overharvesting of certain species and traditional customary laws of indigenous communities prevent overharvesting and helps conserve species.

There is an urgent need for Government agencies and conservationists to merge the traditional knowledge system with modern conservation methods and strengthen participatory conservation management. Existing knowledge gaps on distribution, population status, and rate of change of species that are primarily hunted need to be filled. Sustainability of the existing hunting practices has never been assessed and such research needs to be expedited. Tackling wildlife hunting should be addressed from both the conservation and development perception, and will require an interdisciplinary approach cautiously incorporating social, economic, ecological and political components.

BUTTERFLIES OF THE GARO HILLS OF MEGHALAYA, NORTH-EASTERN INDIA: THEIR DIVERSITY AND CONSERVATION

The northeastern region of India, south of the Brahmaputra River, is part of the globally recognized Indo-Myanmar biodiversity hotspot and is host to a remarkable biodiversity that includes a high proportion of endemic, rare and endangered species. The Garo Hills of the northeastern state of Meghalaya form the north-westernmost limit of the Indo-Myanmar Biodiversity Hotspot. From there the hotspot extends southeastwards to cover the Khasi, Jaintia, Naga, Manipur and Mizo Hills (together encompassing the Patkai Hills) in northeastern India, and all of the Indo-Chinese subregion.

The Indian part of this hotspot is one of the most species-rich regions in the Indian Subcontinent, with considerable endemism at subspecies level. The high species richness and endemism make this an especially important region for butterfly diversity and conservation in India. Early European lepidopterists extensively explored this biodiversity hotspot between 1840 and 1950 and described hundreds of butterfly species and subspecies.

The major taxonomic and natural history work in this region was done in the Khasi and Jaintia Hills in eastern Meghalaya, in Cachar Hills in southern Assam and Bangladesh, and in the Naga-Manipur Hills. The pace of species discovery and accumulation of bionomic information on butterflies of this region has subsequently slowed down as the region has received less attention from lepidopterists with a few notable exceptions. Nevertheless, some areas have historically remained practically unexplored. As far as we know, one area that has never been properly surveyed is the Garo Hills in western Meghalaya.

The Garo Hills are loosely connected in the east with the Khasi and Jaintia Hills in eastern Meghalaya surrounding the Shillong Plateau and Cherrapunji. As mentioned above, the Khasi and Jaintia Hills were intensively surveyed by early European lepidopterists, but those hills have been largely denuded due to coal and limestone mining and agriculture in the past 150 years. Therefore, little forest and associated biodiversity are now to be found in those hills. On the other hand, the Garo Hills still harbor substantial swaths of evergreen and semi-evergreen forests and support a considerable proportion of endangered species such as the Asian Elephant, Bengal Tiger, Hoolock Gibbon and Serow.

A total of at least 85 mammal, 23 amphibian, 33 reptile and 270 bird species have so far been reported from the Garo Hills. However, butterflies in this landscape are poorly known due to lack of surveys. We assume that some information remains unpublished but available on specimen labels in various research collections and museums worldwide. This should be especially true of the Natural History Museum, London, and the National Zoological Collection of Zoological Survey of India, Kolkata, where most of the collections by early British lepidopterists are currently situated. We hope that this information will slowly become available as we continue our work in these museums.

Nonetheless, little is known about current populations, distributions, seasonality and occurrence of butterflies of the Garo Hills, and of the entire northeastern India in general. This information is important for naturalists and ecologists as well as for policy-makers and conservationists.

With this in mind, in the past few years we have been surveying butterfly populations in several northeastern Indian states to fill gaps in our current knowledge of Indian butterflies. As part of this long-term initiative, we have especially focused our attention on surveying the little-known butterfly diversity in the Garo Hills. The work presented below is the first outcome of our surveys in the Garo Hills. This and our subsequent work will generate baseline information on butterflies by intensively surveying populations across seasonal, altitudinal and habitat gradients. We hope that this will be useful in documenting the rich biodiversity of the Garo Hills.

MATERIAL AND METHODS

study area

The Garo hills of western Meghalaya

The Garo Hills cover approximately a third of Meghalaya's total area of 22,429km2. They are distributed among three administrative districts: the East Garo Hills, the South Garo Hills, and the West Garo Hills. So far, we have surveyed butterflies only in the West and South Garo Hills Districts, where several important protected forest areas are situated. The West Garo Hills District is spread over 3,715km2, out of which 2,717km2, or approximately 73%, is forested. More than half of this forest is highly disturbed and the rest is moderately disturbed.

However, evergreen forests are still largely intact in the Nokrek National Park-Tura Peak areas. The South Garo Hills District covers an area of 1,849km2, of which 1,689km2, or approximately 91%, is forested. However, one-third of this is highly degraded forest, and the rest is moderately disturbed by jhum or shifting cultivation. Good forest patches are still found in the Balpakram-Baghmara landscape, where we have done most of our work so far.

A total of approximately 600km2 (presently 64% of its total landmass) of evergreen and secondary semi-evergreen forest of the Balpakram- Baghmara landscape is situated in four protected areas managed by the Meghalaya Forest Department: the Balpakram National Park, Siju Wildlife Sanctuary (6km2), Baghmara Reserve Forest and Rewak Reserve Forest, the rest falls under 36 tribal community lands called Akings. Thus, nearly one-third of the district's area is covered by forests of the Balpakram- Baghmara landscape.

Most of this forest is at low elevations, and may be classified as the Cachar tropical evergreen forest, originally dominated by *Palaquim* spp., *Diospyros topiosa, Dipterocarpus turbinus, Messua ferrea* and other large evergreen trees. Almost all the forest patches now have few very large evergreen trees, and they have a variable proportion of deciduous trees and bamboo depending on the extent of human disturbance, such as the intensity and extent of jhum cultivation. These forest patches are still rich in tropical floral and faunal elements, and the region has one of the highest recorded densities of the Asian elephant in the world.

surveyed localities and dates

KK, SS, BMS, RL and GA surveyed butterflies at several localities in the Baghmara Reserve Forest, the Siju Wildlife Sanctuary, and outskirts of the Balpakram National Park in the vicinity of Gongrot, Taidang, and Halwa Atong akings (akings are Garo tribal villages with the associated community lands). KT surveyed butterflies at the Nokrek National Park and on the Balpakram Plateau within the Balpakram NP. We made four field trips to these areas to survey butterflies, on which we spent 53 days in the field and collected quantitative data on 49 days at the following specific localities.

Baghmara rF

- Karwani, Bhawanipur and Panda (streams in Baghmara RF near Baghmara Town): 2008/05/02,04; 2009/11/16, 21; 2009/12/07– 08, 13, 15, 17, 19–20; 2010/04/30; 2010/05/01-03, 07, 11, 13–14.
- Simsang trail (footpath parallel to the Simsang River in Baghmara RF near Baghmara Town): 2008/05/02; 2009/12/11–12, 21.

Balpakram nP, and Gongrot-halwa atong area

- Taidang, Jidung and Rongrok: 2008/05/03; 2009/11/16–19; 2009/12/05–06; 2010/05/04–06.
- Rani Miksuram (stream near Halwa Atong Village): 2008/05/02; 2009/11/16; 2009/11/20.
- Me Cheng (stream near Halwa Atong Village): 2009/11/20.
- Balpakram Plateau: 2009/11/13–16; 2010/05/15–16.

siju Ws

2009/11/22; 2009/12/03–04; 2010/05/08– 09.

Nokrek nP

2009/11/06–09. The latitudes and longitudes of the major localities were:

- Baghmara town/RF: 25012.543'N & 90038.011'E;
- Gongrot: 25015.838'N & 90043.850'E,
- Balpakram Plateau: 25015.876'N & 90051.837'E,
- Siju WS: 25021.137'N & 90041.187'E; and
- Nokrek NP: 25029.571'N & 90019.460'E.

In addition, KK also briefly surveyed rice fields and the Matcha Nokpante Community Reserve near the Samrakshan Trust's field office in Baghmara Town. We sampled butterflies in several habitats at the above localities: evergreen forest streams, forested hill slopes, and neighborhoods of Gongrot and Halwa Atong villages. Neighborhoods of Gongrot and Halwa Atong included cashew and other orchards, abandoned jhums and extremely disturbed secondary forest, through which we had to walk for 1–2 km to reach excellent patches of evergreen forest on hill slopes and along streams.

SAMPLING AND OTHER METHODS

Our field work usually took place between 0800 and 1700 hr every day. However, the sampling effort was uneven over various visits and by different observers. KK recorded each and every individual butterfly seen during his two visits, all of his observations having been broken down into one-hour butterfly counts from the beginning to the end of each day.

Thus, his data were completely quantitative. SS counted butterflies over several three-hour counts but many of his sightings were outside these counts, so his observations were a mixture of quantitative sampling and all-out searches. BS, RL and GA did not quantify butterfly abundance; all of their records were based on photographs that were later identified by KK. KT usually recorded total numbers for every species seen. Quantitative data presented in Table 5 are summed over all the quantitative observations and all-out searches by all the observers.

For both types of data collection, we followed a fairly uniform method: we walked along forest paths and forest streams, where we have found butterfly abundance to be the highest over years of field work. We followed commonly used paths leading into the forests to survey butterflies in the vicinity of tribal villages. Once we entered forests, we walked either along these paths, waded through forest streams, or followed numerous elephant and other animal trails that criss-cross these forests.

We recorded each and every butterfly species (and every individual in case of KK, SS and KT) that we saw perched overhead, on surrounding vegetation, or in flight at any distance from us. Each record was noted in field notebooks on the spot, and most species, including the commonest ones, were photographed in the field for reference.

However, not all butterflies could be identified from only the upperside or underside as is usually seen in the field. Many species groups have distinctive characteristics on both wing surfaces that need to be checked closely, and it is not always possible to see these without capturing butterflies for a closer look. These characteristics included specific bands and spots, hair pencils, brands, etc., in genera such as *Baoris*, *Pelopidas*, *Jamides*, *Arhopala*, *Rapala*, *Mycalesis* and *Euploea*.

Therefore, we obtained permission from local forest officials to catch butterflies to photograph both their wing surfaces for identification. We caught butterflies with a net, photographed them for relevant distinctive characteristics with digital cameras, and then released them immediately on the spot.

If butterflies could not be identified to a species level without dissecting their male genitalia, we recorded only the genus names or the species group to which they belonged. Thus, several of our records were, e.g., for "*Halpe* spp.", "*Potanthus* spp.", "*Mycalesis* sp.", or "*Neptis nata/soma* group". We hope to obtain permission to collect specimens and dissect their genitalia to determine species in these genera and species groups in the future. Images 3–18 give photographic proof of our butterfly sightings in the Garo Hills so far. We had taken majority of these pictures at the sampling localities mentioned above.

Only a small proportion of species photographs, marked in images 3–18 by asterisks, were taken outside of the Garo Hills. We have included them to illustrate those species for anyone interested in butterflies. These should prove to be a particularly valuable reference for people conducting field work in the Garo Hills or elsewhere in northeastern India in the future.

We paid particular attention to mud-puddling spots where several species could be spotted, and we spent considerable amount of time at these spots because there was a fairly high turnover of butterflies. Some butterfly species were more easily seen on specific food sources such as rotting crabs, which may not always be readily available.

Therefore, we used rotting crabs as bait, which at times attracted over a hundred individual butterflies and dozens of species. The annotated checklist we present below is arranged alphabetically at every systematic level, from family and subfamily names to genera and species.

Taxonomic information, including updated family, subfamily, genus, species and subspecies names, as well as English names of subspecies, was taken from the Butterflies of India website, which is itself based on an upcoming subspecies-level catalogue of Indian butterflies.

Note that parentheses have not been used for authors and years where genus assignments have changed, but the names that we have used should be easily traceable in standard taxonomic works. Further taxonomic details will be found elsewhere.

RESULTS

We recorded 3,804 individuals belonging to 298 species and to an additional eight taxa that could not be identified to species level. These represented 156 genera in 22 subfamilies and six families. A detailed taxonomic breakdown of the Garo Hills butterflies is presented in Tables 1 and 2. The distribution of butterfly species across genera was highly skewed. A large proportion of genera recorded in our surveys were represented by single species, 26 genera by two species, 12 genera by three species, and two genera by four species, the rest by four species or more.

The most prevalent genera—those with five species or more—are listed in Fig. 2. Similarly, the abundance of individual species was highly skewed. The commonest 27 species, i.e., those represented in our sample by 40 individuals or more, or on average at least one individual per count, are shown in Fig. 3.

The season- and locality-wise species richness is given in Table 3, although the differences here may merely reflect our uneven sampling effort. Although we report a substantial number of butterfly species, the actual butterfly species richness in the Garo Hills appears to be much higher. New species accumulated fairly steeply even after reaching 298 species in 49 days of field work.

The steepness of species accumulation based on sampling from only two seasons, and the known butterfly fauna of the nearby Khasi Hills, suggest that another 300– 350 species may still be remaining to be discovered in the Garo Hills.

Nonetheless, the butterfly fauna of the Garo Hills reported here has already proved to be an extremely valuable conservation asset: 48 of the already recorded 298 butterfly species, or approximately 16%, are legally protected in India under the Wildlife Act, 1972. Of these, eight are protected under Schedule I and 33 are protected under Schedule II of the Wildlife Act, 1972.

These species are very important as they receive the highest level of legal protection at the national level. The taxonomic and Schedule-wise breakdown of legally protected butterfly species found in the Garo Hills is given in Tables 1 and 4. Thus, the Garo Hills not only possess high butterfly species richness, but they also support a large number of rare and legally protected species. The Garo Hills should therefore be considered a top-priority, high-value conservation area for long-term preservation of butterfly diversity in India.

AN ANNOTATED CHECKLIST OF BUTTERFLIES OF THE GARO HILLS

In addition to the summary and preliminary analyses of butterfly diversity presented above and in associated tables and figures, we now offer notes relevant to our sightings of butterflies in the Garo Hills. The numbers of individuals recorded for each species, season and general locality are given in Table 5, which would be useful baseline quantitative data for any future work on these butterflies. Also mentioned for comparison is status of these and related species from the neighboring Khasi Hills.

Family hesperiidae subfamily coeliadinae

1. *Badamia exclamationis* Fabricius, 1775 - Brown Awl: Our six records were of individuals resting on the undersides of leaves along forest paths and forest streams and on one occasion, close to human habitation. This is a widely distributed species that has been reported as being common in the Khasi Hills.

2. *Bibasis sena sena* Moore, 1865 - Indian Orangetail Awl: Our record of this species is based on a single specimen spotted late in the evening along the Simsang trail in Baghmara RF in April 2010. It has been reported from the Khasi Hills before. It is legally protected in India under Schedule II of the Wildlife Act.

3. *Burara oedipodea belesis* Mabille, 1876 - Himalayan Branded Orange Awlet: A single specimen was photographed in May 2010 at Siju WS. This species has previously been reported from the Khasi Hills.

4. *Choaspes benjaminii japonica* Murray, 1875 - Narrow Indian Awlking: A widespread species that may be occasionally met with mud-puddling along shaded streams in evergreen and semi-evergreen forests in the Garo Hills. It has previously been reported from the Khasi Hills.

5. *Hasora badra badra* Moore, 1857 - Oriental Common Awl: This is based on a single specimen seen at 0500 hr, just before dawn, in early May 2010 at Siju WS. It has previously been reported from the Khasi Hills.

6. *Hasora taminatus bhavara* Fruhstorfer, 1911 - Himalayan White-banded Awl: Our single record was by KT from the Balpakram Plateau in November 2009. It has previously been reported from the Khasi Hills.

Family hesperiidae, subfamily hesperiinae

7. *Aeromachus jhora creta* Evans, 1949 - Khasi Jhora Scrub Hopper: Our record was based on two individuals that KK saw in May 2008, perched on small herbs beside an open stream outside Halwa Atong Village. It has previously been reported from the Khasi Hills.

8. *Ancistroides nigrita diocles* Moore, 1865 - Bengal Chocolate Demon: A fairly common species that can be seen along forest paths and streams, basking or settling on bird droppings from which it feeds using its remarkably long proboscis. It has previously been reported from the Khasi Hills.

9. *Baoris chapmani* Evans, 1937 - Small Paint-brush Swift: Our record of *Baoris chapmani* was based on a single individual that KK photographed in the Baghmara RF in November 2009, basking on low vegetation along the Karwani stream. "*Baoris penicillata*" has been previously reported from the Khasi Hills, but at that time two taxa had been lumped under "*penicillata*": (a) *Baoris chapmani* Evans, 1937, and (b) *Baoris unicolor* Moore, 1883. The exact identity

of the *Baoris penicillata* specimens recorded from the Khasi Hills will need to be checked from museum specimens mentioned by Cantlie. *Baoris penicillata* Moore, 1881 is Endemic to Sri Lanka, but both *chapmani* and *unicolor* are supposed to occur in northeastern India and we report both from the Garo Hills here.

10. *Baoris farri* Moore, 1878 - Complete Paint-brush Swift: Common in the Garo Hills, frequenting openings along streams in mixed semi-evergreen and evergreen forests. We recorded 10 individuals, eight at Gongrot and two in the Baghmara RF, all in November 2009. This species has previously been reported from the Khasi Hills. It is legally protected in India under Schedule IV of the Wildlife Act.

11. *Baoris unicolor* Moore, 1883 - Black Paint-brush Swift: Our record of *Baoris unicolor* was based on a single individual that KK photographed beside the Karwani stream in mixed semi-evergreen forest in the Baghmara RF in May 2008. See a note under *Baoris chapmani* about the taxonomy and previous records of *Baoris* from the Khasi Hills.

B. unicolor

12. *Caltoris* sp. - Swift: Our record was based on a single specimen that KT photographed in November 2009 on the Balpakram Plateau. Species identifications in this group are based on subtle differences in spotting patterns on the wings and in male genitalia, which could not be investigated closely in our specimen.

Caltoris sp.

13. *Cupitha purreea* Moore, 1877 - Wax Dart: Uncommon in the Garo Hills, occurs along forest paths and streams. Our records are based on only two individuals, one each in May 2008 and November 2009. It has previously been reported from the Khasi Hills.

14. *Halpe* spp. - Ace spp.: We have seen four individuals during both seasons at Gongrot, Baghmara RF and Siju WS. Several species of *Halpe* have been reported from the Khasi Hills, and most of them are expected in the Garo Hills. However, species-level identification of *Halpe* is challenging. So far, we have not dissected male genitalia to determine the species.

15. *Halpe zema zema* Hewitson, 1877 - Sikkim Zema Banded Ace: This species cannot be distinguished from *Halpe zola* Evans, 1937 without dissecting male genitalia, something that we did not do. However, only *Halpe zema* has

been reported from the Khasi Hills before, so we are provisionally assigning the seven individuals that we saw mud-puddling in evergreen forest streams in the Baghmara-Gongrot-Siju landscape to this species. We hope to dissect a few males in the future to confirm this assignment.

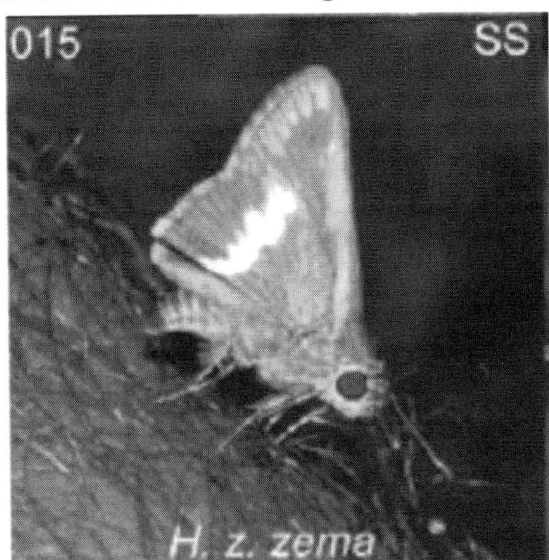

16. *Hyarotis adrastus praba* Moore, 1865 - Bengal Tree Flitter: A single sighting at a forest stream in Panda in December 2009. This subspecies is legally protected in India under Schedule IV of the Wildlife Act.

17. *Iambrix salsala salsala* Moore, 1865 - Eastern Chestnut Bob: very common in the Garo Hills in open forests, along forest edges and around human habitations. Our record is based on 19 individuals recorded from both seasons,

although most of the records were from Gongrot in November 2009. It has been reported from the Khasi Hills before.

18. *Iton semamora semamora* Moore, 1865 - Bengal Common Wight: Our record was based on a single specimen photographed by KT on the Baghmara Plateau in November 2009. This species has apparently not been reported before from the Khasi-Garo Hills complex, so ours is the westernmost record of the species in Meghalaya.

19. *Koruthaialos butleri* de Nicéville, 1883 - Dark Velvet Bob: Our record was based on a single specimen that KK photographed in mixed deciduous forest

in the Baghmara RF in May 2008. This species has been reported from the Khasi Hills before, but it is not common.

K. butleri

20. *Matapa aria* Moore, 1865 - Common Branded Redeye: Most of our records were of specimens frequenting secondary growth in disturbed evergreen forest patches around Gongrot and nearby villages, from November 2009. This species is widely distributed in the Oriental Region and can sometimes be common in mixed deciduous forests and edges of evergreen forests in northeastern India. The species has been reported from the Khasi Hills beforc.

M. aria

21. *Matapa cresta* Evans, 1949 - Fringed Branded Redeye: We recorded this species from two specimens at Jidung stream and one at Me Cheng Chirang at Gongrot, and one at Siju WS, all in November 2009. It has been reported from the Khasi Hills before.

22. *Matapa sasivarna* Moore, 1865 - Black-veined Branded Redeye: KT photographed a single specimen on Balpakram plateau in November 2009. The species has been reported from the Khasi Hills before, but does not appear to be common.

23. *Notocrypta curvifascia curvifascia* Felder & Felder, 1862 - Chinese Restricted Demon: We recorded several specimens in evergreen forest undergrowth at Gongrot in November 2009. It is common in the Khasi Hills.

24. *Notocrypta feisthamelii alysos* Moore, 1865 - Himalayan Spotted Demon: Less common than the previous species, although they seem to share the same habitats and many of their habits. It is not rare in the Khasi Hills.

25. *Notocrypta paralysos asawa* Fruhstorfer, 1911 - Indo-Chinese Common Banded Demon: SS recorded two individuals in Baghmara RF in December 2009. It has been reported to be not rare in the Khasi Hills.

26. *Oriens gola pseudolus* Mabille, 1883 - Oriental Common Dartlet: Our record is based on a single specimen that KK photographed at Rongrok Stream, Gongrot, in November 2009. It has been reported from the Khasi Hills before.

27. *Oriens goloides* Moore, 1881 - Smaller Dartlet: Not uncommon in the Garo Hills. Both species of *Oriens* commonly feed from flowers of small herbs and shrubs, and flit about at forest edges, on paths and in treefall gaps in evergreen and riparian forests. This species has been reported from the Khasi Hills before.

28. *Parnara* sp. - Swift: Three *Parnara* have been reported from India: (1) *Parnara ganga* Evans, 1937, (2) *Parnara guttatus mangala* Moore, 1865, and (3) *Parnara bada* Moore, 1878. All of them have been reported from the Khasi Hills and are expected in the Garo Hills.

However, species in this group can be determined only by dissecting male genitalia. We have not dissected genitalia from any of the specimens that we have encountered so far, but we hope to do so in the future. Of our 118 sightings, 101 were in May 2008 in agricultural fields around Samrakshan Trust's field office at Baghmara, 15 from jhum areas around Gongrot, and only two were from November 2009 at Gongrot.

29. *Pelopidas agna agna* Moore, 1865 - Bengal Obscure Branded Swift: This is based on a single specimen that KT photographed on Baghmara Plateau in March 2009. The species has been reported from the Khasi Hills before.

30. *Pelopidas assamensis* de Nicéville, 1882 - Great Swift: Not uncommon in fallow jhum fields overgrown with shrubs, as well as in small openings inside dense forests. It has been reported from the Khasi Hills before. This species is legally protected in India under Schedule IV of the Wildlife Act.

31. *Pirdana major* Evans, 1932 - Himalayan Green-striped Palmer: Our record from the Garo Hills was based on a single specimen seen by KK at Taidang stream near Gongrot in November 2009. It was a fresh female seen on a clouded afternoon, in one of the most shaded parts of an evergreen forest

stream. It was perched at two meters above ground on a branch overhanging the stream, and was not active. The picture included in image 4 may be the first picture of a live specimen ever taken. This is a very rare species and, as far as we know, it has not been reported in literature from the Garo-Khasi Hills complex before. The Natural History Museum, London, has only one male taken in Sikkim, and eight males and two females taken in "Assam", some of which may have been taken in the Khasi Hills. This species is sometimes included as a subspecies of *Pirdana hyela* Hewitson 1867.

32. *Pithauria stramineipennis stramineipennis* Wood-Mason & de Nicéville, 1886 - Assam Light Straw Ace: Our records are based on two males mud-puddling at Siju WS and a third specimen at Karwani in May 2010. The species has been reported from the Khasi Hills before.

33. *Polytremis lubricans lubricans* Herrich- Schäffer, 1869 - Oriental Contiguous Swift: This species seems to be uncommon in the Garo Hills. Our record was based on a single sighting from Gongrot in May 2009. It has been reported from the Khasi Hills before, and is frequently met with in open areas and secondary vegetation in northeastern India. This subspecies is legally protected in India under Schedule IV of the Wildlife Act.

34. *Potanthus* spp. - Dart spp.: Eleven *Potanthus* species have been reported from the Khasi Hills before: (1) *rectifasciata* Elwes & Edwards, 1897 - Branded Dart, (2) *trachala tytleri* Evans, 1914 - Manipur Broad Bident Dart, (3) *pallida* Evans, 1932 - Pallid Dart, (4) *pseudomaesa clio* Evans, 1932 - Himalayan Common Dart, (5) *juno* Evans, 1932 - Myanmarese Dart, (6) *sita* Evans, 1932 - Sita Dart, (7) *confucius dushta* Fruhstorfer, 1911 - Indo-Chinese Dart, (8) *lydia* Evans, 1934 - Assam Dart, (9) *ganda* Fruhstorfer 1911 - Sumatran Dart, (10) *nesta* Evans, 1934 - Nesta Dart, and (11) *palnia* Evans, 1914 - Palni Dart. Most of them are expected to be found in the Garo Hills. We have come across only two *Potanthus* in the Garo Hills so far and did not dissect their genitalia, so we do not know their specific identities.

35. *Psolos fuligo subfasciatus* Moore, 1878 - Indian Dusky Partwing: Uncommon but widespread in NE India and elsewhere in Indo-China, which we recorded based on two specimens seen by KT from the Balpakram Plateau and Nokrek NP.

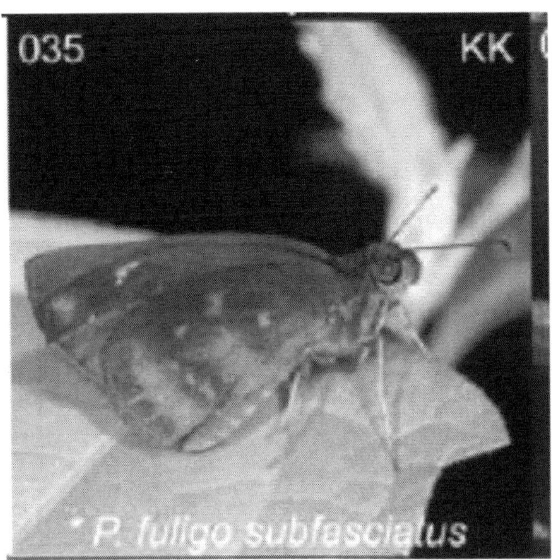

36. *Scobura isota* Swinhoe, 1893 - Khasi Forest Bob: We saw two specimens feeding from a bird dropping inside evergreen forest near Gongrot, and one inside Baghmara RF. The species is not uncommon in northeastern India, and has been reported from the Khasi Hills before.

37. *Sebastonyma dolopia* Hewitson, 1868 - Tufted Ace: Our three sightings were from Siju WS in May 2010. This is a rather uncommon species that has been reported from the Khasi Hills before.

38. *Spialia galba* Fabricius, 1793 - Indian Grizzled Skipper: KT recorded a single specimen on the Balpakram Plateau in November 2009 and SS recorded another specimen near Halwa Atong in May 2010. The species is locally frequent in the Khasi Hills.

39. *Suada swerga swerga* de Nicéville, 1883 - Indian Grass Bob: This was common in the Garo Hills in November 2009. KK recorded five fresh specimens, two of them mating, the rest basking among or near bamboo clumps along streams in semi-evergreen forests.

40. *Telicota bambusae bambusae* Moore, 1878 - Oriental Dark Palm-Dart: We usually saw males of this species mud-puddling or feeding from bird droppings in sunny patches along streams in evergreen forests.

41. *Zographetus ogygia ogygia* Hewitson, 1866 - Sumatran Purple-spotted Flitter: Our record was based on a single specimen that KK photographed in

the Matcha Nokpante Community Reserve outside Baghmara in November 2009. The species has apparently not been reported from the Garo-Khasi Hills complex before.

42. *Zographetus satwa* de Nicéville, 1884 - Purple and Gold Flitter: Our record was based on a single sighting from scrub forest near Botra village in Baghmara RF in December 2009. The species has been reported from the Khasi Hills before, and is not uncommon in northeastern India.

Family hesperiidae, subfamily Pyrginae

43. *Celaenorrhinus asmara consertus* de Nicéville, 1890 - Khasi White-banded Flat: GA, RL and SS photographed a single specimen in Baghmara RF

in May 2010. It has been reported from the Khasi Hills before, but it is an uncommon species in northeastern India.

44. *Gerosis bhagava bhagava* Moore, 1865 - Bengal Yellow-breasted Flat: In Nov. 2009, KK saw two males early in the morning on a sparsely vegetated ridge in the Matcha Nokpante Community Reserve outside the Baghmara Town. The pair was engaged in a fierce contest over closely placed vantage points, which were approximately 3m apart and 1m above the ground on small shrubs. The pair would take off every few minutes, chasing each other at amazingly high speeds, minutes on end, going on for over half an hour. The contestants gave up and departed only when sunlight began to brighten up the surroundings. The species has apparently not been reported from the Khasi Hills before, although it is not uncommon in northeastern India.

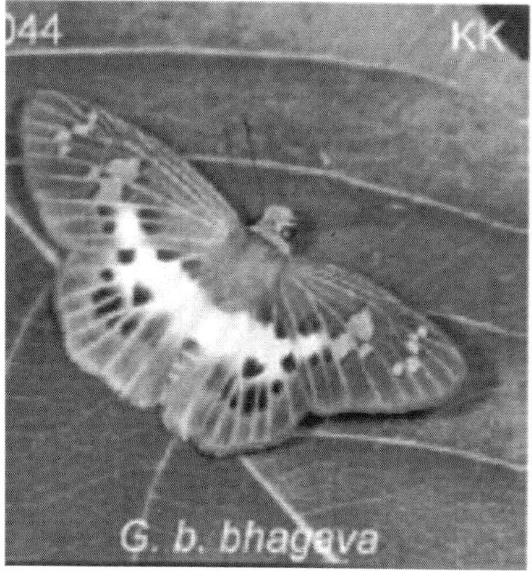

45. *Gerosis phisara phisara* Moore, 1884 - Khasi Dusky Yellow-breast Flat: This species is common in the Garo Hills in evergreen forests, where several individuals were seen mud-puddling. It is also common in the Khasi Hills.

46. *Gerosis sinica narada* Moore, 1884 - Sikkim White Yellow-breasted Flat: Our Garo Hills record is based on a single specimen seen mud-puddling at Taidang stream near Gongrot. It is common in the Khasi Hills.

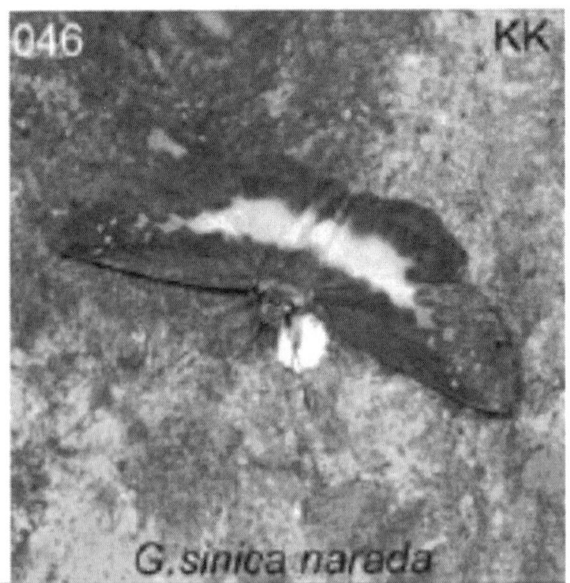

47. *Odontoptilum angulata angulata* Felder, 1862 - Oriental Chestnut Angle: The species was very common in the Garo Hills during the pre-monsoon season when we saw 23 specimens, but none during our November–December 2009

visits. Males were seen mud-puddling or chasing other butterflies from near their vantage points. The species has been reported from the Khasi Hills before.

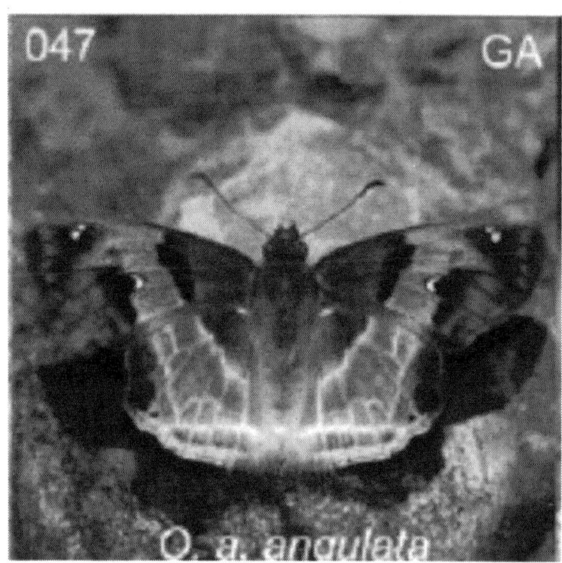

48. *Pseudocoladenia dan fabia* Evans, 1949 - Himalayan Fulvous Pied Flat: We found this to be common in both seasons in disturbed evergreen forests. It has been reported from the Khasi Hills before.

49. *Sarangesa dasahara dasahara* Moore, 1865 - Bengal Common Small Flat: This species frequents forest paths, stream-sides and forest edges in the Garo Hills. It is common in the Khasi Hills

50. *Tagiades gana athos* Plötz, 1884 - Bengal Suffused Snow Flat: It is common inside evergreen forests in the Garo Hills, typically along forest paths and streams. It is also reportedly common in the Khasi Hills.

51. *Tagiades japetus ravi* Moore, 1865 - Himalayan Common Snow Flat: This species is common in the Garo Hills, and shares its habitat and habits with the previous species. It is also common in the Khasi Hills.

52. *Tagiades litigiosa litigiosa* Möschler, 1878 - Sylhet Water Snow Flat: We had a single record of this species from Balpakram Plateau in November 2009. It is common in the Khasi Hills.

Family lycaenidae (Blues, hairstreaks, coppers, etc.)

53. *Curetis bulis bulis* Westwood, 1851: Himalayan Bright Sunbeam: We have so far seen only one specimen of this species near Gongrot in May 2008. It is common in the Khasi Hills, and elsewhere in northeastern India.

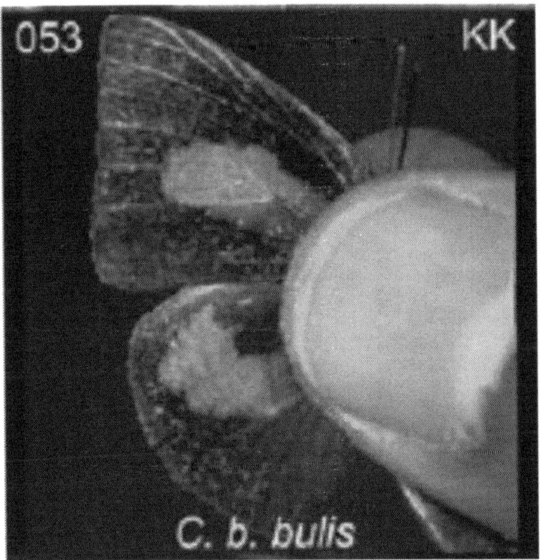

54. *Curetis dentata dentata* Moore, 1879 - Indian Toothed Sunbeam: Our Garo Hills record is based on six specimens that we photographed mud-puddling near Gongrot. The species is "not rare" in the Khasi Hills.

Family lycaenidae, subfamily lycaeninae

55. *Heliophorus epicles latilimbata* Eliot, 1963 - Sikkim Purple Sapphire: This species is common in the Garo Hills on forest paths and at forest edges. Both sexes were frequently encountered basking with their wings partially spread. It is also common in the Khasi Hills, in the eastern Himalaya and elsewhere in northeastern India.

56. *Heliophorus indicus* Fruhstorfer, 1908 – Indian Sapphire: Our Garo Hills record is based on a single male that KT photographed at Nokrek NP in Nov. 2009. The species is distributed widely but is not common anywhere. This is in contrast with the Khasi Hills records, where it is reportedly common. We

suspect that this must be true for *Heliophorus epicles latilimbata*, not *Heliophorus indicus* (Cantlie listed *Heliophorus epicles indicus* as common, but did not mention the commoner *Heliophorus epicles latilimbata*).

Family lycaenidae, subfamily Miletinae

57. *Allotinus drumila drumila* Moore, 1865 - Himalayan Crenulate Mottle: Our sole record for the Garo Hills was from May 2010 near Gongrot. This species is cryptically patterned on the underside and has a habit of perching motionless for hours in exposed spots, and is therefore easily overlooked. Several specimens have been collected in the past from around Cherrapunjee in the Khasi Hills. This species is legally protected in India under Schedule I of the Wildlife Act.

58. *Miletus chinensis assamensis* Doherty, 1891 - Assam Common Mottle: Two specimens of this widespread species were photographed in the Baghmara RF in May 2010.

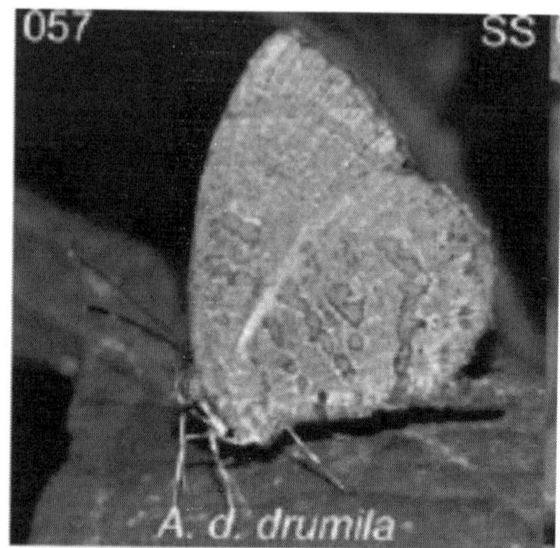

59. *Spalgis epeus epeus* Westwood, 1851 - Oriental Apefly: This tiny species is remarkable for being carnivorous in larval stages, feeding on mealy bugs rather than plants. Its wing coloration is dull and the adults are easily overlooked. We recorded two specimens flying together at Karwani stream in Baghmara RF in May 2010. It was reported to be "not rare but scarce" on the southern side of the Khasi Hills on border with Sylhet.

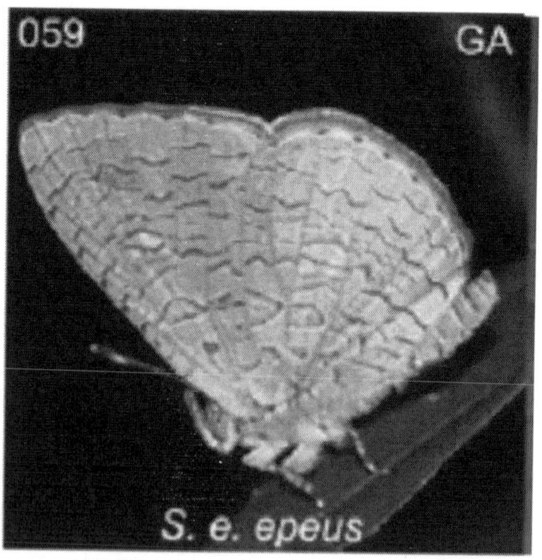

Family lycaenidae, subfamily Polyommatinae

60. *Acytolepis puspa gisca* Fruhstorfer, 1910 - Himalayan Common Hedge Blue: We have recorded several individuals in the Garo Hills, usually mud-puddling along evergreen forest streams. This is a widely distributed and very common species in India and elsewhere in the Oriental Region, including in the Khasi Hills.

61. *Anthene emolus emolus* Godart, 1823 - Bengal Common Ciliate Blue: This is abundant in the Garo Hills, where males were commonly seen either mud-puddling or basking along stream-sides, forest paths and around jhum areas. It is also common in the Khasi Hills.

62. *Anthene lycaenina lycambes* Hewitson, 1878 - Shan Pointed Ciliate Blue: We have recorded four specimens during our surveys so far. The species is somewhat similar to *Anthene emolus emolus*, with which it shares many habits and its habitat.

However, it is much less common compared to *A.e. emolus*, and is also reportedly uncommon in the Khasi Hills. This species is legally protected in India under Schedule II of the Wildlife Act.

63. *Caleta elna noliteia* Fruhstorfer, 1918 - Indo- Chinese Elbowed Pierrot: This species is fairly common in the Garo Hills, and most of our records were of mud-puddling males. It is frequently seen in the Khasi Hills.

64. *Castalius rosimon rosimon* Fabricius, 1775 - Continental Common Pierrot:

This species was common around human habitations and in secondary, fairly open forests. It is common in the Khasi Hills and elsewhere in the Oriental Region.

65. *Catochrysops panormus exiguus* Distant, 1886 - Malay Silver Forget-me-not: This was uncommon in secondary forests, where males were sometimes encountered mud-puddling. It is common in the Khasi Hills.

C. panormus exiguus

66. *Catochrysops strabo strabo* Fabricius, 1793 - Oriental Forget-me-not: This species was uncommon in deciduous forest patches and in secondary evergreen forests, and usually encountered mud-puddling. It is common in the Khasi Hills.

C. s. strabo

67. *Celastrina lavendularis limbata* Moore, 1879 - Eastern Plain Hedge Blue: It was found to be common in the Garo Hills in both the seasons, and especially frequently encountered along evergreen forest streams near Gongrot, where males were usually seen mud- puddling. It has been reported from the Khasi Hills.

C. lavendularis limbata

68. *Chilades lajus lajus* Stoll, 1780 – Indian Lime Blue: It was common around human habitations in the Garo Hills. Several individuals were seen courting and laying eggs around the Samrakshan Trust office in Baghmara. It is also common in the Khasi Hills.

69. *Discolampa ethion ethion* Westwood, 1851 - Oriental Banded Blue Pierrot: BS recorded a single specimen of this species at Taidang stream near Gongrot. This was known from upper and southern Assam but apparently had not been reported from the Khasi Hills proper.

70. *Euchrysops cnejus cnejus* Fabricius, 1798 - Oriental Gram Blue: This species occurs in open, drier habitats, and our only two records were from around human habitations or otherwise degraded habitats. It is also uncommon in the Khasi Hills. This species is legally protected in India under Schedule II of the Wildlife Act.

71. *Jamides alecto eurysaces* Fruhstorfer, 1915 - Himalayan Metallic Cerulean: This was common in the Garo Hills, especially during the pre-monsoon season in the evergreen forests around Gongrot. It is apparently not common in the Khasi Hills.

J. alecto eurysaces

72. *Jamides bochus bochus* Stoll, 1782 - Indian Dark Cerulean: We usually recorded this species in open areas at forest edges. It is common in the Khasi Hills, as elsewhere in India and the Oriental Region.

J. b. bochus

73. *Jamides celeno celeno* Cramer, 1775 - Oriental Common Cerulean: This species was very common around human habitations, along forest streams and at forest edges. The dry and wet season forms are strikingly different, and each was common in the respective season in the Garo Hills. Males were often found mud-puddling, and both sexes were seen feeding from flowers of small shrubs. It is apparently not very common in the Khasi Hills.

J. c. celeno

74. *Jamides elpis pseudelpis* Butler, 1879 - False Glistening Cerulean: Our only record for the Garo Hills was a single individual from Siju WS. It is "not rare" in the Khasi Hills.

75. *Jamides pura pura* Moore, 1886 - Continental White Cerulean: This species cannot be distinguished from *Jamides celeno* without viewing the upperside of the forewings. In *J. celeno* the black border increases in width at the forewing tip and may be fairly broad, whereas it is threadlike and uniformly narrow in *J. pura*. In the Garo Hills, *J. pura* tended to occur in slightly moister habitats but otherwise it was identical to *J. celeno* in its habits. The species is generally uncommon in northeastern India, but KK encountered it frequently around Gongrot in November 2009. It is apparently not uncommon even in the Khasi Hills.

76. *Lampides boeticus* Linnaeus, 1767 - Pea Blue: This species usually appears sporadically in all types of open habitats from human habitations to bare hilltops, and our Garo Hills record was based on a single sighting from the Nokrek NP. It is reportedly common in the Khasi Hills.

77. *Lestranicus transpectus* Moore, 1879 - White-banded Hedge Blue: We have so far seen only a single individual of this uncommon but widely distributed species. It should turn up in more numbers, especially in Nokrek NP and elsewhere at mid-elevations. It has apparently not been recorded in the Khasi Hills before.

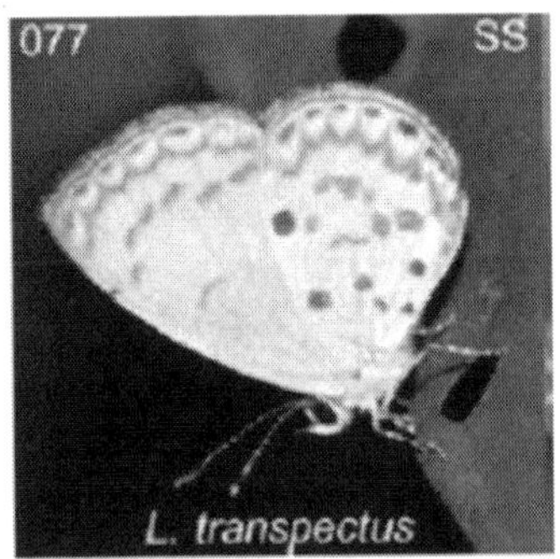

78. *Megisba malaya sikkima* Moore, 1884 - Variable Malayan: We found this species to be very common along forest paths, edges and streams. Males were often seen mud-puddling and both sexes were seen feeding from flowers. It is also common in the Khasi Hills.

79. *Nacaduba beroe gythion* Fruhstorfer, 1916 - Assam Opaque Six-Lineblue: This species is common in the Garo Hills, where males were frequently seen mud-puddling. It is also common in the Khasi Hills.

80. *Nacaduba hermus nabo* Fruhstorfer, 1916 - Assam Pale Four-Lineblue: This and the next species were much less common compared to *N. beroe*. All our sightings were of mud-puddling males. It is also rare in the Khasi Hills.

81. *Nacaduba kurava euplea* Fruhstorfer, 1916 - Sikkim Transparent Six-Lineblue: This was not very common in the Garo Hills, and most of our records were of mud-puddling males. It is reportedly common in the Khasi Hills.

82. *Neopithecops zalmora zalmora* Butler, 1870 - Myanmar Common Quaker: This species was common in May 2010 along forest streams, where males were usually seen mud-puddling, although there were also two records from December 2009. It is common in the Khasi Hills.

83. *Prosotas aluta coelestis* Wood-Mason & de Nicéville, 1886 - Assam Banded Lineblue: This species was fairly common in the Baghmara RF and

near Gongrot, perhaps due to the lower elevation in the Garo Hills, which it seems to prefer. However, it is reportedly uncommon to rare in the Khasi Hills. This subspecies is legally protected in India under Schedule II of the Wildlife Act.

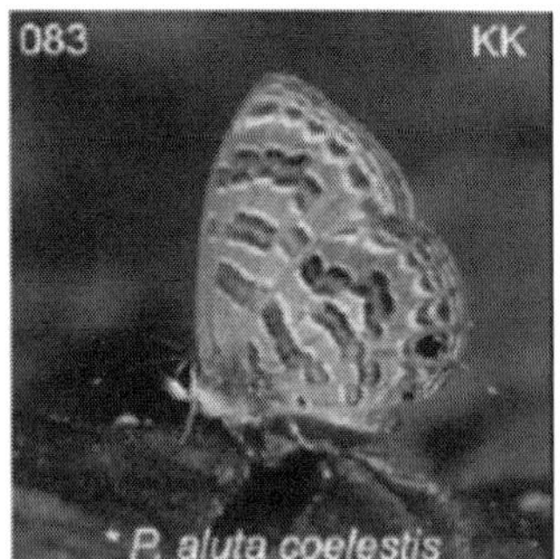

84. *Prosotas bhutea* de Nicéville, 1883 - Bhutia Lineblue: This is an uncommon species, recorded from two males seen along Taidang stream near Gongrot. In appearance and habits this species was very similar to *Prosotas nora*

85. *Prosotas dubiosa indica* Evans, 1925 - Indian Tailless Lineblue: This was very common in the Garo Hills, where we usually recorded males mud-puddling. It is also common in the Khasi Hills.

86. *Prosotas lutea sivoka* Evans, 1910 - Teesta Brown Lineblue: This was common in the Garo Hills, especially during the post-monsoon when males were usually seen mud-puddling. It has also been reported from the Khasi Hills.

87. *Prosotas nora ardates* Moore, 1874 - Indian Common Lineblue: This was common in the Garo Hills, especially during the post-monsoon. Males were sometimes seen mud-puddling, congregated in small groups. It is also very common in the Khasi Hills.

88. *Pseudozizeeria maha maha* Kollar, 1844 - Himalayan Pale Grass Blue: A small but conspicuous butterfly that was usually encountered around human habitations, flying low over herbs and small shrubs. It is also common in the Khasi Hills.

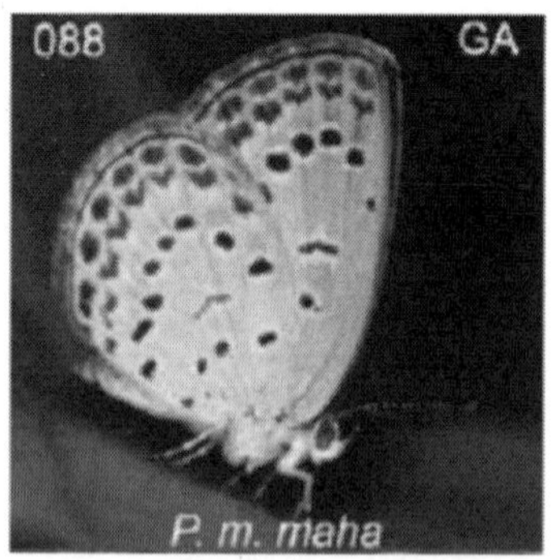

89. *Talicada nyseus khasiana* Swinhoe, 1893 - Khasi Red Pierrot: We only saw two individuals, although this is a highly localized species, which may sometimes be locally common. It is reportedly uncommon around Cherrapunjee and not recorded elsewhere in the Khasi Hills, although it should be present throughout the Garo-Khasi Hills complex.

90. *Tarucus ananda* de Nicéville, 1883 - Dark Pierrot: Our only two Garo Hills records were of mud-puddling males in evergreen forests near Gongrot and in the Baghmara RF. This species is apparently common in the Khasi Hills. It is legally protected in India under Schedule IV of the Wildlife Act.

91. *Tarucus venosus* Moore, 1882 - Veined Pierrot: Unlike the previous species, this is an inhabitant of slightly more open habitats. Our only record was by KT from the Balpakram Plateau.

92. *Udara dilecta dilecta* Moore, 1879 - Himalayan Pale Hedge Blue: Our only record was from Baghmara RF, although this species is apparently common in the Khasi Hills.

93. *Zizeeria karsandra* Moore, 1865 - Dark Grass Blue: We have recorded only one individual around Baghmara in May 2010, and we are surprised that we did not find this species to be common in the Garo Hills. It is widely distributed and common everywhere it occurs, usually in open areas and often around human habitations and cultivated fields. It seems that we have not sampled its habitat properly so far. However, this species is apparently uncommon even in the Khasi Hills.

94. *Zizina otis otis* Fabricius, 1787 - Oriental Lesser Grass Blue: This species occurs in the same habitats as the previous species. Our two records were from the neighborhood of Halwa Atong. It is common in the Khasi Hills.

95. *Zizula hylax hylax* Fabricius, 1775 - Indian Tiny Grass Blue: We recorded a single individual in dry scrub habitat near the Botra Village in December 2009. The species is common in the Khasi Hills.

Family lycaenidae, subfamily theclinae

96. *Amblypodia anita dina* Fruhstorfer, 1907 - Indian Purple Leaf Blue: Our single record was from Rani Miksuram Stream near Halwa Atong Village, by BS.

97. *Ancema blanka minturna* Fruhstorfer, 1912 - Blue-streaked Silver Royal: We came across three males of this species feeding from dead crabs (including on the ones set by us as baits) in Jidung Stream near Gongrot in November 2009. This subspecies is legally protected in India under Schedule II of the Wildlife Act.

98. *Ancema ctesia ctesia* Hewitson, 1865 - Himalayan Bi-spot Royal: SS had a single sighting of this distinctive species from Karwani in December 2009, which needs further confirmation since SS was unable to photograph the specimen. This species is rare in the Khasi Hills and elsewhere in northeastern India.

99. *Arhopala abseus indicus* Riley, 1923 - Indian Aberrant Oakblue: Our single record was based on an individual that was among the congregation of over a hundred *Arhopala* that KK and RL saw in deciduous forest along the Simsang trail in the Baghmara RF in May 2008. This species is rare throughout its range, but has been reported from the Khasi Hills before.

100. *Arhopala ammonides elira* Corbet, 1941 - Assam Little Cerulean Oakblue: Our only record was from the evergreen forest at Karwani, Baghmara RF, on 30 April 2010. Not much is known about this species from India, so this may be a useful spot record.

101. *Arhopala atrax* Hewitson, 1862 - Indian Oakblue: Our two records were from Simsang trail in December 2009 and Karwani stream in May 2010, both in Baghmara RF.

A. atrax

102. *Arhopala centaurus pirithous* Moore, 1883 - Bengal Centaur Oakblue: KK and RL witnessed a remarkable congregation of *Arhopala* from 1100 to 1230 hr on 2 May 2008 in a degraded deciduous forest patch along the Simsang trail in the Baghmara RF. The congregation was composed of over a hundred *Arhopala centaurus pirithous*, only 14 *Arhopala fulla ignara*, and a single *Arhopala abseus indicus*, all intermingled. All the specimens from this congregation that we captured for close inspection turned out to be males, except a female of *Arhopala fulla ignara*. The butterflies had congregated in a relatively dense patch of large shrubs and trees, no larger than approximately 20x20 m, which was more shaded than the surrounding deciduous forest. However, it was not particularly hot or dry that day, so we have no clue why butterflies had congregated there, especially when all the other butterfly species observed around that time in that area were actively mud-puddling, basking or engaged in other usual activities. Some males from the *Arhopala* congregation did bask with wings 3/4th spread, but none were feeding. Most were resting on the upper- or undersides of leaves, both in the open and in shade of the dense vegetation. They were wary, however, and difficult to catch. We hardly saw any *Arhopala* during the post-monsoon, so pre-monsoon seems to be the peak flight period for most *Arhopala* in this area. This species is reportedly "not rare" in the Khasi Hills.

A. centaurus pirithous

103. *Arhopala fulla ignara* Riley & Godfrey, 1921 - Thai Spotless Oakblue: See above under *Arhopala centaurus pirithous* for majority of our sightings of this species. This subspecies is legally protected in India under Schedule II of the Wildlife Act.

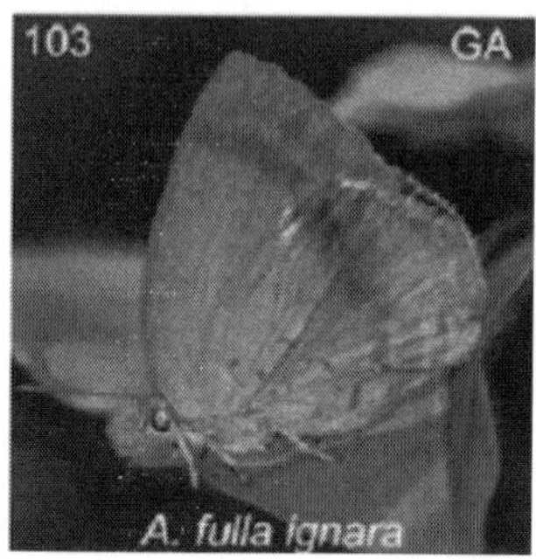

A. fulla ignara

104. *Arhopala perimuta perimuta* Moore, 1857 - Sylhet Yellowdisc Tailless Oakblue: We sighted six individuals at Panda, Gongrot and Balpakram Plateau in November and December 2009, with no pre- monsoon sightings, implying a post-monsoon flight period. The species has previously been reported as "not rare" in the Khasi Hills.

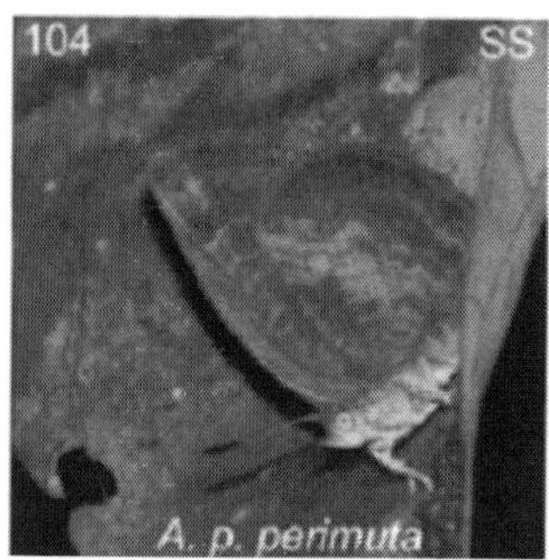

A. p. perimuta

105. *Bindahara phocides phocides* Fabricius, 1793 - Thai Plane: Our two records were from Karwani in December 2009 and Bhawanipur in May 2010, both in Baghmara RF. The species is rare in northeastern India in general, and apparently known only from four specimens in the Khasi Hills. This species is legally protected in India under Schedule II of the Wildlife Act.

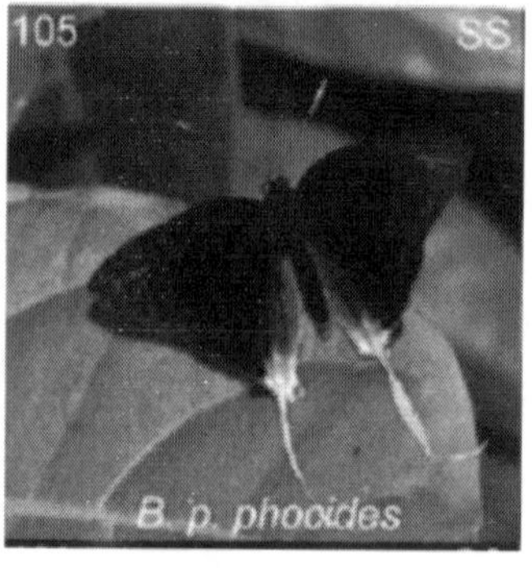

B. p. phocides

106. *Cheritra freja evansi* Cowan, 1965 - Khasi Common Imperial: We have a few records from evergreen forests from Gongrot and Baghmara RF. It is reportedly common in the Khasi Hills.

107. *Chliaria othona othona* Hewitson, 1865 - Oriental Orchid Tit: Our four records were of males mud-puddling along evergreen forest streams at Gongrot, Karwani Stream and Siju WS. It is "not rare but scarce" in the Khasi Hills. This species is legally protected in India under Schedule I of the Wildlife Act.

108. *Creon cleobis cleobis* Godart, 1824 - Bengal Broad-tail Royal: SS recorded a single individual by the roadside near Dabit Chirring in May 2010. The species is not rare in the Khasi Hills.

109. *Dacalana penicilligera* de Nicéville, 1890 - Double-tufted Royal: SS photographed a single individual along the Karwani stream in May 2010.

110. *Flos apidanus ahamus* Doherty, 1891 - Assam Plain Plushblue: This record is based on just the right hindwing that KK found in a dry streambed at Siju WLS on 22 November 2009. This subspecies is legally protected in India under Schedule II of the Wildlife Act.

111. *Horaga onyx onyx* Moore, 1857 - Variable Common Onyx: We have so far seen two individuals in the Garo Hills, one just outside the Baghmara town in an orchard in May 2008, and one in November 2009 at Gongrot. It is rare and known apparently only from three specimens in the Khasi Hills. This species is legally protected in India under Schedule II of the Wildlife Act.

112. *Hypolycaena erylus himavantus* Fruhstorfer, 1912 - Sikkim Common Tit: This was one of the most abundant lycaenids in our sampling. This was seen in both seasons but evidently much more abundant during the post-monsoon, especially near Gongrot and at Karwani Stream. This is also very common in the Khasi Hills.

113. *Loxura atymnus continentalis* Fruhstorfer, 1912 - Continental Yamfly: We saw this commonly basking along forest paths and edges. It is "not rare" in the Khasi Hills.

114. Lycaenid sp.: SS managed to take just one picture of this Thecline at Karwani Stream in December 2009 but we are clueless about what this species may be, or even to which genus it may belong. We have been unable to find a match in any of the books that we have referred to or to any of the specimens available in the Museum of Comparative Zoology at Harvard University. Please contact us if you have any comments or suggestions.

115. *Rapala dieneces dieneces* Hewitson, 1878 - Malay Scarlet Flash: We recorded one individual each at Me Cheng Chirang near Halwa Atong and Balpakram Plateau, both at forest edges. The species is rare in the Khasi Hills.

116. *Rapala manea schistacea* Moore, 1879 - Bengal Slate Flash: We saw three individuals during the pre-monsoon at Baghmara RF and near Gongrot. It is "not rare" in the Khasi Hills.

117. *Rapala pheretima petosiris* Hewitson, 1863 - Indian Copper Flash: This was fairly common in the Garo Hills, where several individuals were seen feeding from flowers of a shrub at the edge of the forest in Baghmara RF. It is "not rare" in the Khasi Hills.

118. *Rapala varuna orseis* Hewitson, 1863 - Sumatran Indigo Flash: We recorded two individuals at Siju WS and Panda Chirring in December 2009. It is "not rare but scarce" in the Khasi Hills. This subspecies is legally protected in India under Schedule II of the Wildlife Act.

119. *Remelana jangala ravata* Moore, 1865 - Northern Chocolate Royal: Our three records were of males mud-puddling in evergreen forest streams. The species has been reported from the Khasi Hills.

120. *Spindasis lohita himalayanus* Moore, 1884 - Himalayan Long-banded Silverline: We saw three males mud-puddling along evergreen forest streams at Gongrot, and a female basking at the edge of the forest in Siju WS. It is "not rare" in the Khasi Hills. This subspecies is legally protected in India under Schedule II of the Wildlife Act.

121. *Spindasis syama peguanus* Moore, 1884 - Pegu Club Silverline: We found it commonly in open spaces at forest edges and in open, dry streambeds, especially around Gongrot. It is "not rare but scarce" in the Khasi Hills.

122. *Surendra quercetorum quercetorum* Moore, 1857 - Himalayan Common Acacia Blue: In our sampling in the Garo Hills, females were much more common than males, which also seems to be true of other populations of this species elsewhere in India. They were mostly seen in open forests and at forest edges or along forest paths where their larval host plants, straggling *Acacia*, were growing. The species is common in the Khasi Hills.

123. *Ticherra acte acte* Moore, 1857 - Himalayan Blue Imperial: Our record of this uncommon species was based on a single specimen seen by SS at Taidang stream near Gongrot. It has been reported from the Khasi Hills.

124. *Yasoda tripunctata tripunctata* Hewitson, 1863 - Sylhet Branded Yamfly: We recorded two individuals, both during the pre-monsoon in evergreen forests at Gongrot and Karwani stream. This rare species was apparently known from the Khasi Hills only from two specimens. This species is legally protected in India under Schedule II of the Wildlife Act.

125. *Zeltus amasa amasa* Hewitson, 1865 - Indian Fluffy Tit: This was one of the most common Lycaenids in our sampling. Dozens of individuals were seen mud-puddling in evergreen forests along Taidang and Jidung streams near Gongrot. It is reportedly "not rare" in the Khasi Hills.

Family Nymphalidae subfamily apaturinae

126. *Apatura ambica ambica* Kollar, 1844 - East Himalayan Purple Emperor: Both our records were of mud-puddling males at Taidang stream near Gongrot. It is common in the Khasi Hills.

127. *Euripus nyctelius nyctelius* Doubleday, 1845 - Sylhet Courtesan: We saw seven males in both seasons, they were perched on vantage points at the tips of branches of shrubs and small trees, from where they chased other butterflies passing nearby. Females of this species are rarely encountered and we did not see any in the Garo Hills. The species is "not uncommon" in the Khasi Hills.

128. *Herona marathus marathus* Doubleday, 1848 - Assam Pasha: This is a very rare species. Our only record was from Nokrek NP by KT. It has apparently not been reported from the Khasi Hills before.

129. *Rohana parisatis parisatis* Westwood, 1850 - Assam Black Prince: We saw three males mud- puddling in evergreen forest streams. It is common in the Khasi Hills.

Family nymphalidae, subfamily Biblidinae

130. *Ariadne ariadne pallidior* Fruhstorfer, 1899 - Large Angled Castor: This species was common in secondary forest, at forest edges and around human habitations in the Garo Hills, especially during the pre- monsoon. It is "not rare" in the Khasi Hills.

131. *Ariadne merione tapestrina* Moore, 1884 - Intricate Common Castor: This species was much less numerous compared to the last species but occurred in the same habitats. It has been reported from the Khasi Hills before.

Family nymphalidae, subfamily charaxinae

132. *Charaxes arja arja* Felder & Felder, 1866 - Bengal Pallid Nawab: This species was recorded in both seasons but was more common during the post-monsoon. It flew in the same places as *Charaxes athamas athamas*: along forest paths, streams and edges. The two species were often seen on the same mud-puddling spots or on baits of rotting crabs around Gongrot. It is presumably common in the Khasi Hills.

133. *Charaxes athamas athamas* Drury, 1770 - Oriental Common Nawab: This species was very commonly seen mud-puddling along forest streams at Taidang, Jidung and Rani Miksuram streams near Gongrot. It was also a major draw on baits of rotting crabs, where nearly a dozen individuals could be attracted at any time of the day. The species is also common in the Khasi Hills.

134. *Charaxes bernardus hierax* Felder & Felder, 1866 - Variable Tawny Rajah: This species was very common in forested areas of the Garo Hills. Males were sometimes seen mud-puddling, but most of the individuals that we recorded were drawn to baits of rotting crabs that we had set out to attract nymphalids. Males of this species are polymorphic in northeastern India, and the individuals that we caught for closer inspection turned out to belong to the following three forms: *hierax*, *pleistoanax* and *hipponax*. The species is reportedly "not rare" in the Khasi Hills.

135. *Charaxes eudamippus eudamippus* Doubleday, 1843 - Himalayan Great Nawab: Our Garo Hills record is based on a single specimen that BS photographed feeding on a rotting crab at Taidang Stream near Gongrot in May 2008. This species may be more common than our sampling suggests so far; we have probably missed its peak flight season in this area, which may be March and April. It is apparently common in the Khasi Hills, and has recently been reported further southwest in Similipal National Park.

136. *Charaxes kahruba* Moore, 1895 - Variegated Rajah: We have so far recorded four specimens in the Garo Hills, most of them around Gongrot, and all of them mud-puddling or feeding on rotting crabs. The species is reportedly very rare in the Khasi Hills, and apparently only two specimens were collected by Parson & Cantlie.

137. *Charaxes marmax marmax* Westwood, 1847 - Sylhet Yellow Rajah: KK recorded three individuals at Taidang and Rani Miksuram streams near Gongrot and Halwa Atong in November 2009. This species is generally rare throughout its range, it is "scarce" in the Khasi Hills, and is legally protected in India under Schedule II of the Wildlife Act.

138. *Charaxes moori sandakanus* Fruhstorfer, 1895 - Margined Malayan Nawab: We have two records of this very rare species, one by BS at Anakpatal, Rongai Stream, Hangsapal, in June 2008, and the other by GA and RL at Taidang stream near Gongrot in May 2010. These sightings are important because this subspecies is legally protected in India under Schedule I of the Wildlife Act.

139. *Charaxes solon sulphureus* Rothschild, 1900 - Sulphur Black Rajah: SS recorded two individuals in Siju WS in May 2010. It is reportedly very rare in the Khasi Hills. This subspecies is legally protected in India under Schedule II of the Wildlife Act.

140. *Prothoe franck regalis* Butler, 1885 - Regal Blue Begum: KK saw two specimens of this species in Jidung and Taidang streams in November 2009. The first one, seen on 18 November, was in dense evergreen forest on the community land that belongs to Gongrot Village. The second one, seen on 19 November, flew from the national park side of Taidang Stream into the evergreen forest on the Gongrot community land across the stream, but it could not be photographed. Our records of this subspecies from the Garo Hills are important for two reasons: (a) this is a significant range extension, and (b) it is legally protected in India under Schedule I of the Wildlife Act. This subspecies has so far been reported only from Upper Assam, Manipur, and N. Myanmar. To our knowledge, there are no previous records either from the Khasi Hills or elsewhere west of Manipur. So this is a significant range extension of this very rare and presumably highly restricted subspecies by nearly 300km, over several mountain ranges. This record nearly doubles its global longitudinal range.

Family nymphalidae, subfamily cyrestinae

141. *Chersonesia risa risa* Doubleday, 1848 – Oriental Common Maplet: This species occurred in both seasons, and it was commonly seen mud- puddling. It is reportedly uncommon in the Khasi Hills.

142. *Cyrestis cocles cocles* Fabricius, 1787 - Thai Marbled Map Butterfly: We found the species to be common in the Gongrot area, although we also saw many individuals in Baghmara RF and Siju WS. Sometimes three or four specimens were seen mud- puddling together along forest streams, occasionally in company of other butterflies, but usually on their own. This species is generally scarce all over northeastern India but it can be locally common. Parsons & Cantlie obtained "many specimens ... from Cherrapunjee professional collectors", but they never saw it in the Khasi Hills. This species is legally protected in India under Schedule II of the Wildlife Act.

143. *Cyrestis thyodamas thyodamas* Boisduval, 1836 - Oriental Map Butterfly: This species was common in the Gongrot area, especially during the pre-monsoon, when it was often seen mud-puddling. It is common in the Khasi Hills.

Family nymphalidae, subfamily danainae

144. *Danaus chrysippus chrysippus* Linnaeus, 1758 - Oriental Plain Tiger: We usually came across this species during the pre-monsoon when males were seen feeding from *Heliotropium* flowers that bloomed in abundance in fallow paddyfields. They were often in company of other danaines in these *Heliotropium* patches. The species is common in the Khasi Hills.

145. *Danaus genutia genutia* Cramer 1779 - Oriental Striped Tiger: Similar to *Danaus chrysippus*, males were commonly encountered feeding from *Heliotropium* flowers in fallow fields and other open areas. The species is also common in the Khasi Hills, although it was earlier reported as *Danais plexippus,* the name that applies to the North American Monarch Butterfly, not to the Indian *Danaus genutia*.

146. *Euploea algea deione* Westwood, 1848 - Bengal Long-branded Blue Crow: All our sightings were of males feeding from *Heliotropium* flowers in the Halwa Atong and Siju areas, or in an all-male, multi-species congregation of *Euploea* that was seen in a patch of open forest near Gongrot. Our records have so far been exclusively from the pre-monsoon. The species is common in the Khasi Hills.

147. *Euploea core core* Cramer, 1780 - Indian Common Crow: We found this species to be common during the pre-monsoon in *Heliotropium* patches in fallow paddyfields of Halwa Atong, usually with males of other *Euploea*. It was also commonly seen in the all-male, multi-species *Euploea* congregation in a patch of open forest near Gongrot. It is common in the Khasi Hills, and was previously reported as *Euploea core vermiculata* Butler, 1866, which is a synonym of the nominotypical subspecies.

148. *Euploea doubledayi doubledayi* Felder & Felder, 1865 - Sylhet Striped Black Crow: Another common species in the Gongrot area, details of our sightings were the same as for *Euploea core core*. The species is reportedly uncommon to rare in the Khasi Hills.

149. *Euploea klugii klugii* Moore, 1858 - Blue King Crow: Our only record for the Garo Hills was from a single male that KK caught, photographed and released in a fallow paddyfield near Halwa Atong in November 2009. It is reportedly rare in the Khasi Hills.

150. *Euploea midamus rogenhoferi* Felder & Felder, 1865 - Assam Blue-spotted Crow: Our record for the Garo Hills is based on a single male that KK caught, photographed and released in the all-male, multi-species *Euploea* congregation in a patch of open forest near Gongrot in May 2009. It was said to be common in the Khasi Hills but Parsons & Cantlie could collect only one specimen, which they reported as *rogenhoferi*'s synonym, *splendens* Butler, 1866. This subspecies is legally protected in India under Schedule II of the Wildlife Act.

151. *Euploea mulciber mulciber* Cramer, 1777 - Bengal Striped Blue Crow: This was the most abundant *Euploea* in the Garo Hills, as is the case elsewhere in northeastern India. It was common in the *Heliotropium* patches of Halwa Atong and in the multi-species *Euploea* congregation near Gongrot, mentioned under *Euploea core core*. Males were also commonly seen mud-puddling and patrolling the streams and paddyfields at Baghmara RF. KT recorded 50 specimens in Nokrek NP. The species is also very common in the Khasi Hills. Surprisingly, this very common subspecies is legally protected in India under Schedule IV of the Wildlife Act.

152. *Euploea radamanthus radamanthus* Fabricius, 1793 - Oriental Magpie Crow: This was another common *Euploea* in the Garo Hills, details of our sightings for this were the same as for *Euploea core core*. It is also common in the Khasi Hills, although previously reported as *Euploea diocletiana diocletiana,* which is a synonym of *radamanthus* commonly used in older literature on Indian butterflies.

153. *Euploea sylvester hopei* Felder & Felder, 1865 - Cachar Double-branded Blue Crow: The details of our sightings of this species were the same as for *Euploea algea deione*. It is reportedly common in the Khasi Hills, although the subspecies was listed under *Euploea harrisi,* which itself is now recognized as a subspecies of *Euploea sylvester* Fabricius, 1793.

154. *Parantica aglea melanoides* Moore, 1883 - Himalayan Glassy Tiger: One of the commonest danaines in our sampling, it was especially numerous at Nokrek NP in November 2009. It is also common in the Khasi Hills.

155. *Parantica melaneus plataniston* Fruhstorfer, 1910 - Himalayan Chocolate Tiger: This species was less common than the last species, but it was also commoner at Nokrek NP in November 2009. It is also common in the Khasi Hills.

156. *Parantica sita sita* Kollar, 1844 - Kashmir Chestnut Tiger: KT found this species to be common at mid-elevations at Nokrek NP in November 2009, although SS also had a single, unconfirmed record from Taidang stream near Gongrot in May 2010. This species is common in the Khasi Hills above 1,000m, where it was previously reported by its synonym, *Danais tytia.*

157. *Tirumala limniace exoticus Gmeìlin,* 1790 - Oriental Blue Tiger: A few males of this species were seen feeding from *Heliotropium* flowers at Halwa Atong, and in forest openings. It is common in the Khasi Hills.

158. *Tirumala septentrionis septentrionis* Butler, 1874 - Oriental Dark Blue Tiger: The details of sightings of this species were the same as the previous species. It is also common in the Khasi Hills.

Family nymphalidae, subfamily heliconiinae

159. *Argynnis hyperbius hyperbius* Linnaeus, 1763 - Chinese Tropical Fritillary: This species is common in the Khasi Hills but must be relatively uncommon at lower elevations of Baghmara and Gongrot. We have recorded only two specimens so far, one from Gongrot and one from Nokrek NP, both in November 2009.

160. *Cethosia biblis tisamena* Fruhstorfer, 1912 - Himalayan Red Lacewing: This species occurs at slightly higher elevations compared to the next species, and we saw it almost exclusively at Nokrek NP, where it was very common. It is also very common at higher elevations in the Khasi Hills.

161. *Cethosia cyane cyane* Drury, 1770 - Bengal Leopard Lacewing: We had numerous sightings of this common species, mostly from Gongrot and Baghmara RF during the pre-monsoon. It is also common in the Khasi Hills.

162. *Cirrochroa aoris aoris* Doubleday, 1847 - Himalayan Large Yeoman: A common species that was frequently seen mud-puddling along evergreen forest streams at Gongrot. It is common in the Khasi Hills.

163. *Cirrochroa tyche mithila* Moore, 1872 - Bengal Common Yeoman: A very common species, which we recorded along evergreen forest streams and paths, mainly at Gongrot. Males were often seen mud- puddling and they were also attracted to our baits of rotting crabs. Interestingly, it is reportedly uncommon in the Khasi Hills.

164. *Phalanta alcippe alcippoides* Moore, 1900 - Himalayan Small Leopard: We recorded a total of six individuals of this species from Jidung Stream near Gongrot and from Karwani Stream in Baghmara RF. It is generally an uncommon species in northeastern India, and has been reported as such in the Khasi Hills.

165. *Phalanta phalantha phalantha* Drury, 1773 - Oriental Common Leopard: We usually recorded this common species in drier, more open forests compared to the previous species, and also in abandoned jhum fields and sometimes around forest villages. It is also common in the Khasi Hills.

166. *Vagrans egista sinha* Kollar, 1844 - Himalayan Vagrant: This species commonly occurs at slightly higher elevations, so it is not surprising that we have recorded only a single specimen in Baghmara RF so far. It is "not rare" in the Khasi Hills.

167. *Vindula erota erota* Fabricius, 1793 - Thai Cruiser: This species can be locally common in evergreen forests but we have so far seen only four specimens mud-puddling along Taidang and Jidung streams near Gongrot. It is common in the Khasi Hills.

Family nymphalidae, subfamily limenitidinae

168. *Athyma asura asura* Moore, 1857 - Himalayan Studded Sergeant: We recorded one or two specimens of this species, always mud-puddling, on most of our field trips, although it was never common. This species is uncommon to rare throughout northeastern India, and it is reportedly rare in the Khasi Hills. It is legally protected in India under Schedule II of the Wildlife Act.

169. *Athyma cama cama* Moore, 1857 - Himalayan Orange Staff Sergeant: We have recorded only two specimens of this species in the Garo Hills. It is "not rare" in the Khasi Hills.

170. *Athyma inara inara* Doubleday, 1850 - Himalayan Color Sergeant: This species can be seasonally common in evergreen forests of northeastern India. We found it to be common in the Gongrot- Baghmara area, especially during the pre-monsoon when both sexes were frequently encountered along evergreen forest streams. Like other *Athyma*, males were usually encountered either mud-puddling or feeding from scats and rotting crabs. It is also common in the Khasi Hills.

171. *Athyma kanwa phorkys* Fruhstorfer, 1912 - Northern Dot-dash Sergeant: Our Garo Hills record was based on a single specimen that SS photographed at Karwani in December 2009. This is a rare species in northeastern India, and it has apparently been recorded from the Khasi Hills based on a single male collected in November from Dauki.

172. *Athyma perius perius* Linnaeus, 1758 - Oriental Common Sergeant: We usually recorded males of this common species on hill-tops or ridges, patrolling areas nearby their vantage points on large rocks. It is reportedly common in the Khasi Hills.

173. *Athyma pravara acutipennis* Fruhstorfer, 1906 - Assam Unbroken Sergeant: We recorded three males mud-puddling along evergreen forest streams near Gongrot during the post-monsoon. It is uncommon in the Khasi Hills. The subspecies is legally protected in India under Schedule II of the Wildlife Act.

174. *Athyma ranga ranga* Moore, 1857 - Himalayan Blackvein Sergeant: This species was not uncommon along evergreen forest streams near Gongrot. It is uncommon in the Khasi Hills, and is legally protected in India under Schedule II of the Wildlife Act.

175. *Athyma selenophora bahula* Moore, 1858 - Sylhet Staff Sergeant: We recorded two individuals at Gongrot and Karwani Stream. It is common in the Khasi Hills.

176. *Athyma zeroca zeroca* Moore, 1872 - Khasi Small Staff Sergeant: An uncommon species in northeastern India, of which we have so far recorded only a single specimen at Gongrot. It is reportedly common in the Khasi Hills.

177. *Bassarona teuta teuta* Doubleday, 1848 - Sylhet Banded Marquis: Our Garo Hills record was based on a single specimen that KT photographed on the Balpakram Plateau in November 2009. It is recorded as "fairly frequent" in the Khasi Hills. The species is legally protected in India under Schedule II of the Wildlife Act.

178. *Bhagadatta austenia austenia* Moore, 1872 - Khasi Grey Commodore: Both our records were from evergreen forests along Taidang Stream near Gongrot during the pre-monsoon. It is uncommon in the Khasi Hills. The species is legally protected in India under Schedule II of the Wildlife Act.

179. *Euthalia aconthea garuda* Moore, 1857 - Northern Baron: So far we have recorded only two individuals—both females—of this species in the Garo Hills. It is "rather uncommon" in the Khasi Hills. Interestingly, this rather widespread and locally common subspecies is legally protected in India under Schedule II of the Wildlife Act.

180. *Euthalia anosia anosia* Moore, 1857 - Assam Grey Baron: SS recorded a single specimen of this rare species at Taidang stream near Gongrot in December 2009. This appears to be only the second record of this species from the Garo-Khasi Hills complex: the only previous record was midway between Guwahati and Shillong, at 600m, in April 1933.

181. *Euthalia lubentina lubentina* Cramer, 1777 - Chinese Gaudy Baron: We had three sporadic records, all females, from the Gongrot-Baghmara areas in both seasons. It is "not rare" in the Khasi Hills. This species is legally protected in India under Schedule IV of the Wildlife Act.

182. *Euthalia monina kesava* Moore, 1859 - Assam Powdered Baron: We recorded several individuals, mostly males, especially during the post-monsoon at Karwani Stream. It is uncommon in the Khasi Hills.

183. *Euthalia phemius phemius* Doubleday, 1848 - Sylhet White-edged Blue Baron: We have so far recorded two females in the Garo Hills in November 2009, one each from Me Cheng Chirang near Gongrot and Balpakram Plateau. The species is fairly common in the Khasi Hills.

184. *Euthalia telchinia* Ménétriés, 1857 - Blue Baron: KT recorded a single female from Balpakram Plateau in November 2009. It is "rather rare" in the Khasi Hills. It is legally protected in India under Schedule I of the Wildlife Act..

185. *Lebadea martha martha* Fabricius, 1787 - Thai Knight: This was very common in both seasons throughout the forested areas of the Balpakram-Siju-Baghmara landscape. We frequently encountered males patrolling

neighborhoods of their vantage points on tall herbs and shrubs along forest paths and streams. The species is common in the Khasi Hills.

186. *Lexias cyanipardus cyanipardus* Butler, 1868 - Sylhet Great Archduke: We had a single sighting of this large and spectacularly colorful species from an evergreen forest fragment among abandoned jhum fields near Gongrot, and four from the Balpakram Plateau, all from November 2009. All the specimens were males. The species is common in the Khasi Hills. It is legally protected in India under Schedule II of the Wildlife Act.

187. *Lexias dirtea khasiana* Swinhoe, 1893 - Khasi Dark Archduke: This species was slightly commoner than the previous species, and most of our sightings were from the pre-monsoon rather than the post-monsoon. It is common in the Khasi Hills. This subspecies is legally protected in India under Schedule II of the Wildlife Act.

188. *Moduza procris procris* Cramer, 1777 - Oriental Commander: This species was fairly common along forest streams near Gongrot, especially during the post-monsoon. It is also common in the Khasi Hills.

189. *Neptis hylas varmona* Moore, 1872 - Indian Common Sailer: We found this species to be especially common in November 2009 in abandoned jhum fields, on paths and in other disturbed areas around Gongrot. It is also common in the Khasi Hills.

190. *Neptis nata/soma* group - Sailer spp.: We must have seen several species from this group but we did not dissect male genitalia, without which species identification was impossible.

191. *Neptis sappho astola* Moore, 1872 - Himalayan Common Glider: Our record is based on a single specimen that was entangled in a spider web near Gongrot Village. The species is common at higher elevation in the Khasi Hills.

192. *Pantoporia hordonia hordonia* Stoll, 1790 - Oriental Common Lascar: This species was common especially during the post-monsoon along forest streams and paths near Gongrot. It is common in the Khasi Hills.

193. *Pantoporia paraka paraka* Butler, 1877 - Oriental Perak Lascar: KK saw one specimen each in evergreen forests along Jidung Stream near Gongrot and Karwani stream in Baghmara RF, both in November 2009. SS saw the third specimen at Karwani Stream in December 2009. The distribution of this species was given in older books as "Assam", which presumably meant the Naga-Manipur Hills and Cachar. Previous spot records are from Sylhet and Cachar in northeastern Bangladesh and southern Assam, 100–200 km east of Balpakram. There are no previous records from the Khasi Hills and our sightings seem to be the first records of the species this far west in northeastern India.

194. *Parthenos sylvia gambrisius* Fabricius, 1787 - Bengal Clipper: This species was common along evergreen forest streams both at Gongrot and

Baghmara RF, especially during the pre-monsoon. It is also common in the Khasi Hills. This subspecies is legally protected in India under Schedule II of the Wildlife Act.

195. *Phaedyma columella ophiana* Moore, 1872 - Sikkim Short-banded Sailer: We have only two records from the Gongrot area. The species is also reportedly rare in the Khasi Hills.

196. *Sumalia daraxa daraxa* Doubleday, 1848 - Sylhet Green Commodore: This species is very common in the Khasi Hills, and should be found in the Nokrek area.

197. *Tanaecia jahnu jahnu* Moore, 1857 - Darjeeling Plain Earl: Our record is based on two males that KK saw at Me Cheng Chirang near Halwa Atong Village in November 2009. The species is "rather rare" in the Khasi Hills.

198. *Tanaecia julii appiades* Ménétriés, 1857 - Changeable Common Earl: This species is generally common in northeastern India, and is reportedly common in the Khasi Hills, so we are surprised that we have so far seen only one male in the Garo Hills.

199. *Tanaecia lepidea lepidea* Butler, 1868 - Himalayan Grey Count: We found this species to be very common in the Garo Hills in both seasons. Males, which made up the majority of our sightings, were usually seen along paths in evergreen forests. The species is also common in the Khasi Hills. This species is legally protected in India under Schedule II of the Wildlife Act.

Family nymphalidae, subfamily nymphalinae

200. *Doleschallia bisaltide indica* Moore, 1899 - Himalayan Autumn Leaf: This record is based on a single sighting in Baghmara RF in May 2010. The species is uncommon in the Khasi Hills.

201. *Hypolimnas bolina jacintha* Drury, 1773 - Oriental Great Eggfly: Both sexes of this female- limited Batesian mimic were very common in the Garo Hills, especially in open forests during the pre- monsoon in Gongrot and Baghmara areas. It is also common in the Khasi Hills.

202. *Hypolimnas misippus* Linnaeus, 1764 - Danaid Eggfly: We recorded several individuals during the pre-monsoon, and this species will prove to be as common in the Garo and Khasi hills as elsewhere in the Oriental and African Regions. Interestingly, no specimens of this species seem to have been reported from the Garo-Khasi Hills before. Surprisingly, this common and widespread species is legally protected in India under Schedule I of the Wildlife Act.

203. *Junonia almana almana* Linnaeus, 1758 - Oriental Peacock Pansy: We found this species to be extremely abundant in fallow paddyfields and along edges of evergreen forests. In fact, it was the most numerous species in our quantitative sampling. This was especially true during the pre-monsoon, although it was present in both seasons. It is also common in the Khasi Hills.

204. *Junonia atlites atlites* Linnaeus, 1763 - Oriental Grey Pansy: This was also a common *Junonia* in our sampling and we found it co-occurring with the previous species especially in fallow paddyfields.

205. *Junonia hierta hierta* Fabricius, 1798 - Oriental Yellow Pansy: This species was less numerous than the previous two *Junonia*, but still very common in and around agricultural fields and other highly disturbed areas. It is common in the Khasi Hills.

206. *Junonia iphita iphita* Cramer, 1779 - Oriental Chocolate Pansy: This species was very common in all kinds of forested areas, especially along forest edges and in natural openings, but also around human habitations. It is common in the Khasi Hills.

207. *Junonia lemonias lemonias* Linnaeus, 1758 - Chinese Lemon Pansy: This was the second-most numerous *Junonia* in our sampling. We found it to be common along major roads and around human habitations, including in agricultural fields. It is very common in the Khasi Hills.

208. *Junonia orithya ocyale* Hübner, 1816 - Dark Blue Pansy: Our record is based on a single specimen that KT photographed on the Balpakram Plateau in November 2009. It is very common in the Khasi Hills.

209. *Kallima inachus inachus* Boisduval, 1836 - Himalayan Orange Oakleaf: We found this species to be common along forest streams and inside evergreen forests, especially near Gongrot during the pre-monsoon. It is also common in the Khasi Hills.

210. *Kaniska canace canace* Linnaeus, 1763 - Chinese Blue Admiral: KT recorded three individuals from Balpakram Plateau in November 2009. The species is common in the Khasi Hills.

211. *Symbrenthia hypselis cotanda* Moore, 1874 - Himalayan Spotted Jester: We have a single record from Nokrek NP. It is uncommon in the Khasi Hills.

212. *Symbrenthia lilaea khasiana* Moore, 1874 – Khasi Common Jester: We commonly encountered this species along evergreen forest streams near Gongrot, either mud-puddling or basking in occasional sunny spots along paths under the canopy. It is also common in the Khasi Hills.

213. *Symbrenthia silana* de Nicéville, 1885 - Scarce Jester: KT recorded a single specimen of this rare species mud-puddling in Nokrek NP. This sighting has previously been reported in literature. Since then, we have come across another old record of this species from this area, a specimen collected 60km away from Shillong, halfway between Guwahati and Shillong, in April 1933. This species is legally protected in India under Schedule I of the Wildlife Act.

214. *Vanessa cardui cardui* Linnaeus, 1758 - Painted Lady: This almost globally distributed species occurs seasonally in many parts of India, and it can be locally common in the right season. We have so far recorded only a single specimen feeding from *Heliotropium* flowers in a fallow paddyfield in Halwa Atong. The species is reportedly very common in the Khasi Hills.

215. *Vanessa indica indica* Herbst, 1794 - Himalayan Red Admiral: BS recorded several specimens from Rongreng Stream, Hangsapal. It is common in the Khasi Hills.

Family nymphalidae, subfamily Pseudergolinae

216. *Dichorragia nesimachus nesimachus* Doyère, 1840 - Himalayan Constable: Our record is based on a single, slightly worn specimen that KK and RL photographed on the sandy bed of Karwani Stream in Baghmara RF in May 2008. It was feeding from a small carnivore scat along with *Charaxes bernardus hierax* on a rainy day. It is reportedly uncommon in the Khasi Hills.

217. *Stibochiona nicea nicea* Gray, 1846 - Himalayan Popinjay: We recorded 14 specimens of this species in both seasons, although majority of sightings were from November 2009 from evergreen forest streams near Gongrot and bamboo patches in mixed semi-evergreen forests around Halwa Atong. The species is also common in the Khasi Hills.

Family nymphalidae, subfamily satyrinae

218. *Amathuxidia amythaon amythaon* Doubleday, 1847 - Sylhet Koh-i-Noor: This species is generally rare at its northwestern range margin in northeastern India. Our Garo Hills record is based on four specimens. The first one was a piece of right forewing that KK discovered in a dry streambed in evergreen forest at Siju WS in November 2009. The remaining three specimens were seen by SS, RL and GA at Karwani in Baghmara RF in May 2010. Only four specimens seem to have been reported from the Khasi Hills before. This species is legally protected in India under Schedule II of the Wildlife Act.

219. *Discophora sondaica zal* Westwood, 1851 - Indian Common Duffer: This is a fairly common species despite its crepuscular habits. We recorded five specimens, all males, in both seasons, and mostly inside evergreen forests at Gongrot. It has been reported from the Khasi Hills before but seldom seen there.

220. *Elymnias hypermnestra undularis* Drury, 1773 - Wavy Common Palmfly: A common species, males of which were especially numerous along Karwani Stream in Baghmara RF in May 2008. It is also common in the Khasi Hills. Females of this sex-limited Batesian mimic are superb mimics of *Danaus genutia* in flight.

221. *Elymnias malelas malelas* Hewitson, 1863 - Bengal Spotted Palmfly: Our record is based on a single specimen that BS photographed at Karwani, Baghmara RF. The species is common in the Khasi Hills.

222. *Elymnias nesaea timandra* Wallace, 1869 - Sylhet Tiger Palmfly: KT recorded one individual on Balpakram Plateau in November 2009, and SS recorded one from Siju WS in December 2009 and another outside Samrakshan's office in Baghmara town in May 2010. The species is not rare in the Khasi Hills.

223. *Elymnias peali* Wood-Mason, 1883 - Brahmaputra Palmfly: This is a slight range extension of the species, and the first record from the Garo Hills. It has previously been reported from upper Assam, and from Namdapha NP in eastern Arunachal Pradesh. The nearest record to the Garo Hills was that of D. Sanders, who took a specimen approximately 60km from Shillong on Guwahati Road in April 1933. That was approximately 100–150 km from the present locality in Balpakram NP. As far as we know, the previous westernmost record north of the Brahmaputra River was that of KK, who recorded a male in February 2001 from near Seijusa in Pakke NP in western Arunachal Pradesh. Our following records from the Garo Hills delineate the westernmost range of this species south of the Brahmaputra River. KK photographed a male from Me Cheng Chirang near Halwa Atong on 20 November 2009. SS recorded one individual from Panda Chirring in December 2009 and another at Karwani Stream in May 2010. The species is generally considered very rare throughout its range, so these three sightings and the range extensions are particularly important. The species is endemic to lowland evergreen forests in and near the Brahmaputra River basin, and it is legally protected in India under Schedule I of the Wildlife Act.

224. *Ethope himachala* Moore, 1857 - Dusky Diadem: This was the third-commonest satyrine and among the most numerous species in our sampling. We saw a total of 61 individuals, nearly 2/3rd of them in November 2009 from Taidang, Jidung and Me Cheng Chirang in the Gongrot-Halwa Atong landscape and from the Karwani Stream in the Baghmara RF. Most of the individuals, of both sexes, were seen basking and chasing each other among somewhat dense vegetation along evergreen forest streams. The species is “not rare” in the Khasi Hills.

225. *Faunis canens arcesilas* Stichel, 1933 - Thai Common Faun: A fairly common species that we encountered in dense undergrowth along paths and small streams under closed canopy of evergreen forests near Gongrot. It is “not rare” in the Khasi Hills.

226. *Faunis eumeus assama* Westwood, 1858 - Assam Large Faun: We recorded this species based on two specimens that GA, RL and SS saw in Taidang Stream near Gongrot in May 2010. It is “not rare” in the Khasi Hills.

227. *Lethe chandica flanona* Fruhstorfer, 1911 - Assam Angled Red Forester: We had two records of this species: a male from Rani Miksuram Stream near Halwa Atong in November 2009, and another male from Nokrek NP in November 2009. It is “scarce” in the Khasi Hills.

228. *Lethe confusa gambara* Fruhstorfer, 1911 - Assam Banded Treebrown: We found this species to be common, although all our sightings were from November 2009 from the Gongrot-Halwa Atong area, and from Siju WS. It is also common in the Khasi Hills.

229. *Lethe europa niladana* Fruhstorfer, 1911 - Himalayan Bamboo Treebrown: Not uncommon, and our sightings were from both seasons and from multiple localities. It is reportedly uncommon in the Khasi Hills.

230. *Lethe mekara zuchara* Fruhstorfer, 1911 - Assam Common Red Forester: A common species that we usually found mud-puddling or visiting animal droppings along various evergreen forest streams near Gongrot and Halwa Atong villages and in Baghmara RF. It was recorded in both seasons. It is "not rare" in the Khasi Hills.

231. *Lethe rohria rohria* Fabricius, 1787 - Himalayan Common Treebrown: Our record is based on a single sighting by KT at Nokrek NP in November 2009. The species is common in the Khasi Hills.

232. *Lethe verma sintica* Fruhstorfer, 1911 - East Himalayan Straight-banded Treebrown: We recorded two specimens from Gongrot in May 2010, and one specimen from Nokrek NP in November 2009.

233. *Lethe vindhya vindhya* Felder, 1859 - Assam Black Forester: Our record of this uncommon species is based on two sightings: one by SS at Panda Chirring in December 2009, and the other by BS near Gongrot. The species is uncommon in the Khasi Hills.

234. *Melanitis leda leda* Linnaeus, 1758 - Oriental Common Evening Brown: This was the second- commonest species in our sampling, with a total of 157 individuals. Specimens of both sexes were commonly encountered in both seasons in evergreen and semi-evergreen forest undergrowth in all localities surveyed. The wet season form was more prevalent in May while the dry season form was more prevalent in November. It is also very common in the Khasi Hills.

235. *Melanitis phedima bela* Moore, 1857 - Bengal Dark Evening Brown: This was overall a common species, but much less common compared to the last species, with which it shared its habitat. It is uncommon in the Khasi Hills.

236. *Melanitis zitenius zitenius* Herbst, 1796 - Himalayan Great Evening Brown: This was the least common *Melanitis* in our sampling. We had three sightings, one near Gongrot and two from Siju WS. The species is not rare in the Khasi Hills. It is legally protected in India under Schedule II of the Wildlife Act.

237. *Mycalesis anaxias aemate* Fruhstorfer, 1911 - Indo-Chinese White-bar Bushbrown: This was commonly seen in dense evergreen forests at Gongrot, Baghmara RF and Siju WS. It was recorded in both seasons. It is uncommon in the Khasi Hills. This subspecies is legally protected in India under Schedule II of the Wildlife Act.

238. *Mycalesis francisca sanatana* Moore, 1857 - Himalayan Lilacine Bushbrown: KT photographed a single specimen at Nokrek NP in November 2009. This species is uncommon at mid-elevations in the Khasi Hills.

239. *Mycalesis intermedia* Moore, 1892 - Intermediate Bushbrown: We had three records of this species based on two individuals seen at Taidang/ Jidung streams near Gongrot and one individual seen at Siju WS, all in November 2009. This species has previously been listed from the Khasi Hills by its synonym, *Mycalesis khasia* Evans, 1912, but without any details. *Calysisme intermedia* Moore, 1892 is the oldest available name for this taxon.

240. *Mycalesis malsarida* Butler, 1868 - Plain Bushbrown: KK saw seven specimens in Nov. 2009 in evergreen forests along the Taidang and Jidung streams near Gongrot and at Karwani Stream in Baghmara RF. It is reportedly "not rare" and "seems scarce" from the Khasi Hills. This species is protected in India under Schedule II of the Wildlife Act.

241. *Mycalesis mineus mineus* Linnaeus, 1758 - Chinese Dark-branded Bushbrown: This is usually common in most forested regions of India, but we have so far recorded only three individuals from disturbed forests around Gongrot. It is very common in the Khasi Hills.

242. *Mycalesis perseus blasius* Fabricius, 1798 - Himalayan Common Bushbrown: This was uncommon in evergreen, semi-evergreen and moist deciduous forests at Me Cheng Chirang near Halwa Atong, in Baghmara RF and Siju WS. The species was initially overlooked and therefore not reported from the Khasi Hills, but a few specimens were subsequently collected.

243. *Mycalesis* spp. - Bushbrowns: Several *Mycalesis* females with distinct phenotypes were seen at all the localities in both seasons but were not collected, and therefore cannot be identified by any means now.

244. *Mycalesis visala visala* Moore, 1857 - Indian Long-branded Bushbrown: We have so far found a single specimen of this species in November 2009 near Gongrot. This is surprising because the species is usually common, and is often among the most abundant *Mycalesis* in places such as Manas and Namdapha national parks in northeastern India. This was reported as "probably uncommon" in the Khasi Hills based on only a few specimens collected.

245. *Orsotriaena medus medus* Fabricius, 1775 - Oriental Medus Brown: This was common in open and/or disturbed forest areas such as around large streams and at forest edges. Both the wet and dry season forms, which differ greatly, were seen in both seasons. It is also very common in the Khasi Hills.

246. *Thaumantis diores diores* Doubleday, 1845 - Assam Jungleglory: This was fairly common, but most of our records were from November 2009, so the post-monsoon seems to be its peak flight period in the Garo Hills. It is also common in the Khasi Hills.

247. *Ypthima baldus satpura* Evans, 1923 - Satpuda Common Five-ring: This was among the most abundant species in the Garo Hills, where we recorded it in both seasons at all the localities surveyed. It was especially common in disturbed habitats such as forest edges, agricultural fields, orchards, and around human habitations. It is also very common in the Khasi Hills. There should be

some *Ypthima affectata* Elwes & Edwards, 1893, the Eastern Five-ring, among our presumed *Ypthima baldus satpura*. However, we did not collect and dissect any *Ypthima*, so we are not sure about all the other species of *Ypthima* that we may have encountered. Cantlie had found *Ypthima affectata* to be "A speciality of the Khasi Hills, discoverable among one's supposed *baldus*." However, *Ypthima baldus satpura* usually outnumbers any other *Ypthima* in this area, just as in forested regions elsewhere in India.

248. *Ypthima huebneri* Kirby, 1871 - Common Four-ring: Another common *Ypthima* species, which was found in more or less the same habitats as the previous species but was comparatively less frequently seen. It is also common in the Khasi Hills.

Family Papilionidae subfamily Papilioninae

249. *Atrophaneura varuna astorion* Westwood, 1842 - Sylhet Common Batwing: This was common in both seasons along wide, open forest streams, where males were encountered mud-puddling. Females were usually seen in denser forests and along evergreen forest paths, where their larval host plant was found. It has previously been recorded as common in the Khasi Hills.

250. *Byasa* sp. - Windmill sp.: KT recorded a single individual of *Byasa*, which could not be photographed and hence we have not been able to identify it to species level. The image included in image 15 for *Byasa* is merely for illustration purposes, it does not represent a specimen seen in the Garo Hills. This image was taken in Ngengpui WS in Mizoram, and is of *Byasa dasarada dasarada* Moore, 1857, the East Himalayan Great Windmill.

251. *Graphium agamemnon agamemnon* Linnaeus, 1758 - Oriental Tailed Jay: This was fairly common in evergreen forests, and was recorded in both seasons. It is uncommon in the Khasi Hills.

252. *Graphium agetes agetes* Westwood, 1843 - Assam Four-bar Swordtail: Our five records were from May 2010 from Karwani, Bhawanipur and Panda Chirring in the Baghmara RF. It is "not rare" at Dauki near the Khasi Hills.

253. *Graphium antiphates pompilius* Fabricius, 1787 - Indo-Chinese Five-bar Swordtail: This species was commonly seen mud-puddling along evergreen forest streams in all the localities surveyed around Baghmara. Most of the sightings were from May 2010, but two were from November 2009. It is also common in the Khasi Hills.

254. *Graphium aristeus anticrates* Doubleday, 1846 - Assam Chain Swordtail: SS recorded one specimen from Siju WS in May 2010, mud-puddling in the company of other *Graphium* and *Papilio*. The Khasi Hills records were based on two specimens taken in April. This subspecies is legally protected in India under Schedule II of the Wildlife Act.

255. *Graphium cloanthus cloanthus* Westwood, 1841 - Himalayan Glassy Bluebottle: Our single record was from Balpakram Plateau in November 2009.

The picture included in image 15 is not from the Garo Hills, it is actually from the Namdapha NP, used here as a reference for this species. The specimen seen on Balpakram Plateau could not be photographed, so this record needs further confirmation. The species is common at higher elevations in the Khasi Hills.

256. *Graphium doson axion* Felder & Felder, 1864 - Himalayan Common Jay: A very common species in evergreen and semi-evergreen forests, whose main flight period in the Garo Hills seems to be the pre-monsoon, to which all our sightings have been restricted so far. It is also common in the Khasi Hills.

257. *Graphium eurypylus cheronus* Fruhstorfer, 1903 - Indo-Chinese Great Jay: This was much less common than the previous species, and was seen mostly in denser evergreen forests. It is uncommon in the Khasi Hills.

258. *Graphium macareus lioneli* Fruhstorfer, 1902 - Khasi Lesser Zebra: Our record is based on a single specimen that SS photographed at Panda Chirring in May 2010. Males of this species are reportedly common in the Khasi Hills.

259. *Graphium sarpedon sarpedon* Linnaeus, 1758 - Oriental Common Bluebottle: This was a very common species, especially during the pre-monsoon. Males were usually encountered mud-puddling along evergreen forest streams near Gongrot and Baghmara RF.

260. *Graphium xenocles xenocles* Doubleday, 1842 - Sylhet Great Zebra: This is very similar to *Graphium macareus lioneli*, with which it shared the habitat but was encountered more frequently in the Garo Hills. It is uncommon in the Khasi Hills.

261. *Lamproptera curius curius* Fabricius, 1787 - Thai White Dragontail: This was a common species, whose males were usually seen mud-puddling along streams in evergreen forests in the Gongrot area. It is also common in the Khasi Hills.

262. *Losaria coon cacharensis* Butler, 1885 - Cachar Common Clubtail: This is generally a very rare species in northeastern India but reportedly common in the Garo Hills and in Cachar, SE Assam. Our Garo Hills record was based on a single specimen seen by KK on 2 May 2008 at Rani Miksuram Stream near Halwa Atong. It could not be photographed, however, so we have used, as a reference, picture in image 16 of an old specimen from the Khasi Hills.

263. *Meandrusa payeni evan* Doubleday, 1845 - Sikkim Yellow Gorgon: Our Garo Hills record is based on a single female photographed by BS at Halwa Ambeng near Gongrot in September 2008. The species is apparently common in the Khasi Hills.

264. *Pachliopta aristolochiae aristolochiae* Fabricius, 1775 - Indian Common Rose: This species was, along with *Papilio polytes romulus*, the most abundant papilionid in our sampling. We recorded 69 individuals in both seasons, although the species was much commoner during the summer. All our sightings were from rural areas and all types of open forest throughout the Garo Hills.

265. *Papilio alcmenor alcmenor* Felder & Felder, 1864 - Khasi Redbreast: Our record is based on KT's single sighting from Balpakram Plateau in November 2009. The species is reportedly very common in the Khasi Hills.

266. *Papilio bianor gladiator* Fruhstorfer, 1902 - Indo-Chinese Common Peacock: Our record is based on a single sighting from Dabit, Baghmara RF, in May 2010. Another subspecies, *Papilio bianor ganesa* Doubleday, 1842, has previously been reported from the Khasi Hills as common. However, *ganesa* occurs north of the Brahmaputra River, and *gladiator* is the correct subspecific name for the populations south of the Brahmaputra River.

267. *Papilio castor castor* Westwood, 1842 - Khasi Common Raven: This was a common species, whose males and females were seen along evergreen forest streams near Gongrot, and in Baghmara RF and Siju WS. However, all our sightings have so far been only from the pre-monsoon, which seems to be its peak flight period in the Garo Hills. The species is reportedly uncommon in the Khasi Hills, especially the female.

268. *Papilio clytia clytia* Linnaeus, 1758 - Oriental Common Mime: This species was common along evergreen forest streams. This is a Batesian mimic with two forms in northeastern India: form *dissimils* mimics *Tirumala*, and form *clytia* mimics brown-and-white *Euploea*. We recorded both the forms in the Garo Hills, although form *dissimilis* was more frequently seen. The species has previously been reported to be common in the Khasi Hills and at Dauki.

269. *Papilio demoleus demoleus* Linnaeus, 1758 - Northern Lime Butterfly: We encountered this species commonly around human habitations, in orchards, and in open forests. It is very common in the Khasi Hills.

270. *Papilio helenus helenus* Linnaeus, 1758 - Oriental Red Helen: This was a very common species, whose males were often seen mud-puddling with other *Papilio* along evergreen forest streams. It is also common in the Khasi Hills.

271. *Papilio memnon agenor* Linnaeus, 1758 - Continental Great Mormon: We recorded 29 individuals, most of them male, during both the seasons. All the males that we saw belonged to the form *agenor*, and all the females belonged to the form *alcanor*, which mimics *Pachliopta aristolochiae*. The species has previously been reported as common in the Garo and Khasi Hills.

272. *Papilio nephelus chaon* Westwood, 1845 - Assam Yellow Helen: In the Garo Hills, habits and habitat of this species were similar to *Papilio helenus helenus*, and it was equally abundant. It is also common in the Khasi Hills.

273. *Papilio paradoxa telearchus* Hewitson, 1852 - Khasi Great Blue Mime: Our record is based on a single individual that SS photographed near Karwani in Baghmara RF in May 2010. The species is reportedly rare in the Khasi Hills. This subspecies is legally protected in India under Schedule II of the Wildlife Act.

274. *Papilio paris paris* Linnaeus, 1758 - Chinese Paris Peacock: We recorded 12 individuals, one each at Baghmara RF and Balpakram NP during the summer, and 10 at Nokrek NP during post-monsoon. Males were seen mud-puddling and patrolling along forest streams and ridges. The species is widely distributed in the Oriental Region, common throughout the Himalaya and northeastern India, and has been reported from the Khasi Hills before.

275. *Papilio polytes romulus* Cramer, 1775 - Indian Common Mormon: We recorded 69 individuals in both seasons, making this one of the commonest species in our sampling, although it was much more abundant during the summer. All our records were from rural/agricultural landscapes as well as inside all forest types at all the sampled localities. The female form *stichius* (also known as the form *polytes* outside taxonomic literature) is an excellent mimic of *Pachliopta aristolochiae*, and all the females that we came across in the Garo Hills belonged to this form. We have not yet come across the non-mimetic female form *cyrus* or the *Pachliopta hector*-mimicking female form *romulus* in the Garo Hills. The species is also very common in the Khasi Hills.

276. *Papilio protenor euprotenor* Fruhstorfer, 1908 - East Himalayan Spangle: KK and RL recorded only two male specimens in May 2008.

277. *Troides helena cerberus* Felder & Felder, 1865 - Khasi Common Birdwing: We recorded 13 specimens of both sexes from Baghmara RF and Balpakram NPin both seasons. These were usually seen flying in the canopy along forest streams and edges. The species is reportedly common in the Khasi Hills.

Family Pieridae subfamily coliadinae

278. *Catopsilia pomona pomona* Fabricius, 1775 - Oriental Common Emigrant: This was very common near human habitations and in deciduous forest patches, and most of our sightings were from the pre-monsoon. It is also common in the Khasi Hills.

279. *Catopsilia pyranthe pyranthe* Linnaeus, 1758 - Oriental Mottled Emigrant: SS recorded this from Karwani in December 2009. It is reportedly common in the Khasi Hills.

280. *Dercas verhuelli doubledayi* Moore, 1905 - Indo-Chinese Tailed Sulphur: This was common during the pre-monsoon, and all our sightings were from Taidang-Jidung streams near Gongrot. The species is reportedly rare in the Khasi Hills.

281. *Eurema andersonii jordani* Corbet & Pendlebury, 1932 - Sikkim One-spot Grass Yellow: This species seems generally uncommon, but KK saw a large group mud-puddling in Taidang Stream, and then two at Siju WS, all in November 2009. The species was not reported from the Khasi Hills.

282. *Eurema blanda silhetana* Wallace, 1867 - Sylhet Three-spot Grass Yellow: This was very common along evergreen forest streams and paths near

Gongrot and in Baghmara RF, especially during the post-monsoon. Males were often seen mud-puddling in small groups. The species is also common in the Khasi Hills.

283. *Eurema hecabe hecabe* Linnaeus, 1758 - Oriental Common Grass Yellow: This species was also very common, usually in the same habitats as the previous species, although it also occurred in more open forests and around human habitations. It was more common during the pre-monsoon. The species is also common in the Khasi Hills.

284. *Gandaca harina assamica* Moore, 1906 - Assam Tree Yellow: This was common along evergreen forest streams near Gongrot, where males were usually encountered mud-puddling. It is also common in the Khasi Hills.

Family Pieridae, subfamily Pierinae

285. *Appias albina darada* Felder & Felder, 1865 - Indian Common Albatross: Our record is based on four males seen mud-puddling and feeding from flowers along evergreen forest streams and forest edges near Gongrot and on the Balpakram Plateau. It is reportedly rare in the Khasi Hills. This subspecies is legally protected in India under Schedule II of the Wildlife Act.

286. *Appias indra indra* Moore, 1857 - Himalayan Plain Puffin: We found this species to be common in mud-puddling assemblages in Taidang and Jidung streams near Gongrot. All our sightings have only been from the pre-monsoon so far, which seems to be its peak flight period at this elevation in the Garo Hills. It is uncommon in the Khasi Hills.

287. *Appias lalage lalage* Doubleday, 1842 - Himalayan Spot Puffin: This species prefers mid- elevation evergreen forests throughout its range, and our only sighting was from mid-elevations at Nokrek NP. It is common in the mid-elevation forests in the Khasi Hills.

288. *Appias lyncida eleonora* Boisduval, 1836 - Indo-Chinese Chocolate Albatross: This species was abundant in both seasons, frequenting deciduous forest patches and large openings in evergreen and semi-evergreen forests in all the localities surveyed by us. It is common in the Khasi Hills, although previously reported by its synonym, *Appias lyncida hippoides* Moore, 1881.

289. *Appias olferna* Swinhoe, 1890 - Eastern Striped Albatross: Our record is based on four individuals seen in Baghmara RF in May 2010. It is uncommon in the Khasi Hills. The taxon was previously treated as a subspecies of *Appias libythea* Fabricius, 1775, the Western Striped Albatross.

290. *Cepora nadina nadina* Lucas, 1852 - Khasi Lesser Gull: This was common in the Gongrot and Baghmara RF areas, especially in evergreen forests during the pre-monsoon. It is also common in the Khasi Hills.

291. *Cepora nerissa nerissa* Fabricius, 1775 - Chinese Common Gull: This species occurred in much more open and drier habitats than the previous

species, and we have only two sightings from the pre-monsoon, one each from Baghmara and Gongrot areas. It is common in the Khasi Hills.

292. *Delias agostina agostina* Hewitson, 1852 – Sikkim Yellow Jezebel: SS recorded a single individual at Baghmara in December 2009. The species is uncommon in the Khasi Hills.

293. *Delias belladonna lugens* Jordan, 1925 - Lushai Hill Jezebel: SS saw two specimens in flight, one in December 2009 at Simsang trail and the other near Gongrot in May 2010. However, these could not be photographed, and our sightings need further confirmation. It is uncommon in the Khasi Hills.

294. *Delias descombesi descombesi* Boisduval, 1836 - Vietnamese Red-spot Jezebel: This species was common during the post-monsoon, when we saw five specimens at the edges of abandoned agricultural fields overgrown with flowering herbs and shrubs along the Rongrok Stream near Halwa Atong. Then several more were seen in Nokrek NP and on Balpakram Plateau. The species is common in the Khasi Hills.

295. *Delias hyparete indica* Wallace, 1867 - Himalayan Painted Jezebel: We had few, sporadic sightings of this uncommon species at Gongrot and in Baghmara RF in November and December 2009. It is also uncommon in the Khasi Hills.

296. *Delias pasithoe pasithoe* Linnaeus, 1767 - Chinese Red-base Jezebel: This species was common, especially during the post-monsoon, in nearly all the localities surveyed by us. Most of the sightings were of mud-puddling males in evergreen forests. It is also common in the Khasi Hills.

297. *Hebomoia glaucippe glaucippe* Linnaeus, 1758 - Oriental Great Orange-tip: This species was common in mud-puddling assemblages in open forests, especially during the pre-monsoon. It is common in the Khasi Hills.

298. *Ixias pyrene familiaris* Butler, 1874 - East Himalayan Yellow Orange-tip: This was common especially in open forests and along the edges of evergreen forests near Gongrot. It is common in the Khasi Hills.

299. *Leptosia nina nina* Fabricius, 1793 - Oriental Psyche: We had relatively few sightings near human habitations and in orchards of this otherwise common and widely distributed species. It is very common in the Khasi Hills.

300. *Pareronia hippia* Fabricius, 1787 - Indian Wanderer: SS had a single record of this species from Karwani in December 2009. This species has not been recorded from the Khasi Hills before, and our sighting needs confirmation since this specimen could not be photographed. Another closely related species, *Pareronia avatar* Moore, 1857, the Pale Wanderer, has previously been reported from the Garo Hills, but not from the Khasi Hills.

301. *Pieris canidia indica* Evans, 1926 - Indian Cabbage White: SS recorded a single individual near Gongrot in May 2010. The species is common in the Khasi Hills.

Family riodinidae subfamily nemeobiinae

302. *Abisara bifasciata suffusa* Moore, 1882 - Indian Double-banded Judy: KT recorded a single individual from Balpakram Plateau in November 2009. This species does not seem to have been recorded from the Khasi Hills before.

303. *Abisara fylla* Westwood, 1851 - Dark Judy: This was common in Nokrek NP. It is also common in the Khasi Hills.

304. *Abisara neophron neophron* Hewitson, 1861 - Khasi Tailed Judy: This is included based on two individuals, one recorded by BS in the Gongrot area and another from Nokrek NP by KT. The species is reportedly uncommon in the Khasi Hills.

305. *Dodona longicaudata* de Nicéville, 1881 - Long-tailed Punch: KT photographed a single individual on Balpakram Plateau in November 2009. This is the westernmost record for this species, perhaps as much as 200km west of its previously known range in the Khasi Hills. This species is generally very rare throughout its range, and reportedly so in the Khasi Hills from where it is known only from three or four specimens. *Dodona longicaudata* has traditionally been listed as a subspecies of *Dodona deodata* Hewitson, 1876. However *longicaudata* has recently been reinstated as a distinct species based on the following diagnosis: "Both sexes have a narrower white band on both wings, reaching 3mm on the male forewing and more infusion of the white areas with darker scaling.... Male genitalia differs from *D. deodata* in the longer tegument, wider valvae, and a longer and squared saccus.". Both *deodata* and *longicaudata* were given as subspecies of *Dodona henrici*, a Chinese species, by Evans.

306. *Zemeros flegyas flegyas* Cramer, 1780 - Himalayan Punchinello: This species was very common in evergreen forests along Taidang and Jidung streams near Gongrot, and near Halwa Atong. Most of our sightings were from November 2009. A female was seen laying eggs on *Maesa* sp., and many caterpillars were subsequently discovered on this plant. The species is also common in the Khasi Hills.

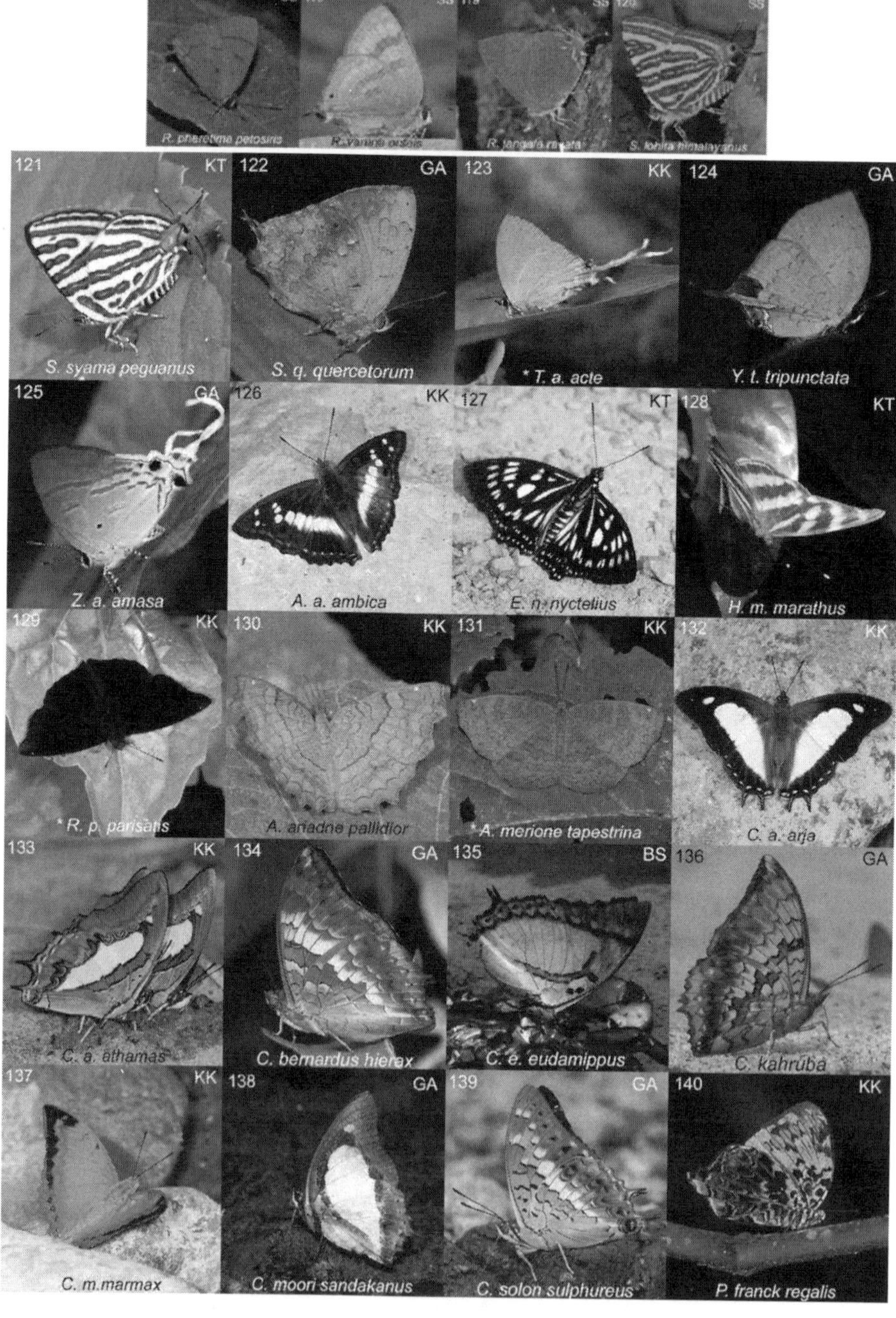
113 KT
L. a. continentalis
114 SS
Lycaenid sp.
115 SS
R. d. dieneces
116 SS
117 SS
R. pheretima petosiris
118 SS
119 SS
120 SS
S. lohita himalayanus
121 KT
S. syama peguanus
122 GA
S. q. quercetorum
123 KK
* T. a. acte
124 GA
Y. t. tripunctata
125 GA
Z. a. amasa
126 KK
A. a. ambica
127 KT
E. n. nyctelius
128 KT
H. m. marathus
129 KK
* R. p. parisatis
130 KK
A. ariadne pallidior
131 KK
* A. merione tapestrina
132 KK
C. a. arja
133 KK
C. a. athamas
134 GA
C. bernardus hierax
135 BS
C. e. eudamippus
136 GA
C. kahruba
137 KK
C. m.marmax
138 GA
C. moori sandakanus
139 GA
C. solon sulphureus
140 KK
P. franck regalis

141 KK C. r. risa
142 GA C. c. cocles
143 SS C. t. thyodamas
144 GA D. c. chrysippus
145 GA D. g. genutia
146 KK E. algea delone
147 SS E. c. core
148 GA E. d. doubledayi
149 KK E. k. klugii
150 KK E. midamus rogenhoferi
151 SS E. m. mulciber
152 GA
153 SS E. sylvester hopei
154 GA P. aglea melanoides
155 KT P. melaneus plataniston
156 KT P. s. sita
157 RL T. limniace exoticus
158 RL T. s. septentrionis
159 KT
160 KT C. biblis tisamena
161 SS C. c. cyane
162 KT
163 GA C. tyche mithila
164 GA P. alcippe alcippoides

165 GA
P. p. phalantha
166 BS
V. egista sinha
167 KT
V. e. erota
168 RL
A. a. asura
169 KT
A. c. cama
170 KK
A. i. inara
171 SS
A. kanwa phorkys
172 KT
A. p. perius
173 KK
A. pravara acutipenni
174 KK
A. r. ranga
175 SS
A. selenophora bahula
KT
A. z. zeroca
177 KT
B. t. teuta
178 KK
B. a. austenia
179 KK
E. aconthea garuda
180 SS
E. a. anosia
181 GA
E. l. lubentina
182 RL
E. monina kesava
183 KT
E. p. phemius
184 KT
E. telchinia
185 GA
L. m. martha
186 GA
L. c. cyanipardus
187 SS
L. dirtea khasiana
188 SS
M. p. procris

189 SS
N. hylas varmona
190 KK
Neptis nata/soma group
191 KK
N. sappho astola
194 SS
P. sylvia gambrisius
192 SS
P. h. hordonia
193 SS
P. p. paraka
195 KK
* P. columella ophiana
196 AP
S. d. daraxa
197 KK
T. j. jahnu
198 GA
T. julii appiades
199 KT
T. l. lepidea
200 KK
* D. bisaltide indica
201 GA
H. bolina jacintha
202 KK
* H. misippus
203 SS
J. a. almana
204 KT
J. a. atlites
205 KT
J. h. hierta
206 KK
* J. i. iphita
207 KK
* J. l. lemonias
208 KT
J. orithya ocyale
209 RL
K. i. inachus
210 KT
K. c. canace
211 KT
S. hypselis cotanda
212 GA
S. lilaea khasiana*

213 KT
S. silana
214 KK
V. c. cardui
215 KK
* V. i. indica
216 RL
D. n. nesimachus
217 KT
S. n. nicea
218 GA
A. a. amythaon
219 KK
D. sondaica zal
220 SS
E. hypermnestra undularis
221 BS
E. m. malelas
222 KT
E. nesaea timandra
223 SS
E. peali
224 GA
E. himachala
225 KT
F. canens arcesilas
226 GA
F. eumeus assama
227 KT
L. chandica flanona
228 KT
L. confusa gambara
229 GA
L. europa niladana
230 SS
L. mekara zuchara
231 KT
L. r. rohria
232 KT
L. verma sintica
233 SS
L. v. vindhya
234 KT
M. l. leda
235 KK
M. phedima bela
236 SS
M. z. zitenius

237 GA
M. anaxias aemate
238 KT
M. francisca sanatana
239 KK
M. intermedia
240 SS
M. malsarida
241 KK
M. m. mineus
242 KK
M. perseus blasius
243 KK
Mycalesis sp.
244 KK
* M. v. visala
245 GA
O. m. medus
246 GA
T. d.diores
247 GA
Y. baldus satpura
248 GA
Y. huebneri
249 KK
* A. varuna astorion
250 KK
B. dasarada
251 RL
G. a. agamemnon
252 GA
G. a. agetes
253 GA
G. anuphates pompilius
254 SS
G. aristeus anticrates
255 AP
G. c. cloanthus
256 SS
G. doson axion
257 GA
G. eurypylus cheronus
258 GA
G. macareus lioneli
259 KK
G. s. sarpedon
260 GA
G. x. xenocles

261 RL
L. c. curius
262
* L. coon cacharensis
263 BS
M. payeni evan
264 GA
P. a. aristolochiae
265 KK
P. a. alcmenor
266 KK
* P. bianor gladiator
267 GA
P. c. castor
268 GA
P. a. clytia
269 KK
* P. d. demoleus
270 GA
P. h. helenus
271 GA
P. memnon agenor
272 SS
P. nephelus chaon
273 RL
P. paradoxa telearchus
274 GA
P. p. paris
275 GA
P. polyt romulus
276 KK
* P. protenor euprotenor
277 KK
T. helena cerberus
278 KK
* C. p. pomona
279 KK
* C. p. pyranthe
280 RL
D. verhuelli doubledayi
281 KK
E. andersonii jordani
282 KK
E. blanda silhetana
283 KK
* E. h. hecabe
284 GA
G. nerina assamica

285 KT
A. albina darada
286 GA
A. l. indra
287 KT
A. l. lalage
288 RL
A. lyncida eleonora
289 RL
A. olferna
290 KK
C. n. nadina
291 SS
C. n. nerissa
292 KK
* D. a. agostina
293 KK
* D. belladonna lugens
294 KK
D. d. descombes
295 SS
D. hyparete indica
296 KK
D. p. pasithoe
297 GA
H. g. glaucippe
298 KT
I. pyrene familiaris
299 BS
L. n. nina
300 KK
P. h. hippia
301 GA
P. canidia indica
302 KT
A. bifasciata suffusa

FOREST AND WILDLIFE RESOURCES

We share this planet with millions of other living beings, starting from micro-organisms and bacteria, lichens to banyan trees, elephants and blue whales. This whole habitat that we live in has immense biodiversity. We humans beside with all living organisms form a intricate web of ecological system in which we are only a part and very much dependent on this system for our own subsistence. For instance, the plants, animals and micro-organisms re-make the excellence of the air we breathe, the water we drink and the soil that produces our food without which we cannot survive. Forests play a key role in the ecological system as these are also the primary producers on which all other living beings depend.

FLORA AND FAUNA IN INDIA

If you seem around, you will be able to discover that there are some animals and plants which are unique in your area. In information, India is one of the world's richest countries in conditions of its vast array of biological diversity, and has almost 8 per cent of the total number of species in the world (estimated to be 1.6 million). This is perhaps twice or thrice the number yet to be exposed. You have already studied in detail in relation to the extent and diversity of forest and wildlife Resources in India. You may have realized the importance of these Resources in our daily life.

These diverse flora and fauna are so well integrated in our daily life that we take these for granted. But, lately, they are under great stress mainly due to insensitivity to our environment. Some estimates suggest that at least 10 per cent of India's recorded wild flora and 20 per cent of its mammals are on the threatened list. Several of these would now be categorized as 'critical', that is on the verge of extinction like the cheetah, pink-headed duck, mountain quail, forest spotted owlet, and plants like *madhuca insignis* (a wild diversity of mahua) and *hubbardia heptaneuron*,(a species of grass). In information, no one can say how several species may have already been lost. Today, we only talk of the superior and more visible animals and plants that have become extinct but what in relation to the smaller animals like insects and plants?

VANISHING FORESTS

The dimensions of deforestation in India are staggering. The forest cover in the country is estimated at 637,293 sq km, which is 19.39 per cent of the total geographical area. (thick forest 11.48 per cent; open forest 7.76 per cent; and mangrove 0.15 per cent). Just as to the State of Forest Report (1999), the thick forest cover has increased through 10,098 sq km since 1997. Though, this apparent augment in the forest cover is due to plantation through dissimilar agencies. The State of Forest Report does not differentiate flanked by natural forests and plantations. So, these reports fail to deliver accurate information in relation to the actual loss of natural forests. categories of existing plants and animal species. Based on the International Union for Conservation of Nature and Natural Resources (IUCN), we can classify as follows –

Normal Species: Species whose population stages are measured to be normal for their survival, such as cattle, sal, pine, rodents, etc.

Endangered Species: These are species which are in danger of extinction. The survival of such species is hard if the negative factors that have led to a decline in their population continue to operate. The examples of such species are black buck, crocodile, Indian wild ass, Indian rhino, lion tailed macaque, sangai (brow anter deer in Manipur), etc.

Vulnerable Species: These are species whose population has declined to stages from where it is likely to move into the endangered category in the close to future if the negative factors continue to operate. The examples of such species are blue sheep, Asiatic elephant, Gangetic dolphin, etc.

Unusual Species: Species with small population may move into the endangered or vulnerable category if the negative factors affecting them continue to operate. The examples of such species are the Himalayan brown bear, wild Asiatic buffalo, desert fox and hornbill, etc.

Endemic Species: These are species which are only establish in some scrupulous areas usually in accessible through natural or geographical barriers. Examples of such species are the Andaman teal, Nicobar pigeon, Andaman wild pig, mithun in Arunchal Pradesh.

Extinct Species: These are species which are not establish after searches of recognized or likely areas where they may happen. A species may be extinct from a local area, region, country, continent or the whole earth. Examples of such species are the Asiatic cheetah, pink head duck.

What are the negative factors that cause such fearful depletion of the flora and fauna?

If you seem around, you will be able to discover out how we have transformed nature into a resource obtaining directly and indirectly from the forests and wildlife – wood, barks, leaves, rubber, medicines, dyes, food, fuel, fodder, manure, etc. So it is we ourselves who have depleted our forests and wildlife. The greatest damage inflicted on Indian forests was throughout the colonial era due to the expansion of the railways, agriculture, commercial and scientific forestry and mining behaviors. Even after Independence, agricultural expansion continues to be one of the major causes of depletion of forest Resources.

Flanked by 1951 and 1980, just as to the Forest Survey of India, in excess of 26,200 sq. km. of forest area was converted into agricultural land all in excess of India. Substantial parts of the tribal belts, especially in the northeastern and central India, have been deforested or degraded through shifting farming (jhum), a kind of 'slash and burn' agriculture. Big-scale development projects have also contributed significantly to the loss of forests. Since 1951, in excess of 5,000 sq km of forest was cleared for river valley projects. Clearing of forests is still continuing with projects like the Narmada Sagar Project in Madhya Pradesh, which would inundate 40,000 hectares of forest. Mining is another significant factor behind deforestation. The Buxa Tiger Reserve in West Bengal is seriously threatened through the ongoing dolomite mining. It has disturbed the natural habitat of several species and blocked the migration route of many others, including the great Indian elephant. Several foresters and environmentalists hold the view that the greatest degrading factors behind the depletion of forest Resources are grazing and fuel-wood collection.

Though, there may be some substance in their argument, yet, the information remnants that a substantial part of the fuel-fodder demand is met through lopping rather than through felling whole trees. The forest ecosystems are repositories of some of the country's mainly valuable forest products, minerals and other Resources that meet the demands of the rapidly expanding industrial urban economy. These protected areas, therefore mean dissimilar things to dissimilar people, and therein lies the fertile ground for conflicts. Habitat destruction, hunting, poaching, in excess of-use, environmental pollution, poisoning and forest fires are factors, which have led to the decline in India's biodiversity.

Other significant causes of environmental destruction are unequal access, inequitable consumption of Resources and differential sharing of responsibility for environmental well-being. In excess of-population in third world countries is often cited as the cause of environmental degradation. Though, an average American consumes 40 times more Resources than an average Somalian. Likewise, the richest five per cent of Indian society almost certainly cause more ecological damage because of the amount they consume than the poorest 25 per cent. The former shares minimum responsibilities for environmental well-being. The question is: who is consuming what, from where and how much? The destruction of forests and wildlife is not presently a biological issue.

The biological loss is strongly correlated with the loss of cultural diversity. Such losses have increasingly marginalized and impoverished several indigenous and other forest-dependent communities, who directly depend on several components of the forest and wildlife for food, drink, medicine, culture, spirituality, etc. Within the poor, women are affected more than men. In several societies, women bear the major responsibility of collection of fuel, fodder, water and other vital subsistence needs. As these Resources are depleted, the drudgery of women increases and sometimes they have to walk for more than 10 km to collect these Resources. This causes serious health troubles for women and negligence of home and children because of the increased hours of work, which often has serious social implications. The indirect impact of degradation such as severe drought or deforestation-induced floods, etc. also hits the poor the hardest. Poverty in these cases is a direct outcome of environmental destruction. So, forest and wildlife, are vital to the excellence of life and environment in the subcontinent. It is imperative to adapt to sound forest and wildlife conservation strategies.

Conservation of Forest and Wildlife in India

Conservation in the background of rapid decline in wildlife population and forestry has become essential. But why do we need to conserve our forests and wildlife? Conservation preserves the ecological diversity and our life support systems – water, air and soil. It also preserves the genetic diversity of plants and animals for better growth of species and breeding. For instance, in agriculture, we are still dependent on traditional crop diversities. Fisheries too are heavily dependent on the maintenance of aquatic biodiversity.

In the 1960s and 1970s, conservationists demanded a national wildlife protection programme. The Indian Wildlife (Protection) Act was implemented in 1972, with several provisions for protecting habitats. An all-India list of protected species was also published. The thrust of the programme was towards protecting the remaining population of sure endangered species through banning hunting, giving legal protection to their habitats, and restricting trade in wildlife. Subsequently, central and several state governments recognized national parks and wildlife sanctuaries in relation to the which you have already studied. The central government also announced many projects for protecting specific animals, which were gravely threatened, including the tiger, the one- horned rhinoceros, the Kashmir stag or *hangul*, three kinds of crocodiles – fresh water crocodile, saltwater crocodile and the *Gharial*, the Asiatic lion, and others.

Mainly recently, the Indian elephant, black buck (chinkara), the great Indian bustard (*godawan*) and the snow leopard, etc. have been given full or partial legal protection against hunting and trade throughout India. The conservation projects are now focusing on biodiversity rather than on a few of its components. There is now a more rigorous search for dissimilar conservation events. Increasingly, even insects are beginning to discover a lay in conservation scheduling. In the notification under Wildlife Act of 1980 and 1986, many hundred butterflies, moths, beetles, and one dragonfly have been added to the list of protected species. In 1991, for the first time plants were also added to the list, starting with six species.

KINDS AND SHARING OF FOREST AND WILDLIFE RESOURCES

Even if we want to conserve our vast forest and wildlife Resources, it is rather hard to manage, control and regulate them. In India, much of its forest and wildlife Resources are either owned or supervised through the government through the Forest Department or other government departments. These are classified under the following categories.

Reserved Forests: More than half of the total forest land has been declared reserved forests. Reserved forests are regarded as the mainly valuable as distant as the conservation of forest and wildlife Resources are concerned.

Protected Forests: Approximately one-third of the total forest area is protected forest, as declared through the Forest Department. This forest land are protected from any further depletion.

Unclassed Forests: These are other forests and wastelands belonging to both government and private individuals and communities.

Reserved and protected forests are also referred to as permanent forest estates maintained for the purpose of producing timber and other forest produce, and for protective reasons. Madhya Pradesh has the main area under permanent forests, constituting 75 per cent of its total forest area. Jammu and Kashmir, Andhra Pradesh, Uttarakhand, Kerala, Tamil Nadu, West Bengal, and Maharashtra have big percentages of reserved forests of its total forest area whereas Bihar, Haryana, Punjab, Himachal Pradesh, Orissa and Rajasthan have a bulk of it under protected forests. All Northeastern states and parts of Gujarat have a very high percentage of their forests as unclasped forests supervised through local communities.

COMMUNITY AND CONSERVATION

Conservation strategies are not new in our country. We often ignore that in India, forests are also home to some of the traditional communities. In some areas of India, local communities are struggling to conserve these habitats beside with government officials, recognizing that only this will secure their own extensive-term livelihood. In Sariska Tiger Reserve, Rajasthan, villagers have fought against mining through citing the Wildlife Protection Act. In several areas, villagers themselves are protecting habitats and explicitly rejecting government involvement.

The inhabitants of five villages in the Alwar district of Rajasthan have declared 1,200 hectares of forest as the Bhairodev Dakav 'Sonchuri', declaring their own set of rules and regulations which do not allow hunting, and are protecting the wildlife against any outside encroachments. Nature worship is an age old tribal belief based on the premise that all creations of nature have to be protected. Such beliefs have preserved many virgin forests in pristine form described Sacred Groves (the forests of God and Goddesses). These patches of forest or parts of big forests have been left untouched through the local people and any interference with them is banned. Sure societies revere a scrupulous tree which they have preserved from time immemorial. The Mundas and the Santhal of Chhota Nagpur region worship mahua (Bassia latifolia) and kadamba (Anthocaphalus cadamba) trees, and the tribals of Orissa and Bihar worship the tamarind (Tamarindus indica) and mango (Mangifera indica) trees throughout weddings. To several of us, peepal and banyan trees are measured sacred.

Indian society comprises many cultures, each with its own set of traditional methods of conserving nature and its creations. Sacred qualities are often ascribed to springs, mountain peaks, plants and animals which are closely protected. You will discover troops of macaques and langurs around several temples. They are fed daily and treated as a part of temple devotees. In and around Bishnoi villages in Rajasthan, herds of blackbuck, (chinkara), nilgai and peacocks can be seen as an integral part of the community and nobody harms them. The well-known Chipko movement in the Himalayas has not only successfully resisted deforestation in many areas but has also shown that community afforestation with indigenous species can be enormously successful.

Attempts to revive the traditional conservation methods or developing new methods of ecological farming are now widespread. Farmers and citizen's groups like the Beej Bachao Andolan in Tehri and Navdanya have shown that adequate stages of diversified crop production without the use of synthetic chemicals are possible and economically viable. In India joint forest management (JFM) programme furnishes a good instance for involving local communities in the management and restoration of degraded forests. The programme has been in formal subsistence since 1988 when the state of Orissa passed the first resolution for joint forest management. JFM depends on the formation of local (village) institutions that undertake protection behaviors mostly on degraded forest land supervised through the forest department.

In return, the members of these communities are entitled to intermediary benefits like non-timber forest produces and share in the timber harvested through 'successful protection'. The clear lesson from the dynamics of both environmental destruction and reconstruction in India is that local communities everywhere have to be involved in some type of natural resource management. But there is still a extensive method to go before local communities are at the centre-stage in decision-creation. Accept only those economic or developmental behaviors that are people centric, environment-friendly and economically rewarding.

2

Tourism Development and Biodiversity

AN OVERVIEW

BACKGROUND

- Visitors are further sub-divided into two categories: tourists; who must stay one or more night in the place visited and same-day visitors; visitors who visit a place and return the same day.
- Comprises many industries like lodging, transportation, entertainment, meals, and financial services, among others.

It is boom time for India's Tourism and Hospitality sector. A 5,000 year history, culture, religion and alternative medicine fascinate both budget and luxury travellers alike. Driven by a surge in business traveller arrivals and a soaring interest in India as a tourist destination, the year 2005 has been the best year till date, with foreign visitor arrivals reaching a record 3.92 million, resulting in international tourism receipts of USD 5.7 billion.

The Department of Tourism's resolve in promoting Indian tourism has strengthened as it recognises its potential. Tourism in India is the third largest foreign exchange earner, accounting for 2.5 per cent of GDP. It also makes a direct contribution to economy with significant linkages with agriculture, horticulture, handicrafts and construction. The outlay on tourism development rose to ₹7,860 million in 2005/2006, from ₹3,500 million in 2003/2004, and continued to focus on the "Atithi Devo Bhavah" campaign, targeted at the inbound foreign tourists in the country. Translated literally this means "Guest is God".

CURRENT STATUS

Commencing with a slow growth at the start of the millennium, the Indian tourism industry has performed quite well in the last couple of years. The Indian tourism industry has out performed the global tourism industry in terms of growth in the volume of international tourists as well as in terms of revenue. The World Travel and Tourism Council (WTTC) has named India along with

China as one of the most fastest growing tourism industries for the next 10 to 15 years. World Travel and Tourism Council (WTTC) the Travel and Tourism Industry contributes 2.1per cent to India's GDP.

The industry employed an estimated 24,349,000 people in 2006 (5.4per cent of total employment, or 1 in every 18.4 jobs). The key driver for this growth in the Indian tourism industry has been a fast growing economy for the last 3-4 years. Despite lagging in the basic infrastructure that supports the tourism industry, Indian tourism industry has been showing an impressive double-digit growth. In order to sustain this growth and meet the expectations, it is essential for the Government of India to invest in infrastructure such as transport and accommodations. Global hotel and hospitality consulting firm, HVS International, the strong performance in tourist arrivals in 2005 can be attributed to a strong sense of business and investment confidence in India inspired by:

- India's strong GDP performance
- Strengthening of ties with the developed world, and
- Opening of sectors of the economy to private sector/foreign investment.

The efforts made by the Ministry of Tourism and Culture in the last few years have had a salutary effect on India's tourism industry:

- Foreign tourist arrivals witnessed a growth of 78 per cent in 2006 over 2001 (last 5 years)
- Growth in foreign exchange earnings was of the order of 122 per cent during this period.
- As per estimates (Ministry of Tourism), on an average, about 3.1 million additional jobs per year have been created directly and indirectly in the tourism sector in the last four years.

India is fast emerging as one of the most enticing destinations for the global leisure traveller. The Readers Travel Awards 2006, conducted by Condé Nast Traveller has recently placed India at number four among the world's must-see countries, up from number nine in 2003. The Incredible India campaign has also been a huge success. As an engine for economic growth, the tourism and hospitality sector cuts across the ruralurban divide, and bridges economic boundaries. The World Travel and Tourism Council's 2006 Travel and Tourism Economic Research, the travel and tourism sector in India generated a total demand of USD 53,544.50 million of economic activity in 2006, accounting for nearly 5.3 per cent of GDP and 5.4 per cent of total employment. The sector grew at a rate of 8.4 per cent in 2006 and is expected to grow by 8 per cent per annum, in real terms, between 2007 and 2016.

THE HOTEL INDUSTRY

The Hotel Industry comprises a major part of the Tourism industry. Historically viewed as an industry providing a luxury service valuable to the economy only as a foreign exchange earner, the industry today contributes directly to employment (directly employing around 0.15 million people), and indirectly facilitates tourism and commerce. Prior to the 1980s, the Indian hotel industry was a slow-growing industry, consisting primarily of relatively static, single-hotel companies. However, the Asiad, held in New Delhi in 1982, and the subsequent partial liberalization of the Indian economy generated tourism interest in India, with significant benefits accruing to the hotel and tourism sector, in terms of improved demand patterns.

Growth in demand for hotels was particularly high during the early 1990s following the initiatives taken to liberalize the Indian economy in FY1991, as per the recommendations of the International Monetary Fund (IMF). The euphoria of the early 1990s prompted major chains, new entrants and international chains to chalk out ambitious capacity additions, especially in the metropolitan cities.

However, most of these efforts were directed realises the business travellers and foreign clientele. In recent years, the hotels sector has grown at a faster rate than GDP. As a result, the share of hotels and restaurants in GDP at current prices has increased from 1.2per cent in FY2000 to 1.5per cent in FY2005.

In constant (1999-2000) prices, the GDP from hotels and restaurants has increased from ₹222.65 billion in FY2000 to ₹335.49 billion in FY2005. As a result, the share of hotels and restaurants in total GDP at constant prices has increased from 1.24per cent in FY2000 to 1.40per cent in FY2005.

STRUCTURE OF THE INDUSTRY

Hotels in India are broadly classified into 7 categories (five star deluxe, five-star, four star, three star, two star, one-star and heritage hotels) by the Ministry of Tourism, Government of India, based on the general features and facilities offered. The ratings are reviewed every five years. As of December 2005.

Premium and Luxury Segment

This segment comprises the high-end 5-star deluxe and 5-star hotels, which mainly cater to the business and upmarket foreign leisure travellers and offer a high quality and range of services. The segment accounted for 29per cent of the total hotel rooms in the country in December 2005.

Mid-Market Segment

This segment comprises 3 and 4 star hotels, which cater to the average foreign and domestic leisure traveller. This segment also caters to the middle level business travellers since it offers most of the essential services of luxury hotels without the high costs since the tax component of this segment is lower compared with the premium segment.

Budget Segment

These comprise 1 and 2 star hotels referred to as 'Budget Hotels'. These categories do not offer as many facilities as the other segments but provide inexpensive accommodation to the highly price-conscious segment of the domestic and foreign leisure travellers.

Heritage Hotels

In the past four decades, certain architecturally distinctive properties such as palaces and forts, built prior to 1950, have been converted into hotels. The Ministry of Tourism has classified these hotels as heritage hotels.

Others

At any point in time, applications for classification are usually pending with the Ministry of Tourism because of which such properties remain unclassified. The number of hotel rooms pending classification has declined from historical 15-20per cent to 5per cent of the total rooms available in the recent past.

KEY CONSUMER SEGMENTS

The market for the hotel industry can be divided into the following key consumer segments based on purpose of visit:

The Business Traveller

The Business Traveller is a businessman or a corporate executive travelling for business purposes. This segment includes corporates, both domestic and foreign, who open offices in the hotel premises during start-ups, corporate executives who make extended stay either for long duration projects or while waiting for permanent accommodation (primarily expatriates) and convention arrivals.

While the senior executives usually stay in 5 star hotels, the middle level executives, who are much larger in number, stay in the budget hotels. This segment offers better realizations, as they demand relatively smaller discounts on room rents (about 10per cent-15per cent), use more of facilities such as PCs, fax multi-media, conference halls. Also, the Food and Beverage (F&B) revenues are better as they usually eat in the hotel itself due to their busy schedules.

The Leisure Traveller

The Leisure Traveller could either be a foreigner or a domestic traveller whose primary purpose of visit is holiday and site seeing. Among non-business foreign tourists the primary motivation for visiting India is largely cultural attraction followed by conferences and conventions, tourist attractions like beaches, wild life, hill resorts etc.

Usually, leisure travellers are part of a package run by a tour operator. The margins offered by leisure travellers tend to be lower because of two reasons. Firstly, they seek higher discounts and also provide less F&B revenues as they usually eat out. The business offered by this segment is highly seasonal and tends to peak in the September to March period.

Airline Cabin Crew

Airline Cabin Crew forms another important segment because of the repetitive and guaranteed nature of the business that they provide. Usually, these are a part of an annual contract whereby, in return for a fixed rate, a certain number of rooms are provided on demand for cabin crews. With discount rates in the range of 40per cent and 50per cent, this represents a low-yield segment for hotels in general.

DEMAND AND SUPPLY SCENARIO

INTERNATIONAL TOURIST TRAFFIC

The foreign tourist arrivals in India increased at CAGR of 5.5per cent from 2.29 million in 1996 to 3.92 million in 2005. Significantly, the bulk of international arrivals into India, both in 2004 and 2005, have been business travellers.

Main reason for this increase has been following fundamental factors:

- Development of infrastructure by the Government
- India's emergence as an outsourcing hub.
- India's growing recognition as an exciting place to visit ('The Readers Travel Awards 2006', conducted by Condé Nast Traveller has recently placed India at number four among the world's must-see countries, up from number nine in 2003) has helped boost its image as a leisure destination.
- India's strong GDP growth.
- Opening of sectors of the economy to private sector/foreign investment.
- Reforms in aviation sector which led to better connectivity with many countries (such as ASEAN) and created additional capacity on existing routes (for *e.g.* USA, Middle East). Also, introduction of low cost airlines also contributed to the demand. The increase in international flights, seat capacity and frequency into the country and the decision to allow private airlines like Jet Airways and Air Sahara to fly overseas has had a positive impact on tourist and business arrivals into India, by way of providing additional seats to key destinations.
- Strengthening of ties with the developed world.
- Success of "Incredible India" campaign and other tourism promotion measures.

SUPPLY SCENARIO

The estimates by HVS International, around 10,856 hotel rooms in Delhi, 9,318 rooms in Mumbai, 7,794 rooms in Bangalore and 7,408 rooms in Hyderabad are expected to be added by 2011.

MAJOR PLAYERS

MAJOR PLAYERS IN THE INDIAN HOTEL INDUSTRY

Hotel Chains

They comprise major players including Indian Hotels Company Limited (the Taj Group) and associate companies, EIH Limited (the Oberoi Group), ITC Hotels Limited (the ITC Welcome Group), Indian Tourism Development Corporation (ITDC) and Hotel Corporation of India (HCI) (the latter two being under the Public Sector). Most of these chains had an established presence in one or more metro cities prior to the tourism boom of the 1980s. Subsequent to the tourism boom, these chains aggressively expanded their presence in other locations. The private players among the hotel chains are industry leaders and have well-established brand identities across the different industry segments.

Small Chains

They are companies that have come up after the tourism boom of the 1980s and 1990s. Due to lack of prior experience in the hotel industry, these players have preferred to opt for operating/management arrangements with international players of repute. Some of the companies in this category are Hotel Leela Venture (with Kempinski), Asian Hotels (Hyatt International Corporation), Bharat Hotels (formerly with Holiday Inn and Hilton and now with Intercontinental). As late entrants, most of these hotel companies have fewer properties, compared with the big chains. However most of these players have initiated expansion plans during the late 1990s.

Public Sector Chains

ITDC and HCI, boast of some of the best locations in major cities but are relative underperformers, as compared with their private sector counterparts.

International Hotel Chains

They are also looking at India as a major growth destination. These chains are establishing themselves in the Indian market by entering into joint ventures with Indian partners or by entering into management contracts or franchisee arrangements. Some of the players who have already entered or plan to enter the Indian market include Marriott, Starwood, Berggruen Hotels, Emaar MGF. Most of these chains have ambitious expansion plans especially with a strong focus on the budget segment and tier II cities.

Localized Hotel Companies

They are mainly comprise early entrants who have an established localized presence and who preferred not to expand during the tourism boom but focus on building and catering to a loyal customer base.

PROFILES OF SOME OF THE MAJOR PLAYERS IN THE HOTEL INDUSTRY

The Indian Hotels Company

The Indian Hotels Company and its subsidiaries are collectively known as Taj Hotels Resorts and Palaces, recognised as one of Asia's largest and finest hotel company. Incorporated by the founder of the Tata Group, Jamsetji N Tata, the company opened its first property, The Taj Mahal Palace Hotel, Bombay, in 1903. The Taj, a symbol of Indian hospitality, completed its centenary year in 2003.

Taj Hotels Resorts and Palaces comprises 59 hotels at 40 locations across India with an additional 17 international hotels in the Maldives, Mauritius, Malaysia, United Kingdom, United States of America, Bhutan, Sri Lanka, Africa, the Middle East and Australia.

The company has had a long-standing commitment to the continued development of the Indian tourism and hospitality industry. From the 1970s through the 1990s, the Taj played an important role in launching several of India's key tourist destinations. Working in tandem with the Indian government, the Taj developed resorts and retreats while the government developed roads and railways to India's hidden treasures.

ITC/Sheraton Corporation

The Indian Hotels Company and its subsidiaries are collectively known as Taj Hotels Resorts and Palaces, recognised as one of Asia's largest and finest hotel company. Incorporated by the founder of the Tata Group, Jamsetji N Tata, the company opened its first property, The Taj Mahal Palace Hotel, Bombay, in 1903. The Taj, a symbol of Indian hospitality, completed its centenary year in 2003.

Taj Hotels Resorts and Palaces comprises 59 hotels at 40 locations across India with an additional 17 international hotels in the Maldives, Mauritius, Malaysia, United Kingdom, United States of America, Bhutan, Sri Lanka, Africa, the Middle East and Australia. The company has had a long-standing commitment to the continued development of the Indian tourism and hospitality industry. From the 1970s through the 1990s, the Taj played an important role in launching several of India's key tourist destinations. Working in tandem with the Indian government, the Taj developed resorts and retreats while the government developed roads and railways to India's hidden treasures.

ITC/Sheraton Corporation

Founded in 1957 by Capt. C.P. Krishnan Nair, the ₹4.5 billion Leela Group is engaged in the business of ready-made garments and luxury hotels and resorts. The Leela Kempinski, Mumbai and The Leela, Goa are two of the best hotels in India, and have also won considerable international acclaim. For this to have been achieved in 12 short years is nothing short of remarkable. Recently in 2001 Capt. Nair fulfilled his longstanding dream of constructing a palace hotel in the garden city of Bangalore.

The Leela Palace Kempinski, Bangalore is built in art deco style recreating the grandeur of The Mysore Maharajas Palace. It is set amidst 8 acres of landscaped garden and waterfalls. It is a palace with the heart of a modern hotel. Its 254 rooms are opulently furnished and are befitting royalty. The newest addition The Leela Kovalam is Kerala's largest resort, built on a rock face cradled between two wide sweeping beaches with a stunning view of the famous Kovalam coastline.

The Bharat Hotels Group

The Bharat Hotels group is a major player in India's tourism and hotel sector. It operates its hotels under 'THE GRAND' banner and its present portfolio of hotels incorporates FOURTEEN luxury hotels in the five-star deluxe segment. These include InterContinental 'The Grand' hotels in New Delhi, Mumbai, Goa and Srinagar and The Grand Ashok Bangalore, The Grand Laxmi Vilas Palace Udaipur and The Grand Temple View Khajuraho. Additionally, soon to open hotels in 2008-09 are – The Grand Great Eastern Kolkata, The Grand Jaipur, The Grand Resort Bekal, The Grand Ahmedabad, The Grand Chandigarh, The Grand Noida and The Grand Fort Dubai. By 2009, the company plans to open hotels in Hyderabad, Amritsar and other key locations.

The EIH Ltd (The Oberoi Group)

Asian elegance is the key to running hotels, if you ask EIH (better known as The Oberoi Group). The company owns and operates about 20 luxury hotels, about 10 mid-range hotels, and two inland cruises; The Oberoi Group operates primarily in India, but also in Australia, Egypt, Indonesia, Mauritius, and Saudi Arabia. Most of the company's luxury properties bear the Oberoi banner. The company in 2004 joined forces with Hilton International to rebrand most of its mid-range hotels as Trident Hiltons (the former Oberoi Towers is now known as the Hilton Towers Mumbai). The Oberoi Group also operates luxury cruises of the Nile River and India's Kerala region.

India Tourism Development Corporation (ITDC)/The Ashok Group

India Tourism Development Corporation (ITDC) was established in 1966 as an autonomous public sector corporation, entrusted with the task of helping develop tourism infrastructure and promoting India as a tourist destination. The ITDC Ashok Group of hotel chains manages some of the best five star and luxury tour hotels in the Indian hospitality industry. The hotels run by the ITDC Ashok Group of hotel chains may be divided into different categories, these are elite hotels, comfort hotels and classic hotels. The ITDC Ashok Group of hotel chains manages 33 hotels in 26 different tourist destinations all over India.

The management of Ashoka Group believes in offering the best in the hospitality industry and the staff at each of the hotels run by the group is especially trained to be courteous and efficient.

The Ashok Group of hotel chains boasts of running some of the best hotels in the Indian hotel industry. The hotels that are a part of the elite and classic category of the ITDC Ashok Group are the Ashok Hotel in New Delhi, the Kovalam Ashok Beach Resort in Kovalam, Kerala, the Agra Ashok in Agra, Hotel Jaipur Ashok in New Delhi and the Qutab Hotel in New Delhi. Most of the hotels managed by the ITDC Ashok Group have had the privilege of playing host to several international and national dignitaries.

The Hotel Corporation of India (HCI)

The Hotel Corporation of India Limited (HCI) is a public limited company wholly owned by Air India Limited and was incorporated on July 8, 1971 under the Companies Act, 1956 when Air India decided to enter the Hotel Industry in keeping with the then prevalent trend among world airlines. The objective was to offer to the passengers a better product, both at the International Airports and at other places of tourist interest, thereby also increasing tourism of India.

Jaypee Hotels Ltd.

Jaypee Hotels Limited primarily engages in the ownership and operation of hotels in India. The company owns three Five Star Deluxe Hotels, namely Jaypee Palace Hotel at Agra, and Jaypee Vasant Continental and Jaypee Siddharth Hotel at New Delhi. It also manages the operation of the hotels Jaypee Residency Manor at Mussoorie and Jaypee Green Resorts. In addition, Jaypee Hotels involves in construction operations. The company is headquartered in New Delhi, India. Jaypee Hotels Limited is a subsidiary of Jaiprakash Associates Limited.

POLICIES AND INITIATIVES

Tourism being a concurrent subject under the Indian constitution, both the central and state governments regulates the hotel industry. The regulations include statutory and regulatory sanctions (or approvals and licenses) from the Central and State departments or agencies. This includes license to operate a restaurant, a hotel license (issued by municipal authorities), license from police (issued by local police) and a bar license (issued by excise department).

TOURISM POLICY

In order to develop tourism in India in a systematic manner, position it as a major engine of economic growth and to harness its direct and multiplier effects for employment and poverty eradication in an environmentally sustainable manner, the National Tourism Policy was formulated in the year 2002.

Broadly, the "Policy" attempts to:

- Acknowledges the critical role of private sector with government working as a pro-active facilitator and catalyst
- Create and develop integrated tourism circuits based on India's unique civilization, heritage, and culture in partnership with States, private sector and other agencies
- Ensure that the tourist to India gets physically invigourated, mentally rejuvenated, culturally enriched, spiritually elevated and "feel India from within".
- Focus on domestic tourism as a major driver of tourism growth
- Harness the direct and multiplier effects of tourism for employment generation, economic development and providing impetus to rural tourism
- Position India as a global brand to take advantage of the burgeoning global travel trade and the vast untapped potential of India as a destination
- Position tourism as a major engine of economic growth

The Government's major policy initiatives include:

- Allowing setting up of Guest Houses
- Immigration services
- Liberalization in aviation sector
- Pricing policy for aviation turbine fuel which influences internal air fares
- Procedural changes in making available land for construction of hotels
- Rationalization in tax rates in the hospitality sector
- Tourist friendly visa regime

The Indian Ministry of Tourism has identified 31 villages across the country to be developed as tourism hubs. The states in which these villages have been identified include Himachal Pradesh, Gujarat, Maharashtra, Bihar, Karnataka, Madhya Pradesh, Andhra Pradesh, Kerala, Tamil Nadu, Orissa, Assam, Sikkim, Rajasthan and West Bengal.

GOVERNMENT'S OPEN SKIES POLICY

The Government's Open Skies policy, permission for domestic airlines to commence international flights, start-up of various low-cost carriers, and fleet expansion by domestic players has created a huge incentive for domestic travellers to explore far-off destinations within and outside India. The booming aviation business is bringing an ever-increasing number of passengers to India, and pulling Indians out of their homes and into hotels.

The numbers, just as to the Ministry of Tourism, speak for themselves:

- The number of domestic and international passengers has increased fifteen-fold to 73.34 million in 2005/06 since 1970.
- Private airlines accounted for 77.0 per cent of the total domestic traffic.
- Domestic air passenger traffic grew by 16.8 per cent in 2005/06 compared to 2004/05.
- International passenger traffic observed a growth of 16.9 per cent in the same period.

FOREIGN TRADE POLICY

The Foreign Trade Policy announced in April, 2006, offered following incentives to the hospitality industry: Hotels and Restaurants are allowed to import duty free equipment and other items including liquor, against their foreign exchange earnings under the Served from India Scheme. As in previous years, this entitlement is 5per cent of previous year's foreign exchange earnings for hotels of one-star and above (including managed hotels and heritage hotels) approved by the Department of Tourism and other service providers in the tourism sector registered with it. The stand-alone restaurants will be entitled to duty credit equivalent to 10per cent of the foreign exchange earned by them in the preceding financial year (instead of the earlier 20per cent). Service exports in Indian Rupees, which are otherwise considered as having been paid for in free forcign exchange by RBI, will now qualify for benefits under the Served from India Scheme.

Also, foreign exchange earned through International Credit Cards and other instruments as permitted by RBI for rendering of service by the service providers shall be considered for the purposes of computation of entitlement under the Scheme. Benefits of the Scheme earned by one service provider of a Group company can now be utilised by other service providers of the same Group Company including managed hotels. The measure aims at supporting the Group service companies not earning foreign exchange in getting access to the international quality products at competitive price and providing services of international standards. This new initiative allows transfer of both the script and the imported input to the Group Service Company. The earlier provision allowed transfer of imported material only.

FDI IN HOTEL AND TOURISM SECTOR

100 per cent FDI is permissible in the sector on the automatic route. The term hotels include restaurants, beach resorts, and other tourist complexes providing accommodation and/or catering and food facilities to tourists. Tourism

related industry include travel agencies, tour operating agencies and tourist transport operating agencies, units providing facilities for cultural, adventure and wild life experience to tourists, surface, air and water transport facilities to tourists, leisure, entertainment, amusement, sports, and health units for tourists and Convention/Seminar units and organizations.

For foreign technology agreements, automatic approval is granted if:

- Up to 3 per cent of the capital cost of the project is proposed to be paid for technical and consultancy services including fees for architects, design, supervision, etc.
- Up to 3 per cent of net turnover is payable for franchising and marketing/publicity support fee, and up to 10 per cent of gross operating profit is payable for management fee, including incentive fee.

OTHER GOVERNMENT INITIATIVES

Government has undertaken following initiatives to attract both inbound and outbound tourists:

- Atethie devo bhava (guests are equal to god) - Under this programme the Government create awareness among Indian people who come in contact with the tourist.
- Encourage religious tourism for instance promote various places in India as Buddhist abodes.
- Incredible India - Under this programme the Government promotes India through various integrated marketing programmes.
- Other projects are the ₹5,400 million National Highways Development Project, the 5,846 km Golden Quadrilateral and the 7,300 km north-south and east-west corridors. Sagarmala project which intends to create a network of seaports, which will change the way people discover and experience real India.
- Various Infrastructure building initiatives

OPPORTUNITIES AND CHALLENGES

OPPORTUNITIES IN THE SECTOR

Considering India's size and unparalleled diversity - natural, geographic, cultural and artistic, there is vast room for growth in tourism industry. As travellers surge into India, the demand for rooms, across segments, has skyrocketed. Hotels in the luxury and business traveller segment are recording nearly 100 per cent occupancy, spiraling tariffs, and a strain on capacity and manpower. Anticipating this demand, around 10,856 hotel rooms in Delhi, 9,318 rooms in Mumbai, 7,794 rooms in Bangalore and 7,408 rooms in Hyderabad are expected to be added by 2011, just as to estimates by HVS International. The expected growth of the industry in future has provided its players with an opportunity to invest in new technologies such as CRM tools and latest security systems, and to venture into niche tourism segments like Medical, Religious, Cruise, Casinos, MICE etc. India can also develop infrastructure to host international conferences and trade shows, thus increasing its share of tourist traffic from such activities

Health Tourism

India is gradually gathering popularity as a health tourist destination. At its current pace of growth, healthcare tourism alone can rake over USD 1.7 billion additional revenues by 2012. Medical tourism is now a USD 299 million industry, as about 100,000 patients come each year. The country needs to exploit the cost advantage it can offer to a health tourist, the study said. The biggest driver for healthcare tourism is the disparity in costs.

- A heart surgery in the US costs USD 30,000 as compared to USD 6,000 in India.
- A bone marrow transplant in the US costs USD 250,000 and USD 26,000 in India.

With yoga, meditation, ayurveda, allopathy, and other systems of medicine, India offers a unique basket of services to an individual that is difficult to match by other countries. Clinical outcomes in India are at par with the world's best centres since India has internationally qualified and experienced specialists.

Critical Success Factors

The key success factors for the Hotel Industry are mentioned as follows:

Site and Location

This can be considered the most critical factor in determining the success of a hotel property. In addition to identifying a city, the site location within the city also assumes significance and issues like distance from the Central Business District (for metro hotels) and connectivity (access to roads, proximity to airports) assume importance.

Positioning

Equally important is the positioning of the hotel just as to the target guest segment. For example, business hotels set up to cater to the high yielding corporate clientele in metro cities would have a distinct competitive advantage over facilities targeted towards leisure travellers in the same city for attracting business travellers.

Financial Flexibility

Development of hotels is a highly capital intensive activity and new hotel properties, typically, have a high break-even point. Therefore, financial flexibility is essential, especially during early years of operations.

Brand Equity

Branded hotels can be further classified into chain hotels and independent hotels. Chain hotels would typically be affiliated to one of the large national or international hotel chains. Association with a hotel chains allows the property to be branded with one of the chain brands. In such cases the property benefits from the equity of the chain brand and promotion and advertising efforts made by the chain no only in India but also overseas. This way the property is able to attract tourists from areas where a independent hotels may not be able to reach effectively.

CHALLENGES

India's poor domestic tourism infrastructure is leading to a threat of loosing foreign tourists to other competing countries. India is highly prone to prevailing socio-economic and political conditions. Like terrorist strikes, riots, epidemics, political uncertainty, slowdown in reforms etc. The growth in the Indian tourism sector is accompanied by the imminent destruction of local ecology and an increase in pollution, which, in the long run, is going to negatively impact the tourism industry of India.

The biggest challenge in the Indian tourism sector is that of entry of new players, the country's growing economy has attracted a host of new players, the number of which is expected to increase further. Aman Resorts, Shangri-la Hotels, Four Seasons Hotels and The Hilton group are some of the international players that are at various stages of establishing presence in India. As the number of player increases, the competitive intensity in the sector is likely to increase. Remarkably, unlike earlier, many new entrants are reportedly considering entry into the mid-market segment, which is currently dominated by non-chain properties.

FUTURE OUTLOOK

The Indian Hospitality sector is expected to show a healthy growth in the medium term. Strong economic growth, increased FDI, greater emphasis on tourism development, favourable Government policies, impending 2010 Commonwealth games, 2011 Cricket World Cup and other international events, will be the major drivers for the growth. There exists a lot of scope for growth in tourism sector.

The Ministry of Tourism, the contribution of tourism to India's GDP is only 5.9 per cent as compared to the worldwide average of 11 per cent. By 2020, the Government of India expects travel and tourism to contribute ₹8,500 billion to GDP, almost four times the value in 2005. With successive Governments committed to reform, a strong manufacturing sector and a private sector that already has a critical mass that is needed to drive growth, it is unlikely that the strong growth in GDP is likely to be reversed. The rising middle class is also becoming increasingly affluent, mobile, Internet savvy and more sophisticated in terms of what is demanded in terms of tourism products and services, and more importantly the price they are willing to pay for it. Entry of international brands through joint ventures and tie-ups is likely to enhance the service levels and will narrow demand-supply gap of rooms. But ICRA expects the shortage in rooms to remain for next five years leading to higher occupancy levels and increase in Average Room Rates (ARR). Currently, just as to industry estimates, there are only 1,05,000 hotel rooms in India while in China the figure is much higher at 7,65,000 rooms. The annual growth rate of hotel rooms in India is only 6 per cent, compared to 22 per cent in China, 18 per cent in Thailand and 15 per cent in Malaysia. Economic growth in tier II and tier III cities have put these on the hospitality industry map.

ARR are likely to harden in these cities in next 2-3 years due to shortage of room. Niche areas like health tourism and spiritual tourism are emerging as lucrative business opportunity for the industry. The overall buoyancy in the market is attracting increased interest from investors and higher inflow of capital in the industry is expected. The growth for hotels is also likely to come from proliferation of Special Economic Zones.

Major impediments to the growth are sensitivity to business cycles and adverse political and social events (including terrorist attacks), high rate of tax, high land price, bureaucracy, and poor infrastructure. For instance, the effective rate of taxation on tourism in India is 21 per cent as compared to 7 per cent in Thailand, 4 per cent in Malaysia and 1 per cent in Hong Kong. Furthermore, owing to high land prices, there are more five star hotels than budget hotels, making India a high cost deluxe destination. Additionally, India still does not have facility of modernised c-visa. The existing visa process is cumbersome and comparatively more expensive than other destinations. Yields are expected to be low in coming years on account of continuing price-cutting and discounts.

The Government is planning to grant infrastructure status to all budget hotels and convention centres set up in Delhi and National Capital Region till 2010 Commonwealth Games. This will enable them to enjoy a 10 year tax holiday as in case of other infrastructure projects such as roads, ports and power.

BIODIVERSITY

Biodiversity encompasses the variety of all life on earth. India is one of the 12-mega diverse countries of the world. With only 2.5% of the land area, India already accounts for 7.8% of the global recorded species. India is also rich in traditional and indigenous knowledge, both coded and informal.

India is a Party to the Convention on Biological Diversity. Recognizing the sovereign rights of States to use their own biological resources, the Convention expects the parties to facilitate access to genetic resources by other Parties subject to national legislation and on mutually agreed upon terms. The

Convention on Biological Diversity recognizes contributions of local and indigenous communities to the conservation and sustainable utilization of biological resources through traditional knowledge, practices and innovations and provides for equitable sharing of benefits with such people arising from the utilization of their knowledge, practices and innovations.

Biodiversity is a multi-disciplinary subject involving diverse activities and actions. The stakeholders in biological diversity include the Central Government, State Governments, institutions of local self-governmental organizations, industry, etc. One of the major challenges before India lies in adopting an instrument,which helps realise the objectives of equitable sharing of benefits enshrined in the Convention on Biological Diversity.

After an extensive and intensive consultation process involving the stakeholders, the Central Government has brought Biological Diversity Act,2002 with the following salient features:-

1. To regulate access to biological resources of the country with the purpose of securing equitable share in benefits arising out of the use of biological resources; and associated knowledge relating to biological resources;
2. To conserve and sustainably use biological diversity;
3. To respect and protect knowledge of local communities related to biodiversity;
4. To secure sharing of benefits with local people as conservers of biological resources and holders of knowledge and information relating to the use of biological resources;
5. Conservation and development of areas of importance from the standpoint of biological diversity by declaring them as biological diversity heritage sites;
6. Protection and rehabilitation of threatened species;
7. Involvement of institutions of state governments in the broad scheme of the implementation of the Biological Diversity Act through constitution of committees.

GEOLOGICAL EVOLUTION

Some 225 million years ago, in the Palaeozoic era, all the present¬day continents were part of one landmass called Pangaea. By about 180 million years ago, in the late Triassic and early Jurassic periods, this super mass started breaking, creating Laurasia (Angara) in the north, and Gondwanaland in the south, with the Tethys Sea in the middle. Gondwanaland then split in the Jurassic period, with South America and Africa drifting to the west, India breaking off from Antarctica, and the southern hemisphere landmasses slowly coming into their presentday positions. By about 45 million years ago, India had begun thrusting into Eurasia, creating the buckling and folding which produced the mighty Himalayan chain. This northwards push of the Indian landmass is continuing even today.

GEOLOGICAL DIVISIONS OF INDIA

India is composed of three major units or earth features, which differ in their physical and geological characters. They are:

1. The Peninsula, i.e., the Deccan plateau south of the Vindhyas;
2. The Himalaya mountains, also referred to as the Extra¬Peninsula, which borders India to the north and east; and;
3. The Indo¬Gangetic Plains, lying between the other two divisions and extends from the Indus valley in the west to the Brahmaputra valley in the east.

Five other distinct but smaller divisions can be distinguished: the deserts of Rajasthan, the islands in the Indian ocean and the Arabian sea, the long coastal stretch, the rivers, and the major lakes.

THE PENINSULA

The Himalayas

The Himalayas are true mountains or 'tectonic' mountains. The rise of the Himalaya mountains (also referred to as the extra¬peninsula) to the north, west and east is the result of the intense squeezing out of the Tethyan geosyncline between Laurasia, advancing from the north, and the Indian Peninsular (Gondwana) Block advancing from the south.These mountains are a weak and flexible portion of the earth's surface and have undergone a lot of deformation. The Himalaya is the result of a series of great orogenic movements separated by periods of relative quiescence. The deformation seems to have been initiated during the Upper Cretaceous and has continued through the Middle Miocene, the end of the Pliocene, and the Pleistocene, until the present time.

The Himalayas were submerged by seas for the greater part of their history. The sedimentation accumulated from the Palaeozoic Era attained an enormous thickness of about 15,200 m, and was accompanied by slow sinking of the seabed. It is covered by marine deposits characteristic of the geological periods commencing with the Cambrian. The rivers in this region are rapid and torrential streams in an immature stage of river development. They are actively eroding their courses and have cut numerous deep gorges.

The Himalayas are not a single continuous range of mountains, but a series of more or less parallel ranges, intersected by enormous valleys and extensive plateaus. The overall width of this region varies from 160 to 400 km, while it is about 2,500 km long. The northern slopes support dense natural vegetation with snow¬covered peaks in the higher elevations. The southern slopes, being very steep, accumulate very little snow and support sparse natural vegetation. The altitude, temperature, and rainfall gradient of this region supports a very high diversity of forest, grassland and aquatic ecosystems, including India's only temperate habitats.

The Himalaya has an enormous influence on the meteorology of the Indian sub¬continent. Its snow¬covered peaks have a moderating influence on the temperature and humidity of northern India.The Himalaya is a tall and continuous wall obstructing the flow of the moisture¬bearing monsoon winds and this causes the precipitation of much of this moisture, either as rain or snow. The numerous Himalayan glaciers fed by this snowfall form the source of several rivers, which lower down also gather much of the monsoon rainfall.

The Himalayan region is classified into three parallel zones:

1. The Great or Inner Himalaya is the northernmost of the ranges, with an average elevation of 6,100 m and much of its upper reaches under perpetual snow.
2. The Lesser or Middle Himalaya lies in the middle and is lower in elevation (ranging from 3,600 to 4,600 m) with an average width of 80 km.
3. The Outer Himalaya (or Shiwalik ranges) lie between the Plains and the Lesser Himalaya. They are a series of low hills with an average elevation of 900 to 1,500 m, and range in width from 8 to 50 km.They are composed of narrow parallel ridges running northwest to southeast, separated by broad valleys called the 'doon'. They are of more recent origin than the rest of the Himalaya.

THE INDO¬GANGETIC PLAINS

The Indo¬Gangetic plains stretch along the southern fringe of the Himalayas. The Plains are the alluvial deposits of the rivers of the Indo¬Ganges system. These deposits owe their origin and fertility to erosion of nutrient¬rich material from the mountains and its deposition in the basin through the river system under the overall influence of monsoonal dynamics. These plains were originally a deep depression lying between the Peninsula and the Himalayas. The region is 250 to 450 km wide, and extends for more than 3,000 km from the Arabian Sea to the Bay of Bengal. The Plains are very flat with a gentle seaward slope. The depth of the alluvium is estimated to be 1980 m and the alluvial filling is of unequal thickness.

The Plains are topographically homogenous for hundreds of square kilometers, but for the ravines formed by gully erosion along river courses like that of the Chambal. Along the outer slopes of the Shiwaliks, a steep gravel slope called the bhabar is often found. In this porous tract the surface waters of most of the rivers tend to disappear. These waters then seep out in the marshy terai areas further south. The Gangetic plains are home to a diversity of dry and moist vegetation types (mostly deciduous) and an extensive network of wetlands.

THE RAJASTHAN AREA

In Rajasthan, the Aravallis are a true tectonic mountain range. The Aravallis form a division between the sands of the 'Thar' desert and the central highlands to the east. They mark the present¬day frontier between the western Asiatic desert region and the true Peninsula of the sub¬continent. The flat lands west of the Aravallis have a mixture of geological characters of the Peninsula and the Himalaya. The geo¬tectonics of this area shows no post

Cambrian folding, which is typical for the Peninsula, but it contains fossil deposits of marine organisms belonging to the Mesozoic and Cainozoiceras, which is typical of the Himalaya. This is the only part of the Peninsula which has been submerged repeatedly by the sea. Prolonged and continued aridity has resulted in desert topography. A thick mantle of sands derived both from weathering of rocks as well as blown in by the winds from the west, cover the Thar region.

Various rocks from the Aravallis have been dated as follows: Bundelkhand granite 2,550 million years, banded gneisses complex 2,300 to 2,400 million years, and post¬Aravalli granites 2,100 to 1,900 million years. (The Aravallis were subjected to folding about 1,900 million years ago.) This region is India's driest, characterised by deserts and semi¬arid ecosystems, including dry deciduous and scrub forests.

THE ISLANDS

Besides the continental landmass, the Indian territory also includes coastal and offshore islands.The former consists of a large number of small islands the largest ones not exceeding 100 ha in size lying mainly in the Gulf of Mannar and the Gulf of Kachchh, though several small islands are to be found off the coasts elsewhere as well.These islands are generally lowlying, with elevations of not more than 100 m or so, and support scrubby vegetation on the exposed and coral reefs on the sub¬littoral regions. Most of the islands of the Gulf of Kachchh also support extensive mangrove patches.Some of the islands in the Gulf of Mannar also have mangroves, but not in abundance.

The offshore islands fall into two categories. In the first are the low¬lying coral atolls of the Lakshadweep archipelago (912° N, 7274° E) in the Arabian Sea.These islands are in fact the emerged parts of the coral atolls growing on extinct submarine volcanoes of the ChagosLaccadives Ridge.The elevation of the islands is generally less than 2 m and the area not exceeding a few sq km. The island vegetation is almost exclusively coconut, besides a few species of sand dune flora and leguminous and ornamental plants imported from the mainland. The aquatic realm is remarkable for the prolific reefs and the diversity of marine life. In the second category are the Andaman and Nicobar islands (614° N, 9294° E), which are the emerged part of a mountain chain that lies on a ridge extending southward from the Irrawaddy delta area of Myanmar. There are approximately 572 islands in the chain, some of which are volcanic. The islands occupy an area of 8293 sq km. All the islands are high islands, with dense forests inland and dense mangrove swamps on the coast. All islands have fringing coral reefs with a great amount of biodiversity.

RIVERS AND RIVER VALLEYS

Due to the differing topography, the river systems of the Peninsula and the Himalaya are very different. In the Peninsula the river systems are very ancient and their channels have approached the last stage of river development, namely base levelling. The valleys are broad and shallow with a very low gradient. Water flowing through these valleys has very little momentum except during the floods. During the non¬flood season these rivers precipitate their silt in parts of their basins, estuarine flats and similar areas, and the stream flow is slow, shallow and meandering. The Western Ghats forms the main watershed for these rivers. The Peninsular rivers are entirely fed by the monsoon rains and are very seasonal in their flow, being normally very dry during the summer. These rivers are often divided into two groups:

1. The coastal rivers, relatively small streams, numbering more than six hundred from Saurashtra to Cape Comorin. They drain the western side of the Western Ghats and cut across the narrow plains before flowing into the Arabian Sea; and,
2. The inland rivers, including the west¬flowing Narmada and Tapti and the east-flowing Mahanadi, Godavari, Krishna and Cauvery.

The drainage system in the Himalaya is of much more recent development. The rivers are still actively eroding, transporting and also depositing these materials as they flow through the plains to the seas. These rivers have contributed to the development of the vast Indo¬Gangetic plains by the deposition of silt eroded from the mountains. There is evidence to suggest that many of these rivers are of greater antiquity than the Himalaya. During the upliftment of the Himalaya these rivers more or less stuck to their original channels but their flowrate was accelerated due to the gradient.These rivers are not dependent on the monsoon rain, but are fed by the melting snow of the Himalaya. The volume of water flowing through these rivers tends to fluctuate seasonally, but they never dry up completely.

Several of the Himalayan rivers (Indus, Sutlej, Bhagirathi, Alaknanda, Kali, Gandak) drain the southern slopes of these mountains and also the northern Tibetan slopes. The watershed of these rivers lies a great distance north of the highest peaks of the Himalaya. Much of the initial drainage is in longitudinal valleys running parallel to the mountains and then these rivers take an acute bend and descend to the plains by cutting across the mountains. This results in very deep gorges ranging in depth from 1,800 to 3,700 m.

The Brahmaputra originates in Tibet, east of Kailas¬Mansarovar. From Assam the Brahmaputra flows into Bangladesh, where it is joined by the Ganga. Further south numerous distributaries are formed, which then constitute the vast Sundarbans mangrove delta prior to flowing into the Bay of Bengal.

LAKES

India's bigger freshwater lakes are found in Sikkim (Yamdok Cho and Chamtodong) and a few in Kashmir and Ladakh (Wular, Dal, Pangkong and Tsomoriri). Nainital, Bhimtal and similar small lakes are found in the Kumaon Himalaya.

The Loktak lake, in the northeastern state of Manipur, is the largest of the phats shallow marshes found in the central valley of the state drained by the Manipur river. This lake is characterized by phoomdi, floating islands of decaying vegetation.

The lakes of northern Kashmir and Ladakh are undergoing a period of marked drying¬up. There are distinct terraces, which are indicative of the retreating waters. This is due to the decreasing inflow of water to these lakes and also the increasing aridity of the entire region, caused in no small measure by the blocking of the monsoon winds by the high Himalaya mountains. Waters of many of these lakes are also showing an increase in their salinity. This is due to the decreasing volume of water in these lakes and the lack of any outlet for drainage. All the salts brought in by the rivers are getting concentrated in these waters.

The Peninsula has a few small freshwater lakes. Rajasthan has four or five saltwater lakes of which the Sambhar lake is most well known (the others include Didwana, Phalodi and Pachbadra). The Chilika and Pulicat lakes are located on the east coast. The Chilika Lake, in the state of Orissa, varies in area from 900 to 1,200 sq km and its salinity varies widely depending on the season. It is only a few metres deep across most of its spread. The lake is cut off from the sea by a long spit of sand which occasionally opens up. Spreading across the coastal states of Andhra Pradesh and Tamil Nadu, Pulicat lake is the second largest lagoon in India after Chilika lake. Its area varies from 250 to 460 sq km. Due to deltaic deposits, the lake is extensively shallow.

COASTS

India has a long coastline stretching along nine states and two archipelagoes. The coastline is comparatively regular and uniform, with only a few inlets and creeks of any significant size. A part of the west coast (Malabar region) has a number of lakes, lagoons and backwaters. These shallow lagoons are inlets of the sea and lie parallel to the coastline. At some places along the coast, extensive mangrove swamps are found, especially along tidal estuaries, salt marshes or river deltas. The western littoral region is remarkable for the relatively low number of rivers (small ones for the most part) draining through it. This is despite the favourable conditions that prevail for the formation of rivers.

The coastal lands along the west coast are relatively narrow, as they are flanked by the Western Ghats for most of their length. At most places the mountains are only 40 to 55 km away from the Arabian Sea.

The coastal plains of the east are typical upland plains of marine erosion. The general lithology and the stratigraphy of the marine deposits on the east coast seem to indicate that, since the latter part of the Palaeozoic Era, the general run of the coastline has never been very far from its present position. The eastern littoral region is very different from the west. The lowland is much wider and much of it is true coastal plain in its structure. In places it is formed of the deltas of major rivers like the Mahanadi, Godavari, Krishna and Kaveri. The coastal lowlands are 100 to 130 km wide. The entire seaboard is surrounded by a narrow submarine ledge where the sea is shallow (the continental shelf). This shelf is broader along the west coast than the east coast. From these shelves the sea suddenly deepens out into the open seas.

Besides the above¬mentioned geological and physical divisions, an analysis of the Indian terrain in terms of the abiotic framework that provides the diverse niches and habitats of biodiversity (both natural and agricultural) would include factors like terrain, drainage, climatic factors and hydrologic cycle.The natural diversity and agro¬biodiversity are influenced, and to a great extent determined, by the combination of these factors.

GEOGRAPHY AND MAJOR BIOMES

India is the seventh largest country in the world and Asia's second largest nation with an area of 3,287,263 square km. The Indian mainland stretches from 8 4' to 37 6' N latitude and from 68 7' to 97 25' E longitude. It has a land frontier of some 15,200 kms and a coastline of 7,516 km. India's northern frontiers are with Xizang (Tibet) in the Peoples Republic of China, Nepal and Bhutan. In the north-west, India borders on Pakistan; in the north-east, China and Burma; and in the east, Burma. The southern peninsula extends into the tropical waters of the Indian Ocean with the Bay of Bengal lying to the south-east and the Arabian Sea to the south-west. For administrative purposes India is divided into 24 states and 7 union territories. The country is home to around 846 million people, about 16% of the World's population.

Physically the massive country is divided into four relatively well defined regions - the Himalayan mountains, the Gangetic river plains, the southern (Deccan) plateau, and the islands of Lakshadweep, Andaman and Nicobar. The Himalayas in the far north include some of the highest peaks in the world. The highest mountain in the Indian Himalayas is Khangchenjunga (8586 m) which is located in Sikkim on the border with Nepal. To the south of the main Himalayan massif lie the Lesser Himalaya, rising to 3,600- 4,600 m, and represented by the Pir Panjal in Kashmir and Dhaula dhar in Himachal Pradesh. Further south, flanking the Indo-Gangetic Plain, are the Siwaliks which rise to 900-1,500 m.

The northern plains of India stretch from Assam in the east to the Punjab in the west (a distance of 2,400 km), extending south to terminate in the saline swamplands of the Rann of Kachchh (Kutch), in the state of Gujarat. Some of the largest rivers in India including the Ganga (Ganges), Ghaghara, Brahmaputra, and the Yamuna flow across this region. The delta area of these rivers is located at the head of the Bay of Bengal, partly in the Indian state of west Bengal but mostly in Bangladesh. The plains are remarkably homogenous topographically: for hundreds of kilometres the only perceptible relief is formed by floodplain bluffs, minor natural levees and hollows known as 'spill patterns', and the belts of ravines formed by gully erosion along some of the larger rivers. In this zone, variation in relief does not exceed 300 m but the uniform flatness conceals a great deal of pedological variety. The agriculturally productive alluvial silts and clays of the Ganga-Brahmaputra delta in north-eastern India, for example, contrast strongly with the comparatively sterile sands of the Thar Desert which is located at the western extremity of the Indian part of the plains in the state of Rajasthan.

The climate of India is dominated by the Asiatic monsoon, most importantly by rains from the south-west between June and October, and drier winds from the north between December and February. From March to May the climate is dry and hot.

WETLANDS

India has a rich variety of wetland habitats. The total area of wetlands (excluding rivers) in India is 58,286,000ha, or 18.4% of the country, 70% of which comprises areas under paddy cultivation. A total of 1,193 wetlands, covering an area of about 3,904,543 ha, were recorded in a preliminary inventory coordinated by the Department of Science and Technology, of which 572 were natural. India's most important wetland areas.

Two sites - Chilka Lake (Orissa) and Keoladeo National Park (Bharatpur) - have been designated under the Convention of Wetlands of International Importance (Ramsar Convention) as being especially significant waterfowl habitats. The country's wetlands are generally differentiated by region into eight categories: the reservoirs of the Deccan Plateau in the south, together with the lagoons and the other wetlands of the southern west coast; the vast saline expanses of Rajasthan, Gujarat and the gulf of Kachchh; freshwater lakes and reservoirs from Gujarat eastwards through Rajasthan (Kaeoladeo Ghana

National park) and Madhya Pradesh; the delta wetlands and lagoons of India's east coast (Chilka Lake); the freshwater marshes of the Gangetic Plain; the floodplain of the Brahmaputra; the marshes and swamps in the hills of north-east India and the Himalayan foothills; the lakes and rivers of the montane region of Kashmir and Ladakh; and the mangroves and other wetlands of the island arcs of the Andamans and Nicobars.

Forests

India possesses a distinct identity, not only because of its geography, history and culture but also because of the great diversity of its natural ecosystems.The panorama of Indian forests ranges from evergreen tropical rain forests in the Andaman and Nicobar Islands, the Western Ghats, and the north-eastern states, to dry alpine scrub high in the Himalaya to the north. Between the two extremes, the country has semi-evergreen rain forests, deciduous monsoon forests, thorn forests, subtropical pine forests in the lower montane zone and temperate montane forests. The distribution of the major evergreen forest formations of the region.

One of the most important tropical forests classifications was developed for Greater India and later republished for present-day India. This approach has proved to have wide application outside India. In it 16 major forests types are recognised, subdivided into 221 minor types. Structure, physiognomy and floristics are all used as characters to define the types.

The main areas of tropical forest are found in the Andaman and Nicobar Islands; the Western Ghats, which fringe the Arabian Sea coastline of peninsular India; and the greater Assam region in the north-east. Small remnants of rain forest are found in Orissa state. Semi-evergreen rain forest is more extensive than the evergreen formation partly because evergreen forests tend to degrade to semi-evergreen with human interference. There are substantial differences in both the flora and fauna between the three major rain forest regions.

The Western Ghats Monsoon forests occur both on the western (coastal) margins of the ghats and on the eastern side where there is less rainfall. The distribution of forest in Kerala State, which contains part of the Western Ghats range. These forests contain several tree species of great commercial significance (e.g. Indian rosewood Dalbergia latifolia, Malabar Kino Pterocarpus marsupium, teak and Terminalia crenulata), but they have now been cleared from many areas. In the rain forests there is an enormous number of tree species. At least 60 percent of the trees of the upper canopy are of species which individually contribute not more than one percent of the total number. Clumps of bamboo occur along streams or in poorly drained hollows throughout the evergreen and semi-evergreen forests of south-west India, probably in areas once cleared for shifting agriculture.

The tropical vegetation of north-east India (which includes the states of Assam, Nagaland, Manipur, Mizoram, Tripura and Meghalaya as well as the plain regions of Arunachal Pradesh) typically occurs at elevations up to 900 m. It embraces evergreen and semi-evergreen rain forests, moist deciduous monsoon forests, riparian forests, swamps and grasslands. Evergreen rain forests are found in the Assam Valley, the foothills of the eastern Himalayas and the lower parts of the Naga Hills, Meghalaya, Mizoram, and Manipur where the rain fall exceeds 2300 mm per annum. In the Assam Valley the giant Dipterocarpus macrocarpus and Shorea assamicaoccur singly, occasionally attaining a girth of up to 7 m and a height of up to 50 m. The monsoon forests are mainly moist sal Shorea robusta forests, which occur widely in this region.

The Andamans and Nicobar islands have tropical evergreen rain forests and tropical semi-evergreen rainforests as well as tropical monsoon moist monsoon forests.The tropical evergreen rain forest is only slightly less grand in stature and rich in species than on the mainland. The dominant species is Dipterocarpus grandiflorus in hilly areas, while Dipterocarpus kerrii is dominant on some islands in the southern parts of the archipelago. The monsoon forests of the Andamans are dominated by Pterocarpus dalbergioides and Terminalia spp.

Marine Environment

The nearshore coastal waters of India are extremely rich fishing grounds. The total commercial marine catch for India has stabilised over the last ten years at between 1.4 and 1.6 million tonnes, with fishes from the clupeoid group (e.g. sardines Sardinella sp., Indian shad Hilsa sp. and whitebait Stolephorus sp.) accounting for approximately 30% of all landings. In 1981 it was estimated that there were approximately 180,000 non-mechanised boats (about 90% of India's fishing fleet) carrying out small-scale, subsistence fishing activities in these waters. At the same time there were about 20,000 mechanised boats and 75 deep-sea fishing vessels operating mainly out of ports in the states of Maharashtra, Kerala, Gujarat, Tamil Nadu and Karnataka.

Coral reefs occur along only a few sections of the mainland, principally the Gulf of Kutch, off the southern mainland coast, and around a number of islands opposite Sri Lanka. This general absence is due largely to the presence of major river systems and the sedimentary regime on the continental shelf. Elsewhere, corals are also found in Andaman, Nicobar, and Lakshadweep island groups although their diversity is reported to be lower than in south-east India.

Indian coral reefs have a wide range of resources which are of commercial value. Exploitation of corals, coral debris and coral sands is widespread on the Gulf of Mannar and Gulf of Kutch reefs, while ornamental shells, chanks and pearl oysters are the basis of an important reef industry in the south of India. Sea fans and seaweeds are exported for decorative purposes, and there is a spiny lobster fishing industry along the south-east coast, notably at Tuticorin, Madras and Mandapam Commercial exploitation of aquarium fishes from Indian coral reefs has gained importance only recently and as yet no organised effort has been made to exploit these resources. Reef fisheries are generally at the subsistence level and yields are unrecorded.

Other notable marine areas are seagrass beds, which although not directly exploited are valuable as habitats for commercially harvested species, particularly prawns, and mangrove stands. In the Gulf of Mannar the green tiger prawn Penaeus semisulcatus is extensively harvested for the export market. Seagrass beds are also important feeding areas for the dugong Dugong dugon, plus several species of marine turtle.

Five species of marine turtle occur in Indian waters: Green turtle Chelonia mydas, Loggerhead Caretta caretta, Olive Ridley Lepidochelys olivacea, Hawksbill Eretmochelys imbricata and Leatherback Dermochelys coriacea. Most of the marine turtle populations found in the Indian region are in decline. The principal reason for the decrease in numbers is deliberate human predation. Turtles are netted and speared along the entire Indian coast. In south-east India the annual catch is estimated at 4,000-5,000 animals, with C. mydas accounting for about 70% of the harvest. C. caretta and L. olivacea are the most widely consumed species. E. imbricata is occasionally eaten but it has caused deaths and so is usually caught for its shell alone. D. coriacea is boiled for its oil which is used for caulking boats and as protection from marine borers. Incidental netting is widespread. In the Gulf of Mannar turtles are still reasonably common near seagrass beds where shrimp trawlers operate, but off the coast of Bengal the growing number of mechanized fishing boats has had the effect of increasing incidental catch rates.

BIODIVERSITY

Species Diversity

India contains a great wealth of biological diversity in its forests, its wetlands and in its marine areas. This richness is shown in absolute numbers of species and the proportion they represent of the world total.

Table. Comparison Between the Number of Species in India and the World.

Group in India(SI)	Number of species the world (SW)	Number of species in (%)	SI/S
Mammals	350(1)	4,629(7)	7.6
Birds	1224(2)	9,702(8)	12.6
Reptiles	408(3)	6,550(9)	6.2
Amphibians	197(4)	4,522(10)	4.4
Fishes	2546(5)	21,730(11)	11.7
Flowering Plants	15,000(6)	250,000(12)	6.0

India has a great many scientific institutes and university departments interested in various aspects of biodiversity. A large number of scientists and technicians have been engaged in inventory, research, and monitoring. The general state of knowledge about the distribution and richness of the country's biological resources is therefore fairly good.

Inventories of birds, mammals, trees, fish and reptiles are moderately complete. Knowledge of special interest groups such as primates, pheasants, bovids, endemic birds, orchids, and so on,is steadily improving through collaboration of domestic scientists with those from overseas. The importance of these biological resources cannot be overestimated for the continued welfare of India's population.

Endemic Species

India has many endemic plant and vertebrate species. Among plants, species endemism is estimated at 33% with c. 140 endemic genera but no endemic families. Areas rich in endemism are north-east India, the Western Ghats and the north-western and eastern Himalayas. A small pocket of local endemism also occurs in the Eastern Ghats. The Gangetic plains are generally poor in endemics, while the Andaman and Nicobar Islands contribute at least 220 species to the endemic flora of India.

WCMC's Threatened Plants Unit (TPU) is in the preliminary stages of cataloguing the world's centres of plant diversity; approximately 150 botanical sites worldwide are so far recognised as important for conservation action, but others are constantly being identified. Five locations have so far been issued for India: the Agastyamalai Hills, Silent Valley and New Amarambalam Reserve and Periyar National Park (all in the Western Ghats), and the Eastern and Western Himalaya.

The 396 known endemic higher vertebrate species identified by WCMC from source references. Endemism among mammals and birds is relatively low. Only 44 species of Indian mammal have a range that is confined entirely to within Indian territorial limits. Four endemic species of conservation significance occur in the Western Ghats. They are the Lion-tailed macaque Macaca silenus, Nilgiri leaf monkeyTrachypithecus johni (locally better known as Nilgiri langur Presbytis johnii), Brown palm civet Paradoxurus jerdoni and Nilgiri tahr Hemitragus hylocrius.

Only 55 bird species are endemic to India, with distributions concentrated in areas of high rainfall. These areas, mapped by BirdLife International (formerly the International Council for Bird Preservation). They are located mainly in eastern India along the mountain chains where the monsoon shadow occurs, south-west India (the Western Ghats), and the Nicobar and Andaman Islands.

In contrast, endemism in the Indian reptilian and amphibian fauna is high. There are around 187 endemic reptiles, and 110 endemic amphibian species.

Eight amphibian genera are not found outside India. They include, among the caecilians, Indotyphlus, Gegeneophis and Uraeotyphlus; and among the anurans, the toad Bufoides, the microhylid Melanobatrachus, and the frogs Ranixalus, Nannobatrachus and Nyctibatrachus. Perhaps most notable among the endemic amphibian genera is the monotypic Melanobatrachus which has a single species known only from a few specimens collected in the Anaimalai Hills in the 1870s. It is possibly most closely related to two relict genera found in the mountains of eastern Tanzania.

Threatened Species

India contains 172 species of animal considered globally threatened by IUCN, or 2.9% of the world's total number of threatened species. These include 53 species of mammal, 69 birds, 23 reptiles and 3 amphibians. India contains globally important populations of some of Asia's rarest animals, such as the Bengal Fox, Asiatic Cheetah, Marbled Cat, Asiatic Lion, Indian Elephant, Asiatic Wild Ass, Indian Rhinoceros, Markhor, Gaur, Wild Asiatic Water Buffalo etc. Summary accounts for some of the globally threatened mammals found in India. The number of species in various taxa that are listed under the different categories of endangerment is shown below in Table.

Table. Globally Threatened Animals Occurring in India by Status Category.

	1994 IUCN Red List Threat Category					
Group	**Endanger -ed**	**Vulnerable**	**Rare**	**Indeter -minate**	**Insufficiently Known**	**Total**
Mammals	13	20	2	5	13	53
Birds	6	20	25	13	5	69
Reptiles	6	6	4	5	2	23
Amphibians	0	0	0	3	0	3
Fishes	0	0	2	0	0	2
Invertebrates	1	3	12	2	4	22
TOTAL	**26**	**49**	**45**	**28**	**24**	**172**

A workshop held in 1982 indicated that as many as 3,000-4,000 higher plants may be under a degree of threat in India. Since then, the Project on Study, Survey and Conservation of Endangered species of Flora (POSSCEP) has partially documented these plants, and published its findings in Red Data Books. A conservation status listing of many of these plants, based on information maintained at WCMC, whilst Table provides summary statistics for this information.

Table. Summary of Plant Conservation Status Information at WCMC.

IUCN Threat category	Number of species
Extinct	19
Extinct/Endangered	43
Endangered	149
Endangered/Vulnerable	2
Vulnerable	108

Rare	256
Indeterminate	719
Insufficiently Known	9
No information	1441
Not threatened	374
TOTAL	**3120**

PROTECTED AREAS NETWORK

Development and History

The protection of wildlife has a long tradition in Indian history. Wise use of natural resources was a prerequisite for many hunter-gatherer societies which date back to at least 6000 BC. Extensive clearance of forests accompanied the advance of agricultural and pastoral societies in subsequent millennia, but an awareness of the need for ecological prudence emerged and many so-called pagan nature conservation practices were retained. As more and more land became settled or cultivated, so these hunting reserves increasingly became refuges for wildlife. Many of these reserves were subsequently declared as national parks or sanctuaries, mostly after Independence in 1947. Examples include Gir in Gujarat, Dachigam in Jammu & Kashmir, Bandipur in Karnataka, Eravikulum in Kerala, Madhav (now Shivpuri) in Madhya Pradesh, Simlipal in Orissa, and Keoladeo, Ranthambore and Sariska in Rajasthan.

Wildlife, together with forestry, has traditionally been managed under a single administrative organisation within the forest departments of each state or union territory, with the role of central government being mainly advisory. There have been two recent developments. First, the Wildlife (Protection) Act has provided for the creation of posts of chief wildlife wardens and wildlife wardens in the states to exercise statutory powers under the Act. Under this Act, it is also mandatory for the states to set up state wildlife advisory boards. Secondly the inclusion of protection of wild animals and birds in the concurrent list of the constitution, has proved the union with some legislative control over the states in the conservation of wildlife. The situation has since improved, all states and union territories with national parks or sanctuaries having set up wildlife wings.

The adoption of a National Policy for Wildlife Conservation in 1970 and the enactment of the Wildlife (Protection) Act in 1972 lead to a significant growth in the protected areas network, from 5 national parks and 60 sanctuaries to 69 and 410 respectively, in 1990. The complete United Nations List of National Parks and Protected Areas for India (1993).

The network was further strengthened by a number of national conservation projects, notably Project Tiger, initiated in April 1973 by the Government of India with support from WWF, and the crocodile Breeding and Management Project, launched on 1 April, 1975 with technical assistance from

UNDP/FAO.

Protected Areas of the Western Ghats

The Western Ghats are a chain of highlands running along the western edge of the Indian subcontinent, from Bombay south to the southern tip of the peninsula, through the states of Maharashtra, Karnataka, Kerala and Tamil Nadu. Covering an estimated area of 159,000 sq. km, the Western Ghats are an area of exceptional biological diversity and conservation interest, and are "one of the major Tropical Evergreen Forest regions in India". As the zone has already lost a large part of its original forest cover (although timber extraction from the evergreen reserve forests in Kerala and Karnataka has now been halted) it must rank as a region of great conservation concern. The small remaining extent of natural forest, coupled with exceptional biological richness and ever increasing levels of threat (agriculture, reservoir flooding plantations, logging and over exploitation), are factors which necessitate major conservation inputs."

There are currently seven national parks in the Western Ghats with a total area of 2,073 sq. km (equivalent to 1.3% of the region) and 39 wildlife sanctuaries covering an area of about 13,862 sq. km (8.1%).

The management status of the wildlife sanctuaries in this part of India varies enormously. Tamil Nadu's Nilgiri wildlife sanctuary, for example, has no human inhabitants, small abandoned plantation areas and no produce exploitation, while the Parambikulam wildlife sanctuary in Kerala includes considerable areas of commercial plantations and privately owned estates with heavy resource exploitation.

MEANING AND IMPORTANCE OF BIODIVERSITY

Meaning: Biodiversity is the sum total of all the varieties of species of plants, animals and micro-organisms living on the earth it also includes the habitat in which they live some scientists estimate that more than 10 million species live on our earth and some believe that this number can be more than 100 million.

In other words, the term biodiversity means the number, variety and variability of living organisms in various ecosystems. All type of life whether terrestrial or aquatic are included in this term.

Biodiversity underlies wide range of activities from food production to medicinal research throughout the world man uses at least 40,000 species of plants and animals everyday. A large number of people around the world still depend on wild species for food, shelter and clothing. All domesticated plants as well as animals came from wild-living ancestral species.

Many organisms have instrumental value for man. Some of the benefits we derive from biodiversity are:

- *Food:* Food is the most important value of biological diversity. Earlier, the plants were consumed directly. With the growth of civilization the wild species became the foundation for agriculture.

- *Medicines:* Medicines are also produced from different plant and animal species. In traditional practices of Ayurveda, many plants and their extracts are directly consumed or applied as medicines.
- *Raw Materials:* Many industrial raw materials are procured from plants as well as animals. A large population still uses firewood as a fuel.
- *Biotechnology:* Biotechnology is the recent development which uses genes of organisms to make new crops. It has led to development of new branch called genetic engineering.
- *Recreation:* Recreation in the form of nature photography, bird watching, trekking wildlife tourism etc. is enabled by biodiversity.

BIODIVERSITY IN INDIA

India is a fortunate country for having rich and varied heritage of biodiversity. It has a variety of habitats ranging from tropical rainforests to alpine vegetation and from temperate forests to coastal wetlands. The two hotspots of biodiversity in India are the Western Ghats and the Eastern Ghats. In 1980's around 8 biodiversity hotspots were identified. Recently, a team of scientists has bought out a list of 25 such hotspots.

Features of India's Biodiversity

- Major realms of biodiversity in India are Indo-Malayan, tropical humid forests, tropical delicious forests and the worm deserts.
- India has ten biogeography regions that include trans- Himalayan, the Himalayan, the Indian desert, the semi-arid Zone (S), the western Ghats, the Deccan peninsula, the Gangetic Plain, North – east India, the is lands and the coasts.
- India is one of the twelve centers of cultivated plants.
- India has five world heritage sites, twelve biosphere reserves and six Ramsar Wetlands. Amongst the protected areas, India has 88 national parks and 490 sanctuaries covering an area of 1.53 lakh Sq. Km.

The restrictedness of Indian biodiversity is very high. About 33% of country's flora and fauna are endemic to the country and are concentrated mainly in four regions: North – East, Western Ghats, North – west Himalaya and the Andaman and Nicobar Islands of 49,219 Plant species, 5150 are restricted or endemic and distributed into 141 genera (Closely related species) under 47 families corresponding to about 30% of the world's recorded flora. This means 30% of the world's recorded floras are endemic to India. Of these endemic species, 3,500 are found in Himalayas and adjoining regions and 1600 in the Western Ghats alone. About 62% of the Known amphibian species are again restricted with majority occurring in Western Ghats.

DIVISIONS OF INDIAN BIODIVERSITY

BIODIVERSITY OF HIMALAYAS

Himalayan Flora

Himalayas are one of the hotspots of India. A variety of plant life grows here as a result of varied climate. Both the vegetation as well as wildlife change with altitude and resulting wildlife climatic conditions. Thousands of species of flora and fauna flourish here which adapt to climate predators and other challenges. However many Himalayan species have become extinct and are threatened on the verge of extinction it is directly attributable to the intervention of man in the ecosystem given below is the brief description of tremendous wealth of the Himalayas.

- Vertical Change in vegetation: Himalayan vegetation varies with altitude and climate. As a result variety of trees grow here in the foothill zone, we can find the tropical delicious forests Tropical delicious forests are found in the areas of lower rainfall. They are mainly found in the slopes of the Himalayas trees of these forests shed their leaves once a year. Teak and Sal are common in the areas of delicious vegetation. In the middle altitudes, the temperate forests grow. Pine, spruce, cedar, fir, juniper are common of middle altitudes. Further high, there are coniferous, subs – alpine and alpine forests. Still above these are areas of permanent grasslands and high altitude melons that gradually disappear in the zone of permanent snowline.
- Horizontal Change in Vegetation: The Himalayan vegetation is marked by the tropical Rainforests of Eastern Himalayas and alpine forests of central and western Himalayas. The tropical rainforests of eastern Himalayas are dense, evergreen and gloomy which resemble the areas of Amazon basin.

In the cold desert of Trans Himalayas we find only sparse desert vegetation Chir Pine grows throughout the Western Himalayas except Kashmir. Other major types of vegetation in western Himalayas are: Chilgoza or pine nut, maple, ash and oak.

Changes Bought by Nan

Just like many other areas on Earth, the Himalayas have also been encroached by man. With the increase in population, the demands for forest products also grew.

The delicate natural balance got disturbed and forest cover started reducing in size. The man cut a large number of trees to meet his domestic and industrial demands. Forests have also been cleared for agriculture. Many species have become extinct and many others are endangered.

Himalayan Fauna

The animal Kingdom in the Himalayas in as diverse as the plant kingdom. The Himalayan wildlife differs greatly from the wildlife of other parts India. The animals live in different habitats, ranging from deciduous forests to alpine.

In the Himalayas, animals of lower altitude too are adapted to warmer conditions whereas, animals of alpine region can live even in the betting cold in the eastern Himalayas, the climate is warm and moist, so the animals adjust accordingly. Seasonal movements with the change in season many animals shift to lower altitudes in winters in search of food. As soon as the winters are over, they migrate to higher reaches animals of extremely cold areas have thick fur and bushy tails. Animals of higher reaches are adapted to rarefied air, therefore, have larger nasal cavities.

Carnivores of Himalayas are elusive of all the mammals of Himalayas some of them are threatened and are rare like snow leopard. It is due to indiscriminate hunting by man. The lower region is an area of bigger mammals like swamp deer, cheetel, hog deer, barking deer, wild boar, tiger, panther, wild dog, black and sloth bear and elephant. Besides, prominent scavengers like hyena and Jackal are also present. The common animals in the higher altitude of Western Himalayas are goat, sheep, yak and wild – ass. Ibex is a famous species of goat. Thar and Marknor are also popular species of goat.

In the Eastern Himalayas, wildlife is significantly different from other parts of Himalayas. Some of animals common in the region are red panda, badgers, porcupines, ferrets etc. the popular goats found in the region are serow, goral and takin.

BIODIVERSITY IN TROPICAL RAINFORESTS

The region of tropical rainforests comprises of Eastern Himalayas, Western Ghats, west Bengal and Andaman and Nicobar Islands. All these regions receive heavy rainfall evergreen trees are prominent feature of these forests. In these forests the upper most storey consists of tall trees and makes the canopy that doesn't allow the sunlight to enter. Trees of comparatively lesser height make the second storey. They remain in shade of trees. This think and dense vegetation provides habitat to a number of animals. These prominent animals are elephant, Nilgiri Langur, Lion tailed macaque, Slender Toris, Malabar civet and spring mouse. Gaint squirrels, civets and bats are also found in the tropical forests. Red panda and golden Langur are typical of the Eastern Himalayas.

Rainforests of Andaman and Nicobar Islands have Characteristic features because they are free from Human interference. Here we can find the most beautiful rainforests of the world more than 200 species of trees grow here some of them are: Padauk, Gurjain, Silver gray etc. the common animals of these islands are: wild Pig, hombill, Andaman teal, Nicobar Pigeon, white beuied sea eagle, Andaman cat Snake, Nicobar legless snake etc.

Mangrove forests in the Sunderban delta in west Bengal are habitat of Bengal tigers. Highest numbers of tigers are found in this part of India other prominent animals spotted are deer, pig, monkey, lizard, water monitor, crocodile, crab and fish. The tigers of these forests can swim in water. It mainly preys on the spotted deer, wild boar and fish Bengal Tigers also attack humans.

BIODIVERSITY IN TROPICAL DECIDUOUS FORESTS

Most parts of India are covered by topical deciduous forests. Trees of this region shed their leaves once in a year. They grow mainly in Peninsular India and Indo-Gangetic Plains. The area under tropical deciduous forests extends from the base of Himalayas to Kanyakumari. The region is home for a variety of flora and fauna.

In the western parts, the region is comparatively dry. The western most part is called the Thar Desert. It receives minimum rainfall. The flora of this region consists of dry tropical, dry mixed deciduous, Thom forests, scrub forests and dry savanna forests. In the extreme west, xerophytes vegetation is dominant. This vegetation has thick outer layer from which evapotranspiration is minimum many of the desert plants are thorny with reduced leaf surface. Cacti and succulents are major plant species of desert area.

Fauna of this region is also diverse the prominent animals are sambhar, wild boar, gaur, Chettal, hog deer, swamp deer or barasingha, nilgai, black buck, elephant, muntjak, common mongoose, wolf, squirrel, hare, wild dog, tiger, leopard, lion, hyena, jackal, jungle cat etc.

Many of the animals are endemic to the region. Animals of desert area are adapted to face the water scarcity and extreme hot conditions. Asiatic wild – ass and black – buck are the main animals of the desert area.

The major national parks of the region are: simplipal in Orissa; ramthambore and Sariska in Rajasthan; Belta in Jharkhand; van Bihar in Madhya Pradesh etc.

AGRO BIODIVERSITY IN INDIA

India is also centre for crop diversity it is the homeland of 167 cultivated species and 320 wild relatives of crop plants. India's record in agro – biodiversity is again very impressive there are 167 crop species and wild relatives. India is considered to be centre of origin of 30,000 to 50,000 species of rice, pigeon pea, mango, turmeric, ginger, sugarcane, goose – berries etc. and ranks seventh in terms of contribution to world agriculture.

Economic Potential of Biodiversity

Both plants and animals are a source of variety of food products. Wheat and rice are the staple food in India. Farmers also grow vegetables, cash crops, cereals etc. orchards are the source of fruit many plants are a source of medicines. Several life saving drugs are obtained from them animals like sheep and goat provide wool. Domesticated animals like horse, camel etc. help in transportation activities. Still in many parts of India, fuel wood is the only source of energy. Forests amount to store of huge potential of fuel wood energy. Biodiversity also helps in making the air clean. Through photo synthesis, plants absorb carbon Dioxide and release oxygen large tracks of forests help in absorbing and decomposing pollutants. They help in maintaining hydrological cycle, protecting and recharging of watershed. It helps in making the water clean.

BIODIVERSITY CONSERVATION

The conservation of biodiversity is of two types: the In Situ conservation and the Ex Situ conservation. Normally, the In Situ conservation is more cost effective however, in some cases the ex-situ conservation has to be adopted.

In Situ Conservation

The major objective of protecting the biodiversity is that the ecosystem and biodiversity are able to flourish and evolve. First of all, in situ conservation requires the identification of areas that are to be protected or that have very high biodiversity it can be done by establishing national parks and national reserves. A reserve is split into patches to provide corridors for the movement of animals.

Various Strategies for in situ conservation are:

- *Surveys:* Data on species diversity populations, locations, extent of habitat, major threats etc. are collected. In our country the 'Ministry of Environment and forests plays a guiding role by pre-paring a list of priority issues and areas.
- *Biosphere Reserve:* A Biosphere reserve is an international conservation designation given by UNESCO. It is created to promote balanced relationship between humans and biosphere. The non-conservation activities are totally prohibited in the biosphere reserve. As on June 2005, there are 482 biosphere reserves in 102 countries of the world.
- *National Park:* It is a reserve of land that is owned and declared by the national government of a country. A National park is usually located in under developed areas and is protected from human developmental activities and pollution. It is a reserve of land to save exceptional native plants and animals, Scenic beauty of landscape, geological formations etc. At present, there are around 4000 national parks throughout the world. In India, there are 89 national parks that cover 1% of the countries land area.

Ex Situ Conservation

The approach of ex-situ conservation is used to preserve biodiversity in an artificial setting. It includes ways like storage of seeds in banks, breeding of animals in 2005, setting up of aquariums, botanical gardens, research institutes etc.

- *Captive Breeding:* It is the process of breeding endangered animals by capturing them from their natural environment and then breeding them in unfavourable conditions. Later, they are realized back to their natural habitat when threats to the animals is lessened or removed. This activity is being practiced in many parts of the world with great success.
- *Botanical Gardens:* The botanical gardens grow a variety of plants purposes. In most cases, they are displayed for public, because they have educative value also many botanical gardens depend on public for funding while some are funded by other institutions or the government. The botanical gardens sent their plant collecting expeditions to various parts of the world and publish their findings.
- *Gene Banks:* Gene Banks is means to preserve the genetic material scientists preserve the plant genetic material in the form of seeds or freezing cuts of plants. The animal genetic material is preserved by freezing the sperms and eggs in zoological freezers. Scientists have thus prevented a gene family from ending.

IMPORTANCE

The increasing use of the term biodiversity is being driven by the fact that, in an ecological context, global biodiversity itself is being lost at an alarming rate. Although it has been shown that the significant global biodiversity loss that has occurred over the timeframe of human existence has not stopped global human population increase, there is clear evidence that biodiversity loss can affect the wellbeing of society and have negative economic impacts.

Biodiversity underpins ecosystem function and the provision of ecosystem services. Biodiversity loss therefore threatens the provision of goods and services provided by ecosystems. Reduction in biodiversity can affect decomposition rates, vegetation biomass production and, in the marine environment, affect fish stocks. It is predicted that a reduction in marine productivity means that fisheries will not be able to meet the demands of a growing global population. In addition to the gradual decline in environmental function linked to reductions in biodiversity, it has been suggested that there is a risk that at some point a threshold will be crossed and a catastrophe may occur. Research has highlighted that biodiversity loss could rival the problems of carbon dioxide increases as one of the major drivers of ecosystem change in the 21st Century. Whether from environmental collapse or gradual decline in function, our ability to adapt to a changing world may be considerably reduced if the environment on which we rely does not contain sufficient biodiversity to evolve and continue to support our needs.

MULTILATERAL ENVIRONMENTAL AGREEMENTS

In response to the current rate of biodiversity loss, and on the grounds that biodiversity is a common concern for humankind, the Convention on Biological Diversity (CBD) was opened for signature in 1992. As of June 2013 it has been ratified by 193 parties (Governments). The CBD provides a global legal framework for action on biodiversity and is considered a key instrument for sustainable development. Its three main goals are:

1. The conservation of biological diversity;
2. The sustainable use of the components of biological diversity;
3. The fair and equitable sharing of the benefits arising from the use of genetic resources.

The CBD's governing body is the Conference of the Parties (COP). It holds periodic meetings to review progress on the Convention targets, and advance its implementation. To support implementation of the CBD, the United Nations General Assembly declared 2011-2020 the United Nations Decade on Biodiversity and adopted the Strategic Plan for Biodiversity 2011-2020. The Strategy is a ten-year framework for action adopted by signatory countries in 2010 in Nagoya, Japan. It builds on the vision that "by 2050, biodiversity is valued, conserved, restored and wisely used, maintaining ecosystem services, sustaining a healthy planet and delivering benefits essential for all people".

The Strategy calls for all countries and stakeholders to effectively implement the three objectives of the CBD by establishing national and regional targets, feeding into the five strategic goals and 20 global targets (collectively known as the Aichi Targets) outlined by the Strategy. The primary framework for action set forth by the CBD is the ecosystem approach, an integrated strategy for the management of biodiversity resources. Biodiversity is also at the centre of a number of other Conventions e.g. the Convention on Migratory Species (CMS), the International Treaty on Plant Genetic Resources for Food and Agriculture (Plant Treaty), The Convention on International Trade in Endangered Species of Wild Fauna and Flora (CITES). It is also the subject of a number of associated Protocols such as the Specially Protected Areas Protocol and the Cartagena Protocol. A new platform, the Intergovernmental Science-Policy Platform on Biodiversity and Ecosystem Services (IPBES), was established by the international community in 2012 and is open to all United Nations member countries. It is an independent intergovernmental body committed to providing scientifically-sound assessments on the state of the planet's biodiversity in order to support informed decision-making on biodiversity and ecosystem services conservation and use around the world.

MEASURING AND MONITORING BIODIVERSITY

Over the last 30 years, many different definitions of biodiversity have been used. As early as 1992, the year the Convention on Biological Diversity was opened for signature at the Rio Earth Summit, it was noted that the definitions of biodiversity are "as diverse as the biological resource". While the CBDdefinition is commonly accepted, the variety of definitions of biodiversity is particularly relevant when it comes to the scientific measurement of biodiversity. For the purposes of detailed analysis, and the creation of indicators to measure or monitor trends, exactly how biodiversity is defined will influence what is measured.

Biodiversity indicators aim at using quantitative data to measure aspects of biodiversity, ecosystem condition, services, and drivers of change. This advances understanding of how biodiversity is changing over time and space, why it is changing, and what the consequences of the changes are for ecosystems, their services, and human well-being. The huge variety of elements included in the definition of biodiversity results in a varied set of methodologies to measure the natural environment. There is no unified metric for quantitative measurement. The variety of metrics employed include:

- Species richness (number of species);
- Population number (number of genetically distinct populations of a particular species defined by analysis of a specific element of its genetic makeup);
- Genetic diversity (The variation in the amount of genetic information within and among individuals of a population, a species, an assemblage, or a community;
- Species evenness (measurement of how evenly individuals are distributed among species); and
- Phenotypic (organism characteristics) variance, (the measurement of the different between the phenotypes within a sample).

BIODIVERSITY MEASUREMENT AND POLICY

To measure biodiversity is an area of discussion particularly relevant at the science/policy interface. The CBD-mandated Biodiversity Indicators Partnership (BIP) promotes the development of indicators in support of the CBD and related Conventions, national and regional governments and a range of other sectors. Indicators initiated under the partnership are linked to the goals of the Strategic Plan for Biodiversity 2011-2020 and include habitat extent, protected areas and species extinction.

3

Economic Perspectives on Nature Tourism

TOURISM: AN INDUSTRY

Tourism industry is the one that deals with the tourists as consumers, the money spent by them, and the resources rendering various goods and services which facilitate the composition of the tourism product. This industry has been named as a 'smokeless industry' because unlike other industries it is invisible and non-polluting. The tourism industry is an extraordinarily complex integration of many industries spread over many sectors.

Tourism is an umbrella industry containing a set of inter-related business participants. For example, industries like Transport, Accommodation, and Travel Companies, Recreation and Entertainment Institutions, Handicrafts business, etc and the provision of the many goods and services demanded by tourists. Interestingly, most of the component industries also get related to varied commercial and non-commercial activities over and above providing their services to the tourists.

Over the years, there has been a growing awareness of tourism as a human activity, an industry, and a catalyst for economic growth and development. Like any other industry the tourism industry draws resources from the economy, adds value and produces marketable products. The only difference here is that no tangible product is produced like in the case of a manufacturing industry. The product in this case is intangible and joint or composite in nature. The tourism industry impacts various auxiliary and ancillary industries as well. Tourism today is undergoing a rapid transformation towards a new industry having far-reaching implications for organizations in the travel and tourism industry in particular, and consequences of import for developing and developed countries in general, growing increasingly dependent on the tourist dollar. The forces driving the change in this industry are many.

In olden times people travelled mainly for commercial and religious reasons and leisure travel was for the rich. Today people travel for a variety of motivations, including business, leisure, religion, culture, visiting friends and relatives, education and health. The means of transportation have become varied and faster and as the transport becomes faster, new travellers emerge and people travel greater distances. Another important force driving the growth within the industry is the growth and expansion of the middle class and an increase in their disposable income. The travel industry is complex in nature and challenging to manage. This is for three main reasons- their process type, cost structure and market features.

In terms of process, most operations are a combination of customer processing operations, material processing operations and information processing operations. There is a mix of cost structures based around provision of service, food, accommodation, sightseeing, airfare etc. Forecasting and packaging are some key market features. Originally segmentation in the industry was based on social class however, currently many factors influence segmentation in the industry.

Now there are products that are specially marketed to specific groups of people or market segments based on lifestyle. Due to segmentation more choice is created for consumers and branding has emerged, major companies are developing brands that are easily recognizable, for example, Thomas Cook holidays, Star Cruises, etc. Tourists are now a sophisticated lot. They are demanding and constantly looking for new variations in the products and newer destinations. In addition, there is growing environmental awareness and travellers are increasingly prepared to shun over-commercialized and polluted destinations for newer and less popular ones. Parallel to all these changes in the market place, there is deregulation of the airline industry, an explosion of technology both for automated reservations and for travel management, and an increasing trend towards concentration of the industry reflected by the large numbers of mergers, takeovers and acquisition of the industry from 'old' to 'new' tourism.

New tourism is a transition from the existing to the tourism of the future typified by:

- Enhanced tourism experiences
- Flexible tourist products
- Management of the tourist industry
- Segmentation
- Thrust towards diagonally integrated organizations and

There are clear and apparent manifestations that the tourist industry is beginning to take on newer dimensions. The emerging new practice is the creation of a number of factors including the system of new information technologies in the tourism industry, deregulation of the airline industry, environmental pressures; technology compensation; changing consumer tastes, leisure time, work patterns and income distribution.

The economics of new tourism is quite different from the old. From system gains, segmented markets, designed and customised holidays the focus now is also on, profitability and competitiveness in tourism. The new tourists show greater care and have a concern for conservation of the natural environment. There has been a shift towards eco tourism, green tourism, rural tourism, farm tourism, sustainable tourism, etc. with perpetual opportunities of benefit from this new tourism. Competitive Strategies for success have to be employed today for survival.

There are new techniques and trends to be followed by the industry players. To gain competitive advantage, the players and participants of the industry will have to

- Be customer friendly,
- Be quality conscious,
- Innovate new and better products,
- Make meaningful value additions.

And for tourist destinations to be competitive, certain key principles need to be incorporated into the policy framework.

Some of these are:

- Be environmentally sensitive,
- Encourage private sector participation,
- Make tourism a leading sector,
- Strengthen the distribution channels in the market place.

Today tourism is sensitive to the environment as well as inhabitants of the region or area, tourism is sustainable, and tourism is capable of transforming tourism-dependent and vulnerable areas' economies into viable entities. Tourism is in a stage of revolutionary change and a new kind of tourism is emerging fast. New tourism promises flexibility, segmentation and diagonal integration. It is driven by information technologies and changing consumer requirements. Today this industry can produce an entire system of value addition and wealth generation.

The objective today is 'tourism should be planned in a manner that it benefits the community as a whole, has benefits for the locals, and optimizes the expectations of the tourists besides taking care of the environment.'

TOURISM IS A GROWTH INDUSTRY

In the 21st century the global economy will be driven by three major service industries–Technology, Telecommuni-cations and Tourism. Travel and tourism will be one of the world's highest growth sectors in the current century. Tourism, just as to experts is expected to capture the global market and become the largest industry in the world. The statistics and projections point to an era of unprecedented growth of tourism around the world. From 70 million international tourist arrivals in the year 1960 the WTO has estimated that international tourism arrivals worldwide would be 1.5 billion by the year 2020. The latest report from the World Travel and Tourism Council "in the year 1999

Travel and Tourism generated about 3.5 trillion US dollars of GDP and almost 200 million jobs across the world economy: approximately.

World travel and tourism GDP is forecast to increase in real terms at 3% per annum in the decade 2000-2010. During the same period employment in travel and tourism is expected to grow at about 2.6% per annum."

World Travel and Tourism Council has summarized some of the highlights concerning worldwide travel and tourism industry as follows:

- The Travel and Tourism Industry contributed 11.7% towards world GDP in 1999;
- Travel and Tourism has emerged strongly from the South- Asian crisis with leisure tourism rising by 4.7% in 1999 and business travel by 4.4%;
- Tourism related spending by international visitors amount to 8% of world exports in 1999 with a further impact by export of Travel and Tourism related goods;
- Travel and Tourism related GDP is forecast to increase at 3% per annum in real terms;
- In the coming years, over 8% of all jobs worldwide will depend upon Travel and Tourism;
- Travel and Tourism will support the creation of over 5.5 million jobs per year over the next decade.

Thus, tourism today is a shining sector and a great economic force. Its status as a major economic activity has been recognized by almost all the nations of the world. During the 1960s there was emphasis on tourism as an earner of foreign exchange, a catalyst of development, and a security against the uncertain fluctuations of commodity prices. Today however, its impact is not only economic but social and cultural as well.

Cultural tourism is a fertile ground for exercising creative talents, fostering special kinds of relations between visitor and the host populations. It enables the tourist to form a view of his present world and a global concept of the historic past. Thus, tourism has wider implications encompassing not only economic benefits but also social and cultural benefits as well.

TOURISM AND DEVELOPMENT

Development can be viewed from various dimensions, however, for the purpose of this current session, we use the following definition of economic development: Economic development is a process of economic transition that involves the structural transformation of an economy and a growth of the real output of an economy over a period of time. It is a long run concept. Structural transformation is achieved through modernization and industrialization and is measured in terms of the relative contribution to gross domestic product of agriculture, industry and service sectors. The potential of tourism to contribute to development is widely recognized in the industrialized countries, with tourism playing an increasingly important role and receiving government support. Tourism along with some other activities like financial services and tele-communications is a major component of economic strategies. Tourism has become a favoured means of addressing the socio- economic problems facing rural areas on one end, while enhancing development of urban areas on the other.

TOURISM AND NATIONAL DEVELOPMENT

Tourism emerged as a global phenomenon in the 1960s and the potential for tourism to generate economic development was widely promoted by national governments. They appreciated that tourism generated foreign exchange earnings, created employment and brought economic benefits to regions with limited options for alternative economic development. National tourism authorities were created to promote tourism and to maximize international arrivals. However, an awareness of the negative environmental, social and some other impacts also increased. The importance of economic benefits at the local level, environmental and social sustainability was also widely accepted. It was observed that tourism presents excellent opportunities for developing entrepreneurship, for staff training and progression and for the development of transferable skills. Tourism development focuses on national and regional master planning. It also focuses on international promotion, attracting inward investment. The primary concern has been with maximizing foreign exchange earnings. These earnings enable the government to finance debt and also to finance some investment in technology and other imports for economic development.

NO TRADE BARRIERS TO TOURISM

Unlike many other forms of international trade, tourism does not suffer from the imposition of trade barriers, such as quotas or tariffs. Mostly, destination countries have free and equal access to the international tourism market. This position has become strengthened by the inclusion of tourism in the General Agreement on Trade in Services, which became operational in January 1995.

REDISTRIBUTION OF WEALTH

Both internationally and domestically, tourism is seen as an effective means of transferring income, wealth and investment from richer, developed countries or regions to less developed, poorer areas. This redistribution occurs as a result of both tourist expenditures in destination areas and also of investment by the richer, tourist generating countries in tourist facilities. Thus it appears as if, the developed countries support the economic growth and development of less developed countries.

TOURISM AND POVERTY REDUCTION

Tourism can contribute to development and the reduction of poverty in a number of ways. Economic benefits are generally the most important element, but there can be social, environmental and cultural benefits and costs as well. Tourism contributes to poverty reduction by providing employment and various livelihood opportunities. This additional income helps the poor by increasing the range of economic opportunities available to them. Tourism also contributes to poverty alleviation through direct taxation of tourism generated income. Taxes can be used to alleviate poverty through education, health and infrastructure development. Some tourism facilities also improve the recreational and leisure opportunities available for the poor themselves at the local level. Tourism is not very different from other productive sectors but it has four potential advantages for pro-poor economic growth:

- It has higher linkage with other local businesses because customers come to the destination;
- It is relatively labour intensive and employs a large proportion of women workers;
- It has high potential in poor countries and areas with few other competitive exports;
- Tourism products can be built on natural resources and culture, which might sometimes be the only assets that people have.

The contribution of tourism to the local economy is also important to note. It has five kinds of positive economic impacts on livelihood, any or all of which can form part of a poverty reduction strategy:

- Collective income which may include profits from a community run enterprise, land rent, dividends from joint ventures. These incomes can provide significant development capital and provide finance for corngrinding mills, a clinic, teachers housing and school books
- Dividends and profits arising from locally owned firms and business units
- Earnings from selling goods and service or casual labour
- Infrastructure gains, for example, roads, water pipes, electricity and communications.
- Wages from formal employment

At this point it must also be mentioned that there are some disadvantages of tourism as well. For example, leakages and volatility of revenue. These are also common to other economic sectors. However, tourism may involve greater trade-offs with local livelihoods through more competition for natural resources, particularly in coastal areas.

STRATEGY FOR DEVELOPING COUNTRIES

Tourism plays a very important role in the economies of many countries. Earnings from tourism-related activities contribute a considerable portion to their

GDPs. Tourism is now being viewed as a significant tool and an important strategy in achieving economic growth in these countries. The WTO is convinced that tourism has considerable potential for growth in many developing countries and Less Developed Countries where it is a significant economic sector and promising high growth rate; and that it has advantages when compared with other economic sectors. This case can be summarized as follows: Comparative Advantages of Tourism as a Development Strategy for Developing Countries.

- Access to international markets is a serious problem for developing countries particularly in traditional sectors like food, agriculture and textiles where they confront tariff and non-tariff barriers. This is not the case for the tourism sector, where barriers would involve visa restrictions and related taxes only. The example of Cuba is instructive in this regard. Whilst Cuba has struggled to find export markets for its sugar and tobacco, it has been much more successful in maintaining a dynamic tourism industry.
- In many developing countries, for example South Africa, China, Philippines and India, domestic tourism is growing rapidly and like international tourism brings relatively wealthy consumers to areas where they constitute an important local market. Domestic tourism can be accessed by people with lower budgets and is often equally valuable to the economy.
- Most export industries depend on financial, productive and human capital. The tourism industry not only depends on these, but also on natural capital and culture, which are sometimes the only assets owned by the poor.
- Tourism has particular potential in many countries with few other competitive exports.
- Tourism is a much more diverse industry than many others and can build upon a wide resource base. This diversity results in wider participation of the informal sector, for example a farming household produces and sells local handicrafts.
- Tourism is consumed at the point of production. This results in great opportunities for individuals and micro-enterprises, in urban or marginal rural areas, to sell additional products or services to the potential consumers.
- Tourism is often reported to be more labour intensive than other productive sectors. Data from six countries with satellite tourism accounts does indicate that it is more labour intensive than nonagricultural activities, particularly manufacturing, although less labour intensive than agriculture.
- Tourism provides various employment opportunities especially to women as compared to some of the other sectors.

Perceived Disadvantages of Tourism as a Development Strategy:

- Foreign private interests drive tourism and it is difficult to maximize local economic benefits due to the high level of foreign ownership, which means that there are high levels of leakages and few local linkages. But that might not be the case many times.
- Many small enterprises and individual traders sustain themselves around hotels and other tourism facilities and these small companies are not foreign owned. There is often confusion about levels of foreign ownership as local ownership is often masked by franchise agreements and management contracts. WTO is studying this issue in collaboration with UNCTAD as part of its poverty elimination research.
- Tourism can impose substantial non-economic costs on the poor. For example, loss of access to resources, displacement from agricultural land, social and cultural disruption and exploitation.
- Many forms of development bring with them disadvantages that need to be managed. The economic and non-economic negative impact needs to be determined and the issues addressed. It is for this reason that the WTO supports a holistic livelihood approach to assessing the impact of tourism-positive and negative–on the poor. Issues like environmental management and planning at local level need to be addressed through the good governance agenda.
- Tourism is a vulnerable industry. It reacts immediately to factors like changes in economic conditions in the originating markets, levels of economic activity in tourism in the destination markets. Thereby affecting international visitor arrivals. It is also very vulnerable to civil unrest, crime, political instability and natural disasters in destination countries.
- It has been observed that the volatility of export markets for tourism is not significantly greater than other commodities. Many times tourism has the advantage noted that it is not subject to tariff or other non-tariff barriers and that the destination has some control over civil unrest, crime and political instability
- Tourism requires highly sophisticated marketing. International tourism marketing is expensive, although there are more efficient and less costly forms of marketing available today. Many government agencies at the national level, tie ups of domestic hotels and resorts with international participants, word of mouth publicity, target marketing are some of the methods used.

Tourism in many developing countries and many LDCs has been growing strongly in recent years and there are strong reasons to think that these trends will continue. Many developing countries have comparative advantages in tourism where tourism constitutes one of their better opportunities for development. The disadvantages, which are often identified in relation to international tourism in developing countries, are few when tourism is compared with other sectors of the economy. WTO believes that tourism is considered alongside other industries as a development option and that where tourism presents the best opportunity for local economic development and antipoverty strategies, development banks, bilateral and multilateral development agencies should back it with determination.

LINKAGES AND LEAKAGES

The term leakage in used to refer to the amount spent on importing goods and services to meet the needs of tourists. Leakages take place across national boundaries that can have impact on the balance of payments of the countries. It results from the economic exchange between the two countries. It also occurs when the local economy is unable to provide reliable, continuous, supplies on the basis of competitive prices of the required product or service and of a consistent quality to meet the market demand.

From a tourism and poverty perspective it is generally more productive to focus on the other side of the coin-linkages. When the local economic linkages are weak, the revenue received from tourism in the local economic area leaks out. In order to reduce such leakages, it becomes necessary to deliver consistently at an appropriate quality and at competitive prices, at the same time, engaging the local suppliers who use local capital and resources.

LEAKAGES

From the perspectives of local economic development and poverty reduction, we are not concerned how much a tourist spends outside the country, but how much he is not spending in the local economy, which means, limiting the benefit to local communities and the poor among them.

Leakages, which have negative impact on the development of local tourism, are:

- Advertising and marketing efforts abroad
- Impact skills, expatriate labour
- Imported commodities, goods and services
- Imported technology and capital goods
- Increased oil imports
- Repatriation of profits
- Transporting tourists to the destination country

However developing local sources of supply, encouraging local ownership and enhancing linkages to the local economy can improve this. The last two of these can create more jobs and opportunities for small and medium enterprises at the same time.

LINKAGES

There are many ways in which local communities can be benefitted by these propositions. The best way is to increase the extent of linkages between formal tourism sector and the local economy. By formal tourism sector we mean hotels, restaurants, lodges, and tour and transport agencies. To the extent linkages to the local economy can be increased, the extent of leakages will be reduced.

The increased integration can further develop strong linkages between tourism and other economic sectors. Not only do agriculture, fisheries, manufacturing, construction and domestic industries get integrated, the auxiliary and ancillary industries are also strengthened.

This in turn provides additional revenue and jobs, which reduces the import content and foreign exchange leakages from the tourism industry. Government and development agencies should create local linkages as part of their overall tourism development strategy in the planning, construction and operational phases.

There are three sets of factors, which are important in enhancing the extent of local linkages:

- The creation of employment at all skill levels and particularly where there is existing capacity.
- The Anti-poverty tourism development strategies have suggested 'new attractions'. The tour operators at the ground level should integrate these. The critical areas include creating mutually beneficial business linkages between the formal and informal sectors. Small and emerging entrepreneurs are often neglected. Local government should ensure that microenterprises and emerging entrepreneurs are promoted while taking local tourism marketing initiatives. Visitor attractions, parks, cultural sites and hotels should be encouraged to provide information about local products and services provided by the poor.
- There is need to understand tourist expectations thoroughly. Also, small enterprises to meet the credit needs and marketing needs are also required. Small enterprises sometimes face difficulties in meeting the requirements of health and safety, licensing and other regulatory requirements. There is a need to systematically educate and train the poor in such a way that they are able to integrate themselves with the growing requirements relating to regulations.

The local market should be geared up to deliver qualitatively reliable and competitive goods and services to tourists. The local business community should be actively involved in the process through partnership approaches. This requires continuous efforts, which is possible through long-term partnership to benefit from linkages. Once planning commission concessions are being granted, private sector companies can be asked to make the development of such linkages part of their bid.

Tourism can help in diversifying other sectors of the local economy and can create new ones, offering additional community livelihood opportunities. Local economic benefits and ownership are likely to be greater, if local communities participate in diversified business activities. Now with the growing awareness governments are adopting policies, to encourage and facilitate participation by the local communities. The participation by the poor in the development of tourism projects may result in increasing employment and growth of complementary products. These benefits can further be maximized through partnerships at the destination level. There is a tremendous possibility of bringing about sustainable development for the local economy if Hotels and tour operators work together with local communities, local government and NGOs.

This can help in reducing poverty and can provide a richer experience to domestic and international tourists. Such partnerships will benefit both the host communities and the tourism industry. This will also help them earn more tourism dollars, euros or pounds without any leakages. This can further be utilized for community development. Through affirmative policies, enterprises can contribute significantly to economic development, in both their constructional and operational phases. Some practical strategies for developing local economic linkages.

Market Access and Enclave Tourism

There is practically no link between local people and tourism market. Tourists are not accessible to the local community when they are within their hotels, coaches, and safari vehicles or inside sites and attractions such as museums. These are all enclave forms of tourism. The local community people who wish to sell their products to tourists don't have access to them. They end up hawking and touting at entry points.

The problem is still more difficult in case of Cruise ship passengers and tourist on "all inclusive" hotel or resort packages where local entrepreneurs hardly interact with them. Access to the market plays major role in involving entrepreneurs in the tourism industry. This is particularly true in the case of the informal sector; where the return on local skills and services is often maximized and where the scale of capital investments is low. There is a need to keep this aspect in mind at the time of tourism planning, as access to tourists for the informal sector is often neglected. Some tourists prefer all-inclusive packages, as they do not always feel safe in a new destination and are happier in a protected environment. They feel protected from the poverty and hassle from beggars, touts and hawkers in some destinations. But there is a way to solve this problem. This requires partnership approach between Hotel and informal traders. This allows informal traders to provide such an environment where tourists feel secure in moving beyond the enclave and to approach "hassle-free" crafts markets. Local guides can also help in establishing contact between tourists and traders by rotation for which they may have agreement among themselves.

This also requires observing certain code of conduct by the local traders and guide. There should be a design to link the informal sector with formal sector so that poor members of community can be helped and tourist market becomes accessible to them. This can help them gain the economic benefit from it. There are a number of strategies that can be used to enhance overall economic benefits and can further reduce poverty.

Growth and Selection

Attracting more of the most appropriate market Segments It has been observed that the tourism sector in the poorest countries is generally highly dependent on international markets, as they do not have significant domestic markets. However, it has also been noted earlier that a significant number of developing countries have strong domestic tourism sectors as well as significant outbound tourists. It becomes imperative that the domestic market should always be considered first by the poorest countries, but in order to maximize foreign exchange revenues, the primary focus continues to be on international arrivals.

There is a challenge to attract larger numbers of those international and domestic tourists who are most likely to benefit the poor, those predisposed to visit local markets and to seek first hand experiences of nature, culture and daily life which are most likely to be provided by poor people. It is worth mentioning the importance of intra-regional tourism in this regard; WTO reported intra-regional tourism as growing in most regions of the world. It is significant that 40% of Africa's tourism comes from neighbouring African countries.

This opportunity can be grabbed by opening up the roads and improving the modes of transport between countries in Africa, which would greatly enhance the movement of people and contribute in reducing poverty. Intra-regional tourism is especially valuable for pro-poor tourism and local economic development.

This is because of the fact that there is greater likelihood of shared cultural values and familiarity with social systems between the people of neighbouring countries. There is no doubt that there is a case for attracting more visitors in order to increase the economic impact. At the same time we must understand that this strategy will only assist in poverty reduction if the additional tourists can be encouraged to spend in ways that benefit the poor and if it results in overall sustainability.

The World Bank's World Development Report recognized that economic growth does not necessarily result in swift poverty reduction. This requires an explicitly pro-poor strategy. This means that there should be constant growth, which favours poor in a disproportionate way.

Some of the key components of broad-based growth which assist in benefiting the poor include:

- Government commitment and responsiveness to the needs of the poor
- The expansion of employment opportunities for the poor
- Improved productivity for the poor,
- Improved access for the poor to credit, knowledge and infrastructure,
- Investment in the human capital of the poor.

Increasing Tourists' Length of Stay

The economic returns can be increased with the same number of tourist arrivals if efforts can be made to extend their stay for a longer period. This results in the development of the product by increasing the numbers of bed nights and the expenditure of tourists on boarding and lodging.

There will be a poverty reduction impact, if the additional bed nights can create extra employment or create greater opportunities for the poor to sell goods and services to the tourists or to the tourism industry.

Increasing Visitor Expenditure

Now-a-days there is a market trend towards more experiential holidays. Tourists want to learn more about the countries they are visiting: the people, their cultures, traditions, cuisine, etc. It is much more than mere holidaymaking. The trend is towards more active holidays, greater personal involvement and active participation instead of passive relaxation. This again has potential for the diversification and enrichment of the tourism product. There is scope to develop more activities and attractions, with increased demand for interpreters and services of guides and transport necessary for their enjoyment. This increases both expenditure and length of stay. Making more extensive use of natural and cultural heritage, at the same time carefully managing the tourism impacts so as to ensue the conservation of resources, can make an important contribution both to economic development and conservation. This leads to growth in "Special interest tourists" who tend to spend more money on and during their holidays and to stay longer, whether those interests are based on natural, archaeological, historical or cultural heritage, or based on adventure and physical challenge.

Developing Complementary Products

Providing a greater variety and richness of attractions and activities at destination can increase tourists' expenditure. This will increase the propensity of travellers to visit various attractions at the destination and may extend their length of stay and increase their expenditure. This translates into creating more promising opportunities for the development of complementary products that enable the poor to engage in the industry and to profit from it. The growth in established industry results in stimulating interest in the development of complementary products: tourism services and goods.

This complements the core tourism facilities of transport, excursions and accommodation. The list of complementary effects goes on increasing. These complementary tourism products often provide experiences that are not provided by the tour operators but which enrich their product. Hoteliers and tour operators can encourage local people to develop tourism products and services and to support them in doing so with training and marketing. This will increase the attractiveness of the destination and increase tourist expenditure in the local economy and will also develop the complementary products.

Local communities can often engage in the provision of complementary products because it requires less capital investment and is therefore less risky. Tourism is often best considered as an additional diversification option for the poor, rather than a substitute for their core means of livelihood. As an additional source of income it can play an important part in improving living standards and raising people above the poverty threshold. The poor can maximize their returns by choosing forms of participation, which complement their existing livelihood strategies. It also helps them earn from their cultural and social assets.

Tourists are interested in the "everyday lives" of local communities and there are a host of smallenterprise opportunities for local people. Local guides and cyclerickshaw driver/guides in India's Keoladeo National Park, and guides and charter-boat operators in Indonesia's Komodo National Park are examples of local people diversifying their livelihood strategies. The boat operators also earn their living from fishing and many of the cycle-rickshaw drivers work in town when the tourist season is low.

Spreading the Benefits of Tourism Geographically

Tourism destinations are geographically diverse in nature. There are different geographical sites like beaches, mountains and urban attractions and holidaymakers can be encouraged to travel further, beyond established destinations, which can enhance and diversify their experience of particular environmental, cultural or natural heritage attractions. Heritage Trails and other similar products have been developed to extend length of stay and to spread the advantages of tourism development to new areas and communities.

They can be used as initiatives, which may benefit the poor. National Parks, cultural sites and World heritage sites are often the major attractions, the primary "tourism magnets" in significant parts of the developing world and they often attract people to marginal rural areas. It can be argued that natural and cultural heritage sites as the major attractions should be taking a wider view of their potential to contribute to tourism development and the well-being of local communities. These areas otherwise are of no interest to tourists.

Changing the way in which tourism is organized in and around attractions can increase the economic development impact. For example, at Kamodo National Park in Indonesia, non-local carriers and package tour operators take away a big slice of tourism trip expenditure, *i.e.*, about 85%, which could have otherwise gone to local economy. Estimates for average local expenditure at Komodo per visitor demonstrate the importance of minimizing enclave tourism.

Cruise ship tourists spent on average US $0, 03 in the local economy, package tourists spent US $52.5 and independent travellers US $97.4. The Parks and other major tourism attractions in rural areas can be developed to assist the development of small-scale, locally owned attractions and tourism services. Nature-based tourism and cultural heritage tourism in rural areas can provide significant local markets and economic development opportunities. It contributes to integrated rural development and offers local employment and supplementary income-generating opportunities for poor people. The development of tourism in such areas can significantly improve incomes for local communities and the poor. For this these flagship attractions can be planned and managed so as to maximize the opportunities for local economic development and poverty reduction.

Infrastructure and Planning Gain

The development of infrastructure and tourism development are interrelated. Tourism can contribute to overall socio-economic development through the provision of roads, telephones, and electricity, piped and treated water supplies, waste disposal and recycling and sewage treatment. Roads developed for tourism provide opportunities for trade and new roads opened to improve trade also bring tourism opportunities if they open access to tourism resources. New economic corridor development projects often create tourism development opportunities for local communities in addition to improving trade linkages.

These facilities enhance opportunities for other forms of local economic development, but more could be done at the local and national level to maximize those benefits, particularly when new projects are licensed. It is possible to maximize the planning gains through appropriate policies by government and tourism planners. The right policy in the right direction will encourage local economic development and benefit the poor.

Local Management of Tourism and Partnerships

Local communities and the poor amongst them are more likely to benefit from planning gain where they are involved in discussions and decisions about tourism developments. Benefits can be maximized where the complementarities between different forms of tourism development and their livelihood strategies are given due consideration. Appropriate planning structures can facilitate effective community participation in the tourism development process and provide a mechanism for capturing planning gain through infrastructure, employment and economic linkages. A planning process should define carrying capacity and set limits of acceptable change.

This will influence local communities' active participation in tourism development and help in achieving anti-poverty goals. It is through participation by these local community people whose traditional and local knowledge can be utilized for empowering them. This will also help in maintaining the environmental, social and cultural integrity of destinations.

Small and Medium Enterprises Development

The increased interest in local tourism experience results in increased opportunities for the development of new locally owned enterprises. This helps in providing competitive and complementary goods and services. This trend is found in developed country destinations. This can be supported by government policy and SME development strategies. The tourism industry offers viable opportunities for the development of a wide range of SME's. Even in the developed countries they contribute to the largest part of local tourism supply.

In Europe small and medium-sized firms meet 70% of tourist accommodation demand. Some estimates for the developing world put the comparable figure as high as 85% In well-established developing country destinations, like Goa, increasing numbers of international tourists are staying in locally owned accommodation. SME's are very important in the provision of restaurants and bars, handicrafts, the supply of furnishings and other consumables to hotels, the provision of transport, local tour operating, guiding and attractions. All this requires access to capital resources and training in business management for SME's. This requirement is critical in the field of marketing. Providing information, advice and mentoring to small and micro enterprises and emerging entrepreneurs can make a significant contribution to their success.

Reducing Seasonality

Seasonality in tourist arrivals is the major cause of seasonal and casual unemployment. There are a number of strategies that can be employed to extend the tourism season. During festivals arranging melas generates curiosity and helps the development of special interest products. Other strategies include developing places for seminars and conventions, and such pricing policies, which specially address senior citizens who have more flexibility to travel in the low season.

These strategies have an overall impact on the local economy. Strategies that reduce seasonality and successfully attract tourists in significant numbers for a larger part of the year, benefit the hotels and tour operators, their employees and those in the destination who earn all or part of their livelihood by direct or indirect sales to tourists or the tourism industry. Those who benefit from this are most often poor.

EMPLOYMENT LINKAGES

The employment impact of tourism is felt by both direct employment in tourism enterprises and indirect employment in those enterprises and micro-enterprises that supply raw material, goods and services to the tourism industry. The demand of direct employment in tourism is dependent upon the scale and level of tourism development and the extent of tourists' engagement in the local economy and with SME's. This helps in maximizing the employment of locals and nationals in tourism, including managerial grades.

Income is also held within the local and national economies and reduces wage and salary leakages. When wages and salaries are remitted or spent outside the local boundaries, it amounts to leakages from the local economy. However, the success of the tourism enterprise will depend upon the delivery of the appropriate level of service, and in this global industry maintaining high levels of training is an important consideration in the economic sustainability of businesses. One of the ways in which the industry can contribute to poverty reduction is by committing to recruit more local poor people and imparting appropriate training and staff development programmes with the belief that those commitments can be met. Tourism can contribute to poverty alleviation through the creation of employment. Certain changes in existing employment practices can bring desirable developments. Pro-poor employment strategies can be pursued, for example prioritizing the employment of women and youth. Tourism is a relatively labour intensive industry providing direct employment in hotels and tour companies, and indirect employment in taxis, bars, restaurants and other indirect service suppliers, where a proportion of employee time serves the tourism industry and tourists.

Tourism can create jobs, which benefit the poor where specific measures are taken to recruit and train workers from amongst the poor. Where tourism enterprises make these efforts, proper estimates should be made; records should be maintained of its effects on employment to determine to what extent local people, and particularly the poor, benefit and to ensure that their efforts are acknowledged. Beyond the hotels, particular efforts should be made to train and employ local guides, artists, performers and craft workers who are able to interpret their heritage and in the process empower youth and women who have considerable control over it. Entrepreneurship development programmes for tourism SME's do complement these efforts.

These programmes typically include developing business opportunity awareness, business planning including project feasibility analysis and training in management skills. Provision of business advisors and mentoring services may be strengthened for emerging entrepreneurs over several years. Many countries already have small business development and credit programmes and tourism SME development can sometimes be attached to these existing programmes.

MOVING BEYOND "TRICKLEDOWN" EFFECT

It has long been established that tourism development projects, if successful, would attract foreign investment, contribute foreign exchange earnings to the national accounts and generate economic development. Through the process of trickledown, the magnitude of benefits would be amplified. Local communities would benefit through employment and local economic development generated by the additional spending and the new entrepreneurial opportunities which this would create. It must be understood that tourism operations need to be profitable in a competitive world market if they are to survive. There are a number of things, which can benefit the local economy in tourist destinations.

The benefits can arise in the following ways:

- Building and complementing existing livelihood strategies through employment and small enterprise development
- Controlling negative social impacts
- Ensuring the maintenance of natural and cultural assets
- Evaluating tourism projects for their contribution to local economic development not just for their national revenue generation and the increase in international arrivals
- Facilitating local community access to the tourism market
- Maximizing the linkages into the local economy and minimizing leakages

ECONOMIC IMPACT OF TOURISM

EARNER OF FOREIGN EXCHANGE

Tourism has major economic significance for a country. The receipts from international tourism are a valuable source of earning for all countries, particularly, the developing. Visitor-spending generates income for both public and private sectors, besides affecting wages and employment opportunities.

Although tourism is sensitive to the level of economic activity in the tourist-generating countries, it provides more fixed earnings than primary products. The income from tourism has increased at a higher rate than primary products. The income from tourism has tended to increase at a higher rate than merchandise export in a number of countries especially in countries having a low industrial base. Now there is practically an assured channel for financial flows from the developed countries to the developing countries raising the latter's export earnings and rate of economic growth. Tourism, therefore, provides a very important source of income for a number of countries, both developed and developing. The figures from World Tourism Organization indicate that, among the world's top 40 tourism earners about 18 were developing countries including India, in the year 1995. Regarding the number of visitor arrivals, in some countries there were more visitor arrivals than the population.

France with a population of 57 million received 74.5 million visitors in the year 2000. Similarly Spain with a population of 37 million received 48.5 million visitors during the same year. Several island countries, like the Caribbean Islands, depend greatly on tourist income resulting from visitor arrivals. These earnings form a major part of the gross domestic product. Even developed countries like Canada which derived over 13 per cent of its gross domestic product from international visitors in the year 1999, rely heavily on income from tourism.

Tourism forms a very important source of foreign exchange, for several countries. Although the quantum contributed in foreign currency per visitor varies from destination to destination, the importance of receipts from tourism in the balance of payment accounts and of tourist activities in the national revenue has become considerable for a number of countries. The major economic benefit in promoting the tourism industry is in the form of earning foreign exchange.

Income from these foreign-exchange earnings adds to the national income and, as an invisible export, may offset a loss of the visible trading account and be of critical importance in the overall financial reckoning. This is truer in the case of developing countries particularly the small countries, which depend heavily upon primary products such as a few basic cash crops where tourism often offers a more reliable form of income. In the case of some European countries, namely Spain, Portugal, Austria, France and Greece, the invisible earnings from tourism are of a major significance and have a very strong positive effect on the balance of payments. Tourism is therefore a very useful means of earning the much-needed foreign currency.

It is almost without a rival as an earning source for many developed as well as developing countries. These earnings assume a great significance in the balance of payment position of many countries.

The balance of payments shows the relationship between a country's total payments to all other countries and its total receipts from them. In other words, it may be defined as a statement of income and expenditure on international account.

Payments and receipts on international account are of three kinds:

- The visible balance of trade relating to the import and export of goods
- Invisible items
- Capital transfers.

The receipts from foreign tourism form an 'invisible export', just like other invisibles which come from transportation and shipping, banking and insurance, income on investments, etc. Because most countries at times have serious problems with their international payments, much attention comes to be focused on tourism because of its potentially important contribution to, and also effect upon, the balance of payments. The receipts from international tourism, however, are not always net. Sometimes expenditures are involved which must be set against them.

Net foreign exchange receipts from tourism are reduced principally by the import cost of goods and services used by visitors, foreign exchange costs of capital investment in tourist amenities and promotion and publicity expenditure abroad. Peters, "Certain imports associated with tourist expenditures must be deduced... the importation of material and equipment for constructing hotels and other amenities, and necessary supplies to run them; foreign currency costs of imports for consumption by international tourists; remittances of interests and profits on overseas investment in tourism enterprises, mainly hotel construction; foreign currency costs of conducting a tourism development programme, including marketing expenditure overseas". Reliance on imports to meet the tourist's needs does not, in any way deny developing countries the opportunity of earning foreign exchange in supplying such goods and services. Imports are, to a large extent, essential to the operation of the tourist sector as to that of other sectors. The important question is whether the value added domestically on an item or service in is maximized? Maximization of import substitution without due regard to the effect on overall tourism receipts may be counter-productive.

Also, differences in the pattern and level of reliance on imported goods and services, capital equipment and manpower are very wide, depending upon the level of development of a country. In some cases, this reliance is simply due to a lack of resources that transform into items which are to be sold by the industry. In others, the industry has not yet drawn on such supply potential, for which it may be an important stimulus. There is a general need for careful programmes of positive import substitution.

MULTIPLIER EFFECT

The discussion in earlier paragraphs clearly indicates that earnings from tourism occupy an important place in the national income of any country. Without taking into account receipts from domestic tourism, international tourism receipts alone contribute to a great extent. The flow of money generated by tourist spending multiplies as it passes through various parts of the economy. In addition to an important source of income, tourism provides a number of other economic benefits, which vary in importance from one country to another; depending upon the nature and scale of tourism. The benefits from infrastructure investments, justified primarily for tourism such as airports, roads, water supply and other public utilities, may be widely shared by the other sectors of the economy. This enables us to understand how tourism impacts development in the economy. Tourist facilities such as hotels, restaurants, museums, clubs, sports complexes, public transport, and national parks are also used by domestic tourists and visitors, businessmen and residents, but still a significant portion of the costs are sometimes borne by international tourists. Tourists also contribute to tax revenue both directly through sales tax and indirectly through property, profits and income taxes.

Tourism provides employment, develops infrastructural facilities and may also help regional development. Each of these economic aspects can be dealt with separately, but they are all closely related and are many times considered together. Let us first look at the income aspect of tourism. Income from tourism cannot be easily measured with accuracy and precision. This is because of the multiplier effect. The flow of money generated by tourist spending multiplies as it passes through various parts of the economy through the operation of the multiplier effect. The multiplier is an income concept. The Concept: The 'multiplier' measures the impact of extra expenditure introduced into an economy by a person. It is, therefore, concerned with the marginal rather than average changes.

In the case of tourism, this extra expenditure in a particular area can take the following forms:

- Spending on goods and services by tourists visiting the areas
- Investment of external sources in tourism infrastructure or services;
- Government spending
- Exports of goods stimulated by tourism

The expenditure can be analysed as follows:

- *Direct Expenditure*: In the case of tourism, this expenditure is made by tourists on goods and services in hotels and other supplementary accommodation units, restaurants, other tourist facilities like buses, taxis coaches, railways, domestic airlines, and for tourism-generated exports, or by tourism related investment in the area.
- *Indirect Expenditure*: This covers a sum total of inter-business transactions which result from the direct expenditure, such as purchase of goods by hoteliers from local suppliers and purchases by local suppliers from wholesalers.
- *Included Expenditure*: This is the increased consumer spending resulting from the additional personal income generated by the direct

expenditure, *e.g.*, hotel workers using their wages for the purchase of goods and services. Indirect and induced expenditure together are called secondary expenditure.

There are several different concepts of the multiplier. Most multipliers in common use incorporate the general principle of the Keynesian model.

The four types of multipliers are intrinsically linked as follows:

- *Sales Multiplier*: This measures the extra business turnover created by an extra unit of tourist expenditure. Output Multiplier: This is similar to the sales multiplier but it also takes into account inventory changes, such as the increase in stock levels by hotels, restaurants and shops because of increased trading activity.
- *Income Multiplier*: This measures the income generated by an extra unit of tourist expenditure. The problem arises over the definition of income. Many researchers define income as disposable income accruing to households within the area, which is available to them to spend. However, although salaries paid to overseas residents are often excluded, a proportion of these salaries may be spent in the local area and should therefore be included.

  Income Multipliers can be expressed in two ways:
  - The ratio method which expresses the direct and indirect incomes generated per unit of direct income;
  - Normal method, which expresses total income generated in the study area per unit increase in final demand created within a particular sector.

Ratio multipliers indicate the internal linkages which exist between various sectors of the economy, but do not relate income generated to extra sales. Hence, on their own, ratio multipliers are valueless as a planning tool. Employment Multiplier:

The employment multiplier can be expressed in one of the two ways:

- As a ratio of the combination of direct and secondary employment generated per additional unit of tourist expenditure;
- Direct employment created by tourism per unit of tourist expenditure. Multipliers can be further categorized by the geographical area which is covered by the research, such as local community, a region within a country or the country as a whole.

The multiplier mechanism has also been applied to tourism and, in particular, to tourist expenditure. The nature of the tourism multiplier and its effect may be described in the example: "The money paid by a tourist in paying his hotel bill will be used by the management of the hotel to provide for the costs which the hotel had incurred in meeting the demands of the visitor, *e.g.*, such goods and services as food, drink, furnishing, laundering, electricity, and entertainment. The recipients, in turn, use the money they have thus received to meet their financial commitments and so on. Therefore, tourist expenditure not only supports the tourist industry directly but also helps indirectly to support many other industries which supply goods and services to the tourist industry. In this way money spent by tourists is actually used several times and spreads into various sectors of the economy. In sum, the money paid by the tourist, after a long series of transfers over a given period of time, passes through all sectors of the national economy, stimulating each in turn throughout the process".

On each occasion when the money changes hands, it provides 'new' income and these continuing series of exchanges of the money spent by the tourists form what economists term the multiplier effect. The more often the conversion occurs, the greater its beneficial effect on the economy of the recipient country.

However, this transfer of money is not absolute as there are 'leakages' which occur. Such leakages may occur as a result of importing foreign goods, paying interest on foreign investments, etc.

The following are some examples of such leakages:

- Payment for goods and services produced outside, and imported into, the area;
- remittance of incomes outside the area, for example, by foreign workers;
- indirect and direct taxation where the tax proceeds are not re-spent in the area;
- savings out of income received by workers in the area.

Any leakages of these kinds will reduce the stream of expenditure which, in consequence, will limit and reduce the multiplier effect. Income generated by foreign tourist expenditure in countries possessing more advanced economies, which generally are more self-sufficient and less in need of foreign imports which are less self-sufficient and need to support their tourist industries by substantial import. If the developing countries are desirous of gaining maximum economic benefits from tourism, they should strictly control the imported items for tourist consumption and keep foreign investment expenditure at a reasonable level. If the leakages are not controlled then the benefits arising from tourism will be greatly reduced or even cancelled.

The most important leakage would arise from expenditure on import of agricultural products like food and drink. In a primary macro-economic approach to the prospects opened up by tourism establishment in a developing country, it is regarded as advantageous that a good portion of tourist consumption should consist of food products. It is estimated that the major part of these products can be found in those countries, whose economic structure is largely agricultural in character. In this sense tourist consumption, derived from international flow, can offer an assured outlet to a production which is already active within the domestic economy, without raising problems connected with export of such products and could thus be substituted for imported foodstuffs and a significant saving effected thereafter. The host country derives maximum economic benefits from the tourism industry as these savings help in increasing the benefits from the tourism multiplier. This aspect of the question is all the more important as the multiplier effect maintains its efficacy and effectiveness as long as no importation takes place. It follows that if the national economy is to derive the maximum benefit from the impact of international and national tourism, there is an elementary obligation to find all those products needed for tourist consumption. The dynamics of agricultural production in recent years confirms the ability of developing countries to produce the major part of their agricultural products required for tourist consumption without resorting to massive imports. The tourist economy of any country, if it is to remain healthy, must rely upon local agricultural production and this condition seems today to be on its way to realization in most of the developing countries.

Multiplier of Tourism Income

To sum up, Multipliers are a means of estimating how much extra income is produced in an economy as a result of initial spending or after cash is injected. Every time the money changes hands it provides new income and the continuing series of conversion of money spent by the tourists form the multiplier effect. The more often the conversion occurs, the greater its beneficial effect on the economy of the recipient country.

GROWTH OF INFRASTRUCTURE

A significant benefit of tourism is development and improvement of infrastructure. The benefits from infrastructure investments, justified primarily for tourism–airports, roads, water supply and other public utilities–may be widely shared by the other sectors of the economy. In addition to development of new infrastructure, the improvements in the existing infrastructure which are undertaken in order to attract tourists are also of great importance. These improvements may benefit the resident population by providing them with amenities which they desire. Furthermore, the provision of infrastructure may provide the basis or serve as an encouragement for greater economic diversification. A variety of secondary industries may be promoted which may not directly serve the needs of tourism.

Therefore, it is evident that tourist expenditure is responsible for stimulating other economic activities. One of the characteristics of under development is that of deficiencies in the basic infrastructures, which lie at the root of a series of problems related to the development of tourism. Development of infrastructure requires a certain size of investment. Tourism provides the size of demand which justifies the development of infrastructure. On the basis of this minimum demand for such facilities and for such social capital, the size of such infrastructural services evolves. Construction of primary infrastructures represents the foundation of any future economic growth, even though they are not directly productive. The tourism industry shows the elementary need for basic infrastructure.

It has today the important benefit of being able to profit from the existing infrastructures and thus to make a decisive contribution to the growth of the national economy. The international and national tourist traffic, moreover, represents a reward for the capital invested and can now contribute to the financial efforts required for maintenance. The satisfactory degree of development achieved in this specific sector now permits major tourist progress, while also giving further proof of the complementary character of tourism in relation to other economic sectors. Creation of basic infrastructures for tourist usage will also be of service to the other sectors of the economy such as industry and agriculture. This results in better equilibrium of general economic growth.

TOURISM AND TAXATION

Tourism also results in tax revenues both at national and local levels. Taxes can provide the financial resources for the development of infrastructure, enhancing and maintenance of some types of attractions and other public facilities and services, tourism marketing and training required for developing tourism, as well as to help finance poverty alleviation programmes by governments both at local and national levels.

In addition, tourism-related tax revenues help finance general community improvements and services used by all residents. WTO's 1998 report on tourism taxation emphasizes that taxation policies in a country must be carefully evaluated in an integrated manner to ensure that tourism-related taxes are giving the necessary substantial revenues. However, taxes should not be so high for the country's international competitive position to be counter productive and produce a loss of tourist traffic.

The aim should be to strike a balance between, a level of taxation that maintains a competitive position for the country and reasonable profits for the industry, and, receiving adequate revenues to support investment in and maintenance of the tourism sector, and to contribute towards general community welfare.

BALANCED REGIONAL DEVELOPMENT

Another important domestic effect relates to the regional aspects of tourist expenditure. Such expenditure is of special significance in marginal areas, which are relatively isolated, economically underdeveloped, and have unemployment problems. The United Nations Conference on International Travel and Tourism held in Rome in 1963 stated that tourism was important not only as a source of earning foreign exchange, but also as a factor determining the location of industry and in the development of underdeveloped regions. It further stated that in some cases the development of tourism may be the only means of promoting the economic advancement of less-developed areas lacking in other resources. In fact underdeveloped regions of the country usually greatly benefit from tourism development. Many of the economically backward regions contain areas of high scenic beauty and of cultural attractions. These areas, if developed for use by tourists, can bring in a lot of prosperity to the local people.

Tourism development in these regions accordingly becomes a significant factor in redressing regional imbalances in employment and income. Tourist expenditure at a particular tourist area helps the development of the many areas around it. Many countries both developed as well as developing have realised this aspect of tourism development and are contemplating developing tourist facilities in underdeveloped regions with a view to bringing prosperity there. Khajuraho in India, which is now an internationally famous tourist spot, is an example of one such region.

To show, Khajuraho, a remote and unknown small village about forty years ago, is now on the world tourist map which attracts thousands of tourists, both domestic as well as international. Today, Indian Airlines flies a jet plane between the capital city of New Delhi and Khajuraho and seats are not easy to come by.

Thousands of tourists visit the place by air, rail and road transport every month to see the architectural beauty of temples and erotic sculptures whose creators were the Chandela kings, who ruled in North India from the 9th to the 13th centuries. Today 22 glorious temples remind us of the classic Indian architecture and culture of those times and represent the finest expression of the art of medieval India. The area around Khajuraho is well developed and full of life. The place has provided employment to hundreds of local people in hotels and shops.

There is a thriving clay-model industry devoted to making replicas of the famous temple sculptures and a number of shops dealing with items of presentation, handlooms and handicrafts, have created jobs for many. Tourists love to purchase various souvenirs to take home.

Thus local people are recipients of additional income which has increased the prosperity of the region. Subsequently areas around Khajuraho have also prospered and reaped the benefits from the tourist multiplier. There is no dearth of areas which could, after they are developed for tourism, become great assets to the region in particular and to the country as a whole. The French government has created a series of new resorts particularly to bring prosperity to the areas which traditionally have been underdeveloped. The Italian government is likewise attempting to develop tourism in Southern Italy in order to help redress the economic imbalances which have long existed between the northern and the southern parts of Italy. Tourism is to be regarded not as an area of peripheral investment whose benefits will help in creating employment opportunities and in the regeneration of backward regions. In India a similar approach needs to be adopted to develop areas with great tourism potential.

GENERATION OF EMPLOYMENT

Employment is an important economic effect of tourism. The problems of unemployment and under-employment are more active in the developing countries. Tourism can be looked upon in this light as a major industry which employs manpower on a large scale.

The problems which the industrialized countries face in recruiting manpower for the tourists industry confirm that, in any productive process consisting of services, human labour remains the basic need. If a comparison is to be drawn with the productive sector none of the technological progress achieved has succeeded in rendering the human factor less indispensable than in this sector, and this is true to an absolutely indisputable extent.

The high social impact of the tourist industry is well known, for it has repercussions in every other national economic sector through the multiplier effect, which is particularly marked in those services that are complementary to the tourist accommodation industry. The tourist industry is a highly labour-intensive service industry and hence is a valuable source of employment. It employs a large number of people and provides a wide range of jobs which extend from the unskilled to the highly specialized. In addition to those involved in management there are a large number of specialist personnel required to work as accountants, housekeepers, waiters, cooks and entertainers, who in turn need a large number of semi-skilled workers such as porters, chambermaids, kitchen staff, gardeners, etc. Tourism is also responsible for creating employment outside the industry in its more narrowly defined sense and in this respect those who supply goods and services to those directly involved in tourism are beneficiaries from tourism.

Such indirect employment includes, those involved in the furnishing and equipment industries, souvenir industries and farming and food supply. Construction industry is another very big source of employment. The basic infrastructures-roads, airports, water supply and other public utilities and also construction of hotels and other accommodation units create jobs for thousands of workers, both unskilled and skilled. In many of the developing countries, where chronic unemployment often exists, the promotion of tourism can be a great encouragement to economic development and, especially, employment.

However at this point it is, necessary to consider the seasonal nature of the tourism industry. Where general diversification alternatives are scarce, a combination of heavy dependence on tourism and highly marked seasonality calls for measures to develop off -season traffic. Employment multiplier: This multiplier is similar to the Income Multiplier except that in this case a multiplier impact on employment is observed.

Employment Multiplier can be expressed in the following two ways:

- As a ratio of the combination of direct employment. At the destination, the jobs are directly created in the industry there.
- As a ratio of secondary employment generated per additional unit of tourist expenditure to direct employment. The workers and their families require their own goods and services giving rise to further indirectly created employment in shops, schools, health care institutions, etc.

OTHER DIMENSIONS

The World Tourism conference which was held at Manila, Philippines in October 1980, considered the nature of tourism phenomenon in all its aspects. The role tourism is bound to play in a dynamic and vastly changing world was also identified. Convened by the World Tourism Organization the conference also considered the responsibility of various states for the development and enhancement as more than a purely economic activity of nations and peoples.

The significance of tourism was discussed in during the conference. The participants in the World Tourism Conference attached particular importance to its effects on the developing countries. It stated its conviction "that the world tourism can contribute to the establishment of a new international economic order that will help to eliminate the widening economic gap between developed and developing countries and ensure the steady acceleration of economic and social development and progress in particular of the developing countries."

4

Zoo Tourism

INTRODUCTION

Zoos are perhaps the oldest form of wildlife tourism; efforts to tame and keep wild animals in captivity are nearly as old as human society itself. The first documented examples were the animal collections associated with places of worship in Ancient Egypt around 2,500BC. These were simply glorified 'menageries', a term used pejoratively to describe collections of captive animals kept solely for the purposes of display, religion, or for the aggrandisement of the owner. In ancient Egypt, the animals were kept primarily for their religious significance.

Later, other ancient societies including the Greeks, Romans and Chinese also established menageries to display the wealth and prestige of the owners, and to provide for exotic hunting and entertainment. The tradition of gathering and holding impressive animal collections by royal and noble families continued into the 18th century in different parts of the world. The history of the modern zoo began in the late 18th and early 19th centuries with the formation of the first 'public zoos', open to all. The first of these new zoos was the Jardin des Plantes, opened in 1793 in Paris. It was followed by similar establishments in London, Amsterdam, Berlin and Central Park, New York. These zoos represented a significant change, for in addition to public display they were established to support scientific endeavour and public education.

For instance London Zoo was based on the philosophical foundation of scientific advancement and didactic enlightenment. It was immediately popular, and soon became the most fashionable venue in London. The scientific principles on which it was founded and its setting in a large public open park with informal, naturalistic landscaping were to be the pattern of development for new zoos all over the world for the next hundred years. However, by the 1960s, many zoos were in a parlous state: old fashioned, badly run and increasingly out of touch. Their survival depended upon them becoming seen as an integral and relevant part of today's society, and in developed countries particularly, zoos began to respond to growing environmental and animal welfare concerns. As Knowles explains: 'The zoo person of the second half of the century became a conservationist and it was this new philosophy that was to drive the many changes that have occurred in the last decade'.

These zoos now strive to become conservation centres, and in so doing, they have embraced three justifications and objectives for keeping wild animals in captivity: conservation, education and research. Thus the evolution of zoos from menagerie, through zoological garden to conservation centre, can be seen as an illustration of the history of the Western World, in which civilisation has slowly come to appreciate, value and conserve nature. The history and development of captive animal displays can also be understood by reference to first, second and third generation exhibits. The label first generation refers to the barred cages used in the 18th and 19th centuries to display exotic animal species, which were designed primarily to display the animals in isolation to the visiting public.

As Martin explains, large size, bizarre appearance or assumed ferocity was sufficient reason in themselves for displaying the animal, rather in the mode of a stamp stuck on an otherwise blank page of an album. In the 20th century these cages were replaced with larger, more open cement enclosures often surrounded by moats. However, over time it became clear that these too were unsuitable for the animals kept in them and a rising concern over animal welfare meant that they were no longer acceptable to the visiting public. From the middle of the 20th century many zoos developed more naturalistic enclosures that sought to replicate aspects of the displayed animals' natural habitats. These third generation exhibits provided more space for the animals, and typically used more vegetation and disguised barriers to separate the animals from their visitors. At the start of the 21st century, exhibit design continues to develop, as zoos seek to better fulfil their conservation and education objectives.

The latest generation of exhibits combines technology, new construction techniques and a variety of additional interpretive media to create what has been referred to as an immersion experience. Unfortunately, there are still zoos in the world which have failed to develop and improve, and where the standards of animal welfare are still of concern. For instance, less scrupulous zoos in the west have yet to embrace accepted standards of husbandry and care, while in developing countries, many zoos might be said to provide inferior living standards for their animals. The continued existence of such institutions illustrates the both the diverse nature of the zoo industry, and the continual battle to balance public expectations with commercial reality. As Hediger and Mitchell point out, in addition to conservation, education and research, zoos have to have a fourth justification: recreation. They provide a pleasant setting for tourists, local visitors and family outings, and can be an integral part of the social and cultural life of the community. Cherfas goes further, and asserts that this recreational role is critical to zoos. His view is that if people do not pass through the metaphorical turnstile, the zoo is not a zoo: it may be a school, a breeding station, an experimental laboratory, but it is not a zoo, and without people it will not survive. This, then, is the major quandary for today's zoos – how to attract and entertain their visitors, without compromising their other objectives– education, conservation and research.

Although zoos have been a popular and traditional part of society, their future is by no means assured. Many are seen to be traditional and old-fashioned with little scope for change, competing in a tourism industry with innovative and exciting new destinations. The welfare of zoo animals is still controversial while the role of zoos in conservation is yet to be fully understood or appreciated. London Zoo is a typical, traditional city zoo, which has struggled to maintain its place in society. The characteristics and history of this zoo are summarised. The discussion so far has addressed zoos without reference to their role in tourism. Zoos are unusual amongst wildlife tourism destinations in that, while the proportions may vary, most visitors to most zoos are local residents, not tourists. For instance, of the estimated 8 million people to visit Australian zoos each year, approximately 5 million were domestic with the remainder being from overseas. Swarbrooke and Mothershaw have provided similar evidence for the UK by reference to Chester Zoo, where most zoo visitors were drawn from the local area or region, and where the zoo is consequently a vital component of the city's economy and sustainability.

Perhaps as a consequence of this, zoos in the past generally have not seen themselves as being in the tourism industry, but rather as an integral part of their local communities. However, as they have become more business oriented, zoos are now marketing themselves as wildlife tourism destinations. Today, zoos are organisations seeking to satisfy multiple stakeholders with limited resources, and consequently zoo managers must tackle a number of important challenges. These include maintaining a satisfactory balance between running the zoo as a tourism business and a conservation organisation; generating sufficient finance and funding; effectively communication their roles in order to attract an optimum number of visitors; managing the demands of the animal collection and attaining cultural status on the basis of their conservation work. To do this effectively will require zoos to be efficient, competitive businesses within the broader wildlife tourism market.

THE ZOO INDUSTRY

However, as the World Zoo Conservation Strategy explains, there are two characteristics that all such institutions have in common:

- Zoos possess and manage collections that primarily consist of wild animals, of one or more species, that are housed so that they are easier to see and to study than in nature.
- Zoos display at least a portion of this collection to the public for at least a significant part of the year, if not throughout the year.

Consequently, regardless of the composition of their collections, their official name (zoo, aquarium, sanctuary, fauna park etc.) and their type of ownership, all these zoological institutions will be known by the general term 'zoo' in this chapter. With such a diversity of facilities, it is very difficult to calculate the exact number of zoos throughout the world although it has been estimated that there are more than 10,000. The International Zoo Yearbook provides an annual list of zoos of the world and the 2003 edition includes 922 zoos from 85 countries.

However, this is by no means a comprehensive list, because the information is supplied voluntarily by the zoos and does not include many smaller institutions. For instance, the Australian listing includes just 17 zoos while there are an estimated 209 captive wildlife facilities in that country. Nevertheless, such a list does demonstrate the extraordinary geographic range and diversity of zoos across the world. Each zoo is unique and they may be characterised in terms of size, location, management and marketing expertise, organisational structure, number and variety of species displayed. They include institutions under private or public ownership, and exist in both developed and developing countries. Thus zoos are perhaps the most widespread and available form of wildlife tourism in the world being marketed across all cultures and socio-economic levels.

As such a significant segment of the tourism industry, zoos can make a considerable contribution to the economy of their local region, city or even nation. Through their business activities, zoos create employment, purchase goods, materials and services, earn foreign exchange through their visitation by overseas tourists, and generate operating surpluses which are usually reinvested in zoo development projects. For instance, the Australian zoo industry with eight million paid admissions per year, has an annual turnover of some $143 million, generates an operating surplus of $16 million, and employs almost 2,000 people.

The majority of zoos are found in cities, where they have the potential to attract large numbers of visitors. These metropolitan zoos typically display a large number and diversity of species, in relatively small groups and enclosures. The modern trend for presenting animals in their natural physical and social environments has resulted in the development of safari parks and open-range zoos. These represent a minority of zoos, but are becoming increasingly popular. Typically located outside major cities, they are set on a larger area but attract fewer visitors than their city counterparts. They tend to display a greater number of individuals from fewer species, to simulate natural social groupings and behaviour. The World Zoo Conservation Strategy reckons there to be approximately 1,200 'core' zoos in the world. These are so categorised because they are organised as members of recognised zoo associations, of which there are currently 50 throughout the world.. The umbrella organisation for the world zoo community is the World Association of Zoos and Aquaria, with about 200 institutional members, while another 1000 are linked through their membership in a regional or national

Association member. All members of the WAZA Network are obliged to comply with its Code of Ethics and Animal Welfare. They agree to work together at a global level to build cooperative approaches to common needs and issues, to share information and knowledge, and represent the zoo community in other international bodies such as the World Conservation Union. Consequently, the most accurate and complete information and data about the zoos of the world come from these 1200 'core' zoos. Operating zoos is acknowledged as being a highly expensive business and the closer they come to the concept of a conservation centre, the costlier they become. Consequently, zoos often have difficulty in generating the necessary annual revenue from visitor admissions to cover the substantial costs of housing and maintaining and staffing their collection.

Zoos in the UK that closed down during the 1990s did so largely because of a lack of sufficient visitors and revenue. Even for well-established and popular zoos, levels of visitation can vary from year to year in response to a number of factors over which the zoo has little or no control. These may include the state of the economy (particularly the international tourism market), weather conditions (especially during school holidays) and increased competition from other tourist attractions. In addition, other extraordinary factors can also impinge severely on a zoo's ability to generate revenue and balance its budget. For instance, the Foot and Mouth Disease outbreak in the UK in 2001 cost their zoo industry AUD$20 million and was particularly severe in its effect on zoos that had to close their gates for its duration. Consequently, in addition to gate receipts, zoos have increasingly used a number of other means of generating additional income.

These include attracting sponsorship from local, national and international companies, membership schemes and season tickets (often through 'Friends of the Zoo' societies), animal adoptions and sponsorships and retailing and catering activities. More recently, many zoos have introduced after-hours or 'valueadded' events to increase admissions incomes, such as after-hours and 'behind-thescenes' tours, concerts, corporate evenings and private functions. This is a trend which developed in the USA but which is now increasingly seen in zoos in other parts of the world. Another recent development that has impacted upon the zoo industry and its activities has been the trend towards 'economic rationalism'. This philosophy asserts that a prosperous economy depends on efficiency, and the greatest efficiency occurs when open competition in a free market determines outcomes.

The effect on zoos has been twofold. Firstly, public zoos have received less and less government support. These institutions are being told that they need to become more efficient and economically viable by reducing their dependence on 'government handouts' and more fully developing their commercial potential. Secondly, the managerial values of private industry have been increasingly forced upon zoos. This has meant that the majority of new senior staff positions created for zoos have been in the fields of marketing, development and management, and that these vacancies tend to be filled by business professionals rather than people with an animal or zoo background.

This, according to Mazur, has signalled a shift in values beyond simply occupational changes. Zoo leaders, she claims, are now more likely to see their organisation first as a business that must operate 'efficiently', and therefore to apply performance criteria, such as budgeting measures that assess accountability via cost – answerability and economic efficiency. As Chris Larcombe, former Chief Executive Officer of the Zoological Board of Victoria and Director of Melbourne Zoo, explained at an Australasian regional zoo conference in 1995: 'We must come to terms with the increasing financial pressures on the operations of our properties. What we are talking about here is a sustainable base of economic support and leveraging of resources in order to continue to develop our properties.... But we will only be able to continue to deliver this potential if we have organisations of sustainable financial viability'. However, while the desire to increase revenue, efficiency and sustainability is both necessary and desirable, the challenge for zoos is in how to achieve it without losing sight of their fundamental objectives. As van Linge says, 'animal management must never be made subordinate to the pleasure of the visitors'.

THE MARKET

Zoos are a popular and traditional part of wildlife tourism. In many countries, zoos are amongst the most popular destinations for a day out. For instance Mexico City zoo receives more than 12 million visitors per year, Beijing 11 million, Moscow 3.5 million, San Diego 3.3 million and Tokyo 1.5 million. The nine major Dutch zoos are visited yearly by a combined total of approximately 6 million people, with the majority being local residents. The total number of people visiting zoos annually is even harder to estimate than the total number of zoos, and can only realistically be estimated for the 1,200 core zoos mentioned above; at least six hundred million visits are made to these zoos every year. This represents approximately ten per cent of the world's population, and provides a reasonable indication of the popularity and size of the captive wildlife market. In the USA, for instance, zoo attendances exceed all professional sports events combined, with almost 50% of the total population visiting zoos on an annual basis, and more than 90% of Americans having been at least once in their lifetime. This data comes from the 1,200 'core' zoos.

Yet in spite of this popularity, zoos find themselves within an increasingly competitive market servicing an audience that is becoming more discerning.

The past 20 years have seen unprecedented growth in the number of stand-alone visitor attractions, such as museums, heritage properties, farm parks (which display domestic animals), and theme parks. In many countries the number has more than doubled in this period, and has included a wide range of innovative leisure products. Consequently, Hunter-Jones and Hayward suggest that the attractions market is in serious danger of becoming oversupplied. Evidence suggests that in real terms, demand for traditional attractions such as zoos is actually now in decline. For instance, in the U.K. visits to a constant sample of zoos rose by just 4% between 1976 and 1997, while during the same period visits to all other attractions rose by 34%.

(British Tourism Authority (BTA)/ English Tourist Board. A similar stagnation of visitor numbers has been found in Australian zoos. Compares the annual attendance for a number of selected zoos for 1978 and 1998. A number of reasons for this wavering zoo popularity have been given. These include demographic changes resulting in an aging population, not traditionally the main audience of zoos, changes in numbers of leisure consumption, poor marketing techniques employed by zoos limited rejuvenation of the role of the zoo, lack of funding and issues of animal welfare. However, Hunter-Jones and Hayward believe that the overriding reason is simply that zoos are now part of an increasingly competitive leisure market. To compete effectively, they argue, zoos must appreciate their own place in the tourism market and strive to gain a better understanding of the motivations and attitudes of their visitors.

THE ZOO IN THE COMMUNITY

Zoos can play an important role in the life of their local community. Beyond their economic and conservation contributions, zoos can also reflect and participate in the culture of a society. Mullan and Marvin have discussed this aspect of zoos in some detail in their book 'Zoo Culture'. They maintain that zoos have many of the same elements as art galleries and museums, particularly through their history and their place in our cultural traditions. However, they also argue that in one important aspect zoos are different: whereas art galleries and museums entered the realm of high culture, zoos have become essentially popular because they do not intimidate people; visitors can enjoy themselves without having to possess much knowledge about the animals they are viewing.

This has led not just to a higher visitation rate, but also to a perception of zoos as being more 'entertaining', friendlier and more likely to attract both public scrutiny and support. Consistent with this are the results of studies that have examined who visit zoos. Studies from both the US and from Europe have found that visiting zoos is a social experience, with few people visiting alone.. This is supported by similar findings in Australia. The great majority of respondents in all these studies indicated that they were visiting with either close friends or relatives, children were often included and most tended to be frequent visitors. Less clear are the attitudes of these people both to their own visit, and to the role of the modern zoo.

THE ATTITUDES OF ZOO VISITORS

Despite the importance of zoos as tourist attractions, until recently there has been little research to investigate the nature, attitudes and motivations of zoo visitors.. The nature of the zoo as a recreational setting and the preference of visitors to be in social groups would imply that enjoyment is a primary motivating factor, and this is supported by a number of studies across many countries. For instance in a survey of visitors at Woodland Park Zoo Seattle, Fielder and Wheeler found that nearly three quarters considered the zoo to be about entertainment with 92 per cent visiting as a family or social group.

In the U.S., the U.K. and Australia that examined why people visited zoos in those countries. All these studies agree that while people visit zoos for a number of different reasons, paramount amongst them seems to be recreation. In addition, Turley has found children to be particularly significant in the decision: they both facilitate and in their absence inhibit, zoo visiting, with their presence increasing the enjoyment of the visit. Similar findings have come from the U.S. where it was also found that adults who visited zoos as children were more likely to revisit later in life, and to show them greater commitment and support. However, while such research may indicate why people like zoos, the reasons for not visiting have been seldom considered. A major concern still appears to be the perception of captivity and captive conditions. For instance, Turley conducted a small national survey of latent visitors to U.K. zoos in which 40% associated traditional zoos with bars and unnatural conditions, whilst over one third (35%) indicated that not liking to see animals in captivity was a reason for not visiting. Perhaps of even greater significance for zoo managers is the fact that conservation does not appear to be a major motivation for zoo visitors, and is supported by Turley who found that of the three key objectives pursued by zoos (recreation, education and conservation), conservation had the least influence on the desire to visit.

However, although zoo visitors appear to be influenced mainly by motives of enjoyment, many also believe that zoos do have a key role to play in conservation and education. Of those questioned at Woodland Park, Seattle, 68% claimed that they considered the purpose of the zoo to be primarily educational. This is supported by the studies of Australian zoos by Mazur and Ford who also found that the great majority of visitors expected to learn about environmental issues at the zoo. Thus zoos seem to be faced with a contradictory situation: people visit them mainly for recreation, but they believe that their main role is actually in conservation. This dilemma has important implications for zoo management in their search for more revenue: can conservation attract visitors? Will it make money for the zoo, or merely remain a net cost? Turley suggests that conservation may provide people with a justification for visiting the zoo, and therefore does influence attendance level indirectly.

However, there is no evidence to support this yet. Conversely, as Mazur points out, it is not known if visitors will actually go to a zoo less if more conservation programs are implemented and promoted. Such unanswered questions point to a need for more research in this area. So far most has been short term and marketing based, and there has been little deeper evaluation of visitor behaviour. This view is supported by Mason who believes that there is a great deal still to be understood about the nature of zoos as tourist attractions, the characteristics of zoo visitors and visitor satisfaction. In particular their interpretation and understanding of the zoos' conservation, educational, scientific and entertainment roles need to be addressed as a part of this tourism research. For an industry committed to supporting conservation, it is clear that more information is needed about the role of conservation in supporting the industry.

THE WILDLIFE

One million, with the majority comprising 3,000 vertebrate species. Thus, while the majority displays a broad range of species and includes mammals, birds and reptiles, some zoos specialize in the fauna of a particular region or habitat (such as marine parks or desert zoos) and others display only one or two classes of animal (such as bird parks or primate sanctuaries). For any one zoo, the choice of what species to hold may depend on many factors including:

- Zoo legislation which may restrict what a zoo may hold, both for exotic and native species
- The cost of maintaining a particular species
- The conservation status of a species and the zoo's desire to contribute to a particular captive breeding program or conservation activity
- The marketability of the species in terms of its ability to attract visitors.
- The zoo's own stocking policy, or master plan for future development and the availability of suitable enclosure space, facilities and relevant expertise
- The availability of a species from another captive facility that may preclude a zoo from obtaining it.

The final collection may then be a mixture of common and endangered species, and may ultimately represent a compromise between what species the zoo would ideally like to exhibit, and the species that are actually available and appropriate. The primary attraction of zoos is of course, their animals. However, while they are still places of recreation and entertainment, changes in public expectations and the zoo's own objectives mean that today there is far more scrutiny of the way in which their animals are being managed and utilised. In particular, this involves consideration of two important and related factors: the ethics of zoos and the role of zoos in conservation.

THE ETHICS OF ZOOS

Although zoos are popular places to visit, the relationship between the zoo and its public can still present problems. Not only do some people believe that zoos are basically cruel and evil places, but visitors often express negative attitudes towards the animals' captive environments and the way in which they are perceived to be treated. Furthermore, Wolf and Tyitz found that most zoo visitors were primarily concerned for the comfort of the animals, and for their health and happiness. Such attitudes may then be reflected in zoo attendance levels. For instance Brown, believes that the failure of UK zoos to attract more visitors through the 1980's was in part due to a growing concern for animal welfare. Despite their improvements in captive animal management and adoption of conservation objectives, zoos are still seen by some as being superficial, expensive, unnecessary and therefore indefensible.

For instance, the Australian and New Zealand Federation of Animal Societies is opposed to keeping wild animals in captivity, believing that zoos in their present form provide stressful conditions and are unnecessary. Similarly, the Born Free Foundation continues to campaign strongly in the UK and Europe for the abolition of 'the confinement of wild animals for human entertainment', while in the U.S., organisations such as the Society for the Prevention of Cruelty to Animals and People for the Ethical Treatment of Animals provide a consistent and vocal voice for the anti-zoo lobby. Others are simply sceptical of the conservation claims of zoos, believing them to be merely window dressing. As Scott writes: 'Despite their protestations to the contrary, zoos are still menageries. The only difference is that their Public Relations are more efficient and some of them do a little serious captive breeding and research on the side.' In addition, according to Hutchins there is likely to be a continued growth in animal welfare and rights organizations, as well as concern by the public for the welfare of animals in captivity.

Thus zoos actually provoke two ethical considerations. Firstly some people hold the belief that because animals in the wild live in an environment of great complexity with much spatial and temporal variation, no captive environment can be appropriate or suitable. To these people zoos are philosophically unacceptable, and cannot be justified on any grounds. As Hanson explains, this is an elaboration of the idea that 'wild animals ought to roam free', a statement about the authentic state of wilderness. Secondly, the history of zoos as menageries of animals in cramped conditions and maintained largely for human amusement has left a lasting impression on some people of poor animal welfare. As Stevens and McAlister explain: 'It is quite apparent that, for the most part until fairly recent times, the way in which wild animals were kept is something of which humankind should be embarrassed and ashamed.' This combined with the fact that they are constantly in the public gaze, has brought zoos under close scrutiny over the past 20 years. In July 1994, the World Society for the Protection of Animals and the Born Free Foundation (BFF) issued The Zoo Inquiry. Whilst anti-zoo movements have been alive and well in many parts of the world and particularly North America, because WPSA and BFF are UK-based, the major concentration of argument centred on UK and Irish zoos. Although critical of zoos, this document was significant in that it also made some constructive recommendations regarding animal welfare standards, and the role of zoos in conservation. In the ten years since this report, many of these recommendations have actually been adopted by the zoo industry, at least in developed countries.

This has come about through a combination of zoo legislation, and codes of practice. Zoo Legislation that requires zoos to be licensed and inspected now exists in most developed and many developing countries around the world. Although their content varies from country to country and the terminology and its use are not uniform, there are some basic provisions that are common to all. Some of the most recent legislation now requires zoos to justify their existence. For instance a European Union Directive requires zoos in member countries to have conservation objectives, and to address the behavioural needs of its animals. This Directive also provides for the partial closure of a zoo in the event of its failure to comply with conditions imposed in its licence. Codes of Practice represent a form of industry self-regulation and have been developed over the past decade by a number of regional zoo associations to try to raise the standards of animal care and welfare in their member institutions.

In some regions these codes are enforced by the terms of membership of the association itself, with expulsion as the penalty for non-compliance, while in others they are only morally enforced using self-regulation. More recently, these codes have been supplemented by a Code of Ethics developed by the World Association of Zoos and Aquaria. Amongst other things, WAZA demands that members assist in achieving the conservation and survival of species and promote the interests of wildlife conservation and animal welfare.

Members are further asked to act in accordance with all local, national and international laws, and to strive for the highest standards of operations. Stevens and McAlister in their review of the development of the WAZA Code of Ethics have recognized that writing it proved difficult. It had to accommodate both established zoos in developed countries, which required that the proposed code was sufficiently rigorous, and newer zoos in developing regions of the world, which had to be able to attain the requirements of the document. Nevertheless the authors also urge the zoo industry to treat the code seriously: 'It behoves all those involved in the zoo profession to adhere to a strict code of ethics. To do otherwise is to give more ammunition to those who say that zoos are a 'nineteenth century anachronism'.

THE ROLE OF ZOOS IN CONSERVATION

Modern zoos regard conservation as being one of their key objectives, and regard themselves as being 'conservation centres' rather than simply collections of captive wild animals. The actions required by them to dedicate their potential to conservation have been defined in the WZCS, while the Zoo Futures 2005 paper guides zoos in implementing it. These documents are currently being reviewed and updated by the WAZA, and are expected to be republished in 2004. However, their conservation actions can be summarised here as including:

- *Ex situ* Conservation Activities (the conservation of biological diversity outside their natural habitat) such as the maintenance of sustainable captive populations through the genetic management and captive breeding of their collections, conservation education, and research.
- *In situ* Conservation Activities particularly in developing countries, such as endangered species rescue, habitat protection and restoration, and the reintroduction to the wild of captive bred animals. Perhaps the best example of the contribution of an individual institution to *in situ* conservation is Jersey Zoo.

While zoos invest considerable amounts of money in the pursuit of their conservation objectives, most have great difficulty finding additional resources to become involved in conservation programs. As Mallinson points out, in recent years the increase in personal mobility and choice of attractions for a day out have seen many zoos experience falling attendances which, in turn has affected their capacity to contribute to conservation. To help combat this, Larcombe believes that zoos must not only contribute to conservation, but must also be seen to be doing so.

As Bartos and Kelly argue, 'a summary of measurable contributions by zoos in the areas of education, conservation, research and tourism is of critical importance in demonstrating their contribution to the whole community'. However, such suggestions assume that zoo visitors are interested in wildlife conservation, and will visit zoos to learn about it. Unfortunately there is little evidence to support this. As Mason points out, there is an urgent need for more zoo research to determine more clearly not only what the visitors want, but also how zoos can better combine their role in conservation with their commercial imperative.

TOWARDS SUSTAINABLE ZOO TOURISM

Zoos are a popular and important part of wildlife tourism, and they can continue to capitalize on this popularity through the upgrade of existing facilities and the development of new displays and exhibits. However, rather than merely improving what they already have and do, it is likely that zoos of the future will require a more radical shift in the way that their managers, staff, and visitors, see them. As Mazur and Clark conclude: 'While the zoo community should be congratulated for their efforts at modernising their institutions, increasing environmental degradation will ensure continued societal demands for more fundamental changes in zoos than what have transpired so far'.

The opportunity and challenge for zoos today is to transform themselves from traditional static animal collections into true conservation centres, where their message is delivered more effectively through a combination of both entertainment and education. As Mazur and Clark point out, this will involve developing and implementing appropriate policies, economic and organisational procedures, and nurturing and encouraging zoo personnel in the achievement of change. Such a zoo will not be bound by its existing physical boundaries and activities, but will seek to entertain, involve and educate their visitors. In so doing, it will also address and balance its two potentially conflicting obstacles: commercial viability and ethical credibility.

COMMERCIAL VIABILITY

In order to compete effectively and improve their revenue base, zoos must develop and implement strong and innovative marketing strategies that provide a solid financial base while also supporting their conservation, education and scientific goals. This will involve a combination of the following activities:

- Gaining a better understanding of zoo visitor attitudes, expectations and levels of satisfaction and a willingness to broaden their appeal and target other visitor groups such as the expanding seniors market.
- Greater integration and development of other zoo facilities, such as the restaurant and souvenir shop. Traditionally, these have been seen as an adjunct to the zoo, secondary to the animal displays. However, they can be upgraded to become destinations in their own right, and hence another reason for revisiting the zoo. Changing patterns of leisure behaviour over the past ten years have resulted in the growth and demand for leisure shopping, eating and drinking as essential components of a day trip. According to Stevens, shopping for pleasure has now become one of the most important out-of-home activities in the UK, while in the US; there is a close relationship between shopping and visiting attractions among overseas visitors.
- The development of more collaborative links and strategic alliances with other components of both business and government. In this way, zoos are more likely to develop new marketing opportunities, raise funding for their capital works projects, and contribute to and promote their contribution to wildlife conservation.

- Zoos should begin to position themselves more strongly with the donor community in order to take advantage of unprecedented current levels of corporate and personal charitable giving. However, to do so effectively, they must also be more businesslike in their operations, including tighter budgeting and financial reporting.
- Zoos can enhance the experience of their visitors by continuing to develop new and innovative exhibits. As van Linghe explains, zoos can no longer rely solely on the presence of exotic animals to put over their educational message or to attract their share of visitors. Instead, zoos should seek to incorporate more naturalistic settings for their animals with interactive and interpretive displays and presentations that involve and excite the visitors. There may also be opportunities for themed displays, promoting a particular aspect of wildlife and conservation. Possibly these will be linked to other events occurring outside the zoo, either natural or human-made. These displays can be constantly changing, creating an incentive for revisits to the zoo.
- Zoos can further bridge the gap between captive and free-range wildlife by developing greater links with *in situ* conservation activities and ecotourism. In fact, Mason argues that zoos can make a significant contribution within the ecotourism market by acting as a 'taster', providing the stimulus for visitors to make lengthy journeys to more distant locations to see wildlife in their natural settings.

ETHICAL CREDIBILITY

Zoos are now seeking credibility as scientific institutions devoted to conservation and education. Yet this must still be achieved against a backdrop of hostility from the antizoo lobby. As Luoma explains, zoos must confront the suspicion that all the talk of conservation is no more than window dressing to subdue criticism. Turley sees acceptance of their conservation role as vital if zoos are to attain credible cultural status, and that this will be an important part of their sustainability. To achieve it they must be seen as proponents of good animal welfare as well as wildlife conservation. Appropriate actions may include:

- They must adopt, embrace and promote world-class standards of animal care and husbandry by ensuring that both the physical and psychological needs of their animals are fully met.
- Exhibits should be designed which are not only aesthetically pleasing to the public but also replicate critical aspects of their natural environment, thus allowing them to display their full range of normal behaviours.
- Expert veterinary care and nutrition should be provided, and zoos

will participate in and follow the recommendations of cooperative breeding programs.

- Zoos should also be committed to strong conservation objectives through a broad range of activities. These may include public education, scientific research, development of relevant technologies, professional training, conservation planning and captive breeding for reintroduction. However, as Hutchins points out, simply sustaining captive populations of wild animals, whether they are endangered or not, should not by itself be considered conservation. Zoos of the future will need to establish stronger links with *in situ* conservation projects and organisations, and so become more involved with activities such as ecological restoration, the direct support of national parks and the reintroduction and post-release monitoring of wildlife to these areas.
- Finally, zoos must endeavour to use their strong public relations and educational skills to communicate clearly their mission, goals and achievements to the public and to relevant key decision makers.

In this way, zoos can balance the twin challenges of commerce and ethics, and in so doing develop a stronger revenue base, more effectively achieve their conservation objectives and attain credible, cultural status in the community. Zoo tourism may then become truly sustainable

5

Hunting and Fishing

HUNTING AND FISHING TOURISM

As road networks and industrial agriculture expand, and people become more affluent, wildlife resources are diminishing, forcing hunters and fishers to travel further for their quarry, whether it is to the next lake or forest, or to the other side of the globe. The increasing urbanisation of society, combined with the extensive range of quarry, has created a demand and supply situation in which various strategies have been pursued to provide clients with their desired experience, and to derive profit for the fishing and hunting industry. The main target species for hunting tourism include larger ungulates, rodents, and waterfowl, but also incorporate carnivorous species such as bears, wolves, foxes, felids, mustelids, and crocodiles. Fishing focuses on a wide range of marine/estuarine fish, molluscs, crustaceans, and a variety of freshwater species in rivers and lakes. Not all hunting/fishing falls under tourism, but much of it incorporates the following defining elements of tourism:

- Travel to and from a particular destination
- The presence of a tourism service industry (outfitters, tour guides, hunting farms)
- The exchange of money for services
- Overnight, to several months, stays at destinations
- A service industry
- Aspects of leisure and recreation

There is a wide range of products available, varying between over US$100,000 for a hunting trip to a few dollars for a fishing license in Australia. How important is the industry worldwide, how many people engage in it and what is the total economic value of the hunting market?. This was conducted in order to gain at least a coarse measure of tourism-related hunting and fishing activities. If one assumes that particular tourism sectors, including wildlife tourism, are represented equally on the web, and in proportion to the size of the actual industry, then it is possible to gain an understanding of their relative size. Hunting and fishing account for 29 per cent of all the websites connected with tourism (a total of approximately six million hits). In almost one third of cases, the concept of being immersed in nature was associated with hunting or fishing. International hunting tourism, as an industry, has developed in the wake of the European expansion. The affluent British gentleman-adventurer, often also a naturalist, travelled to remote places, to explore first-hand the wonders of the tropics, the confronting dangers of a tiger or elephant hunt, the thrill of a safari, or the quiet pastime of the insect collector.

It is not surprising that such a person would take home a trophy, such as skins, horns, teeth, dried penises, skulls or tails, in order to verify their adventures. Although, in later years, photographic evidence could have replaced this method of verification, tiger skins and elephant tusks had, by that time, become such an essential part of a residential display that its waste would have been unthinkable. Much of this would have occurred during the 19th Century in Africa and Asia, and thus international trophy hunting was born. Trophy hunting was never restricted to the European gentry. In the 1960s, for example, the King of Bhutan, a Buddhist, succumbed to a heart attack while enjoying a hunting-safari in the heart of Africa. In 2003, there is a wide, and increasing, range of potential destinations for hunters and fishers depending on their interests in prey and costs. Hofer et al., distinguished between the demand and supply countries. There are fishers and hunters in all parts of the world, however there are distinct places where the supply outweighs the demand. It is to these destinations that most fishers and hunters travel.

Hunting and fishing, including in their tourism form, are important land uses and are a part of the essential cultural heritage for many societies. In Europe hunting remains of great cultural significance, as it does in many other parts of the world, particularly for indigenous people. The hunting language in Germany and Scandinavia forms an essential part of the Germanic cultural heritage; even music has its own hunting history. Although not required for subsistence, hunting and fishing for recreation play an important role in the economy of western countries, and may even bring significant commercial benefits. Recreational hunting is a multibillion dollar industry in the US and in Europe. Statistics suggest that in Australia every third person goes fishing, and in the state of New South Wales 27 per cent of estuarine waters are now "free of commercial fishing". At present around 6 million wild ungulates are harvested in the northern hemisphere every year, instigated by a complex framework of tradition, commerce, and social values. In Germany, one of the most industrialised countries in the world, hunting remains an important land use and tradition. The result is a harvest of nearly 1.2 million ungulates, equalling approximately 50,000 tons of venison every year. Fishing, more so than hunting, has been an important aspect of the lives of a large part of society. Its origins and pursuit have been much less questioned, and there has been generally little controversy surrounding its practice.

Many people holiday on the coast, on islands, or by the riverside so that they can take their fishing rod, hand line, or crab basket. Whilst this may not be an independent industry, it is an essential part of holidaymaking. The emergence of a more specific and targeted fishing-tourism sector was probably connected to a rise in mobility, an increase in the number of recreational fishers, and the emergence of service providers (such as guides, boat owners, land owners, and resort owners) who could take advantage of the increase in fishers by offering special experiences, locations, and species, and constructing a price for it. We suspect this industry was a response to declining fish resources.

The more expensive end of the market, big game fishing, which targets species such as sharks, marlin, and tuna, started as an elite industry in the US but has spread from there to many other countries. Hunting and fishing are treated in this chapter as the harvesting of aquatic or terrestrial wild animals. By combining hunting and fishing we also want to overcome the contrasts between the relative social indifference towards fishing, and the frequently negative public attitude towards hunting. Hunting and fishing both use wildlife, both can be humane and professional, or cruel and destructive, and both can only be justified, as Caughley and Sinclair express it, "...if they are sustainable...". By using a Triple Bottom Line concept (i.e. being socially, economically and environmentally accountable) hunting/fishing can contribute to a holistic and sustainable conservation approach, as recent examples such as CAMPFIRE demonstrate. From an ecological viewpoint, the sustainability of hunting and fishing relies on the principles of wildlife harvesting.

Well-managed hunting can have a wide range of benefits for conservation, which by its very nature is opposed to modern and intensive agriculture and forestry. There is emerging support from those formerly subscribing to the protectionist-conservationist attitude, who now proclaim that rich trophy-hunting tourists might be the saviour of Africa's wildlife. Hunting tourism seems to have become acceptable again, after many years of discredit by the conservation movement (of which many hunters consider themselves a professional part). For example countries such as Zambia, Tanzania, Zimbabwe, South Africa, and Namibia, which are safe-havens for Africa's magnificent wildlife, derive significant income from commercialised Safari hunting.

This tourism form has been instrumental in the development of highly successful community conservation models such as CAMPFIRE in Zimbabwe. Recreational hunting and fishing, a vast industry in the "rich countries", may provide increasingly important income to the poorer countries as consumptive wildlife tourism. This industry, however, still raises many questions for conservationists from western countries, while many non-western societies simply view it as an opportunity for income through consumptive wildlife use. In this Chapter we mainly focus on the consumptive hunting and fishing aspects of the tourism industry, although the majority of the following is also applicable to the non-consumptive "catch and release" fishing. This review attempts to explain how this tourism industry works, estimates its volume and trends, identifies problems of sustainable hunting and fishing, and suggests improvements towards sustainability of the industry, including conservation and community development.

CLASSIFICATION OF CONSUMPTIVE WILDLIFE TOURISM

This review combines hunting with fishing tourism, and describes them as having distinct features, marketing, income, and biological characteristics. One feature of the tourism industry is the indistinct boundaries between its subcategories; many tourists like to mix hunting and fishing. In our attempt to classify the wide range of activities we separate hunting tourism into three different market segments: (1) the 'big game' hunters with their various subdivisions, all targeting the experience, adventure, potential danger, and acquisition of a trophy; (2) the 'small game' hunters, more interested in the hunting experience and skill displayed (two Olympic disciplines have emerged from this sport, trap and skeet shooting) and (3) skill hunting, which we classify separately by its highly specific use of certain hunting tools (eg. bow, muzzle-loader, and various traps). The overlap between fishing categories is even more fluid, as freshwater fishing for example includes spear fishing, and charter-boat fishing may take place in marine or freshwater environments.

UNDERSTANDING RECREATIONAL HUNTERS' AND FISHERS' MOTIVATIONS & PERSPECTIVES

What types of people go hunting and fishing for recreation, and why do some spend significant funds on the activity? These questions do not have simple answers. Sociological research shows that people from all social strata, religions, and cultures, hunt and fish. Most of us have, at some stage of our lives, been holding a fishing rod or a simple hand line, dreaming of or even catching a fish.

For many these early starts have grown into a life-long obsession, and in Australia a staggering 4.5 million people claim to be recreational fishers. The situation is similar in Europe and North America, where individually, or in organised fishing clubs, people spend time and money to pursue the hobby, which has a number of specialised branches. Some of this fishing, the pursuit of the great, the magnificent, and the deadly, such as with the giant black marlin, tuna species, or the great white shark, has obtained the same status as safari big game hunting, and is actually called 'big game fishing'. Whilst the raw, and elemental nature of this fishing has been immortalized in Ernest Hemingway's "The Old Man and the Sea", it persisted mainly as the pursuit of the very rich. More recently it has gained popularity as society has generally become more affluent.

Most fishing and hunting, however, is less grand and is simply immersion in an elemental behaviour, ingrained in our genes through millions of years of evolution. From an evolutionary perspective it was essential for our primal nutritional needs, and it is always sure to give us a thrill, a moment of excitement, pride in our skill, and the feeling of achievement. Hunting is not significantly different from fishing, as many people perceive it to be. In fact much of it is a sort of terrestrial fishing, carried out with traps, nets, snares, and lines. Most hunts and fishing tourism trips follow a certain pattern. The first step is to get your equipment together. The equipment needs care, replacement from time to time, and some follow the latest fashions and techno-innovations.

For most, equipment has to be individual, age generally improves it and it becomes precious to us. The equipment might be a fishing rod, it might be a net, a trap, or it might be a bow or a spear, a boomerang or a firearm. While most of it is simply functional, much of it has acquired a status of its own, or is supposed to reflect the status of its owner. In western society these tools of the trade are now a huge industry and market. In Australia, for example, most small towns in regional areas have a shop or a petrol station selling fishing rods, ammunition, rifles, rabbit traps, crayfish baskets, fishing line, or bait. The majority of business, for these stores, is from the tourists, who arrive from urban centres in search of the great outdoors, their dream of self-sufficiency, their desire for adventure, for honing their childhood skills, or simply having a good time with their mates and their family. The ability to provide a meal from wildlife reflects on a person's status within a family, and having been the provider of meals from wildlife -we might assure the reader lacking this experience- that it feels good. Social aspects of hunting are, although poorly researched, of great importance.

ECONOMICS AND MARKETS

The number of hunters, in many parts of Europe, continued to increase during the seventies, but has remained stable or slightly declined from 1980 onwards. This trend is reflected in the US where fishers and hunters combined declined by 2.2 million to 37.8 million from 1991 to 2001. Interestingly, however, expenditure has increased significantly even though there is a smaller number of hunters and fishers. There has been a rather dramatic rise in outbound trophy hunting in North America, and a small rise in Europe. Trophy hunting is a form of hunting tourism that targets species depending on their size and body characteristics, such as antlers, tusks, or horns. It features very prominently in connection with tourism from Canada, the US, and Australia, with Africa being an important supply country as the high exports of Convention on International Trade in Endangered Species of Wild Fauna and Flora listed species indicate.

DEMAND AND SUPPLY COUNTRIES

In most western countries, with the exception of Canada, Australia, and New Zealand, the demand for hunting and fishing generally far outstrips the supply. In parts of Europe this trend has resulted in fishing clubs with virtually closed membership, and stringent criteria to join. In central, and increasingly parts of Eastern Europe with the Hunting District System, many hunters without district access choose to go overseas. The importance of some regions, for hunting and fishing, stood out in the website analysis. North America is important in this industry as it serves supply and demand, while the circle size for Canada, Mexico, and South Africa, represents mostly supply countries.

Despite its small size, New Zealand stands out for its relatively high representation due to a high number of introduced ungulates, which have become the basis of a very successful recreational and tourist hunting industry. The absence of advertisements from former Russian countries reflects the lack of Internet use in advertising in these countries, not the absence of a market. The frequencies express the importance of this industry for each country. The biggest demand and supply can be found in the largest consumer nation, the US. The large hits for Canada, Australia, and NZ, despite relatively low population numbers, suggests that these nations play a special role in offering fishing products, which are mostly charter-boat trips. This analysis included 14 advertisers with 1–2 different charter offers. Australian charters offer the highest number of species in the catch, Alaska the lowest. Coastal and marine fishing have the highest proportion of hits. Spear and charter-boat fishing are in much lower proportions, which may also reflect legal restrictions for spear fishing and the high capital costs for the charter-boat business.

THE HUNTING AND FISHING INDUSTRY

The hunting and fishing industry constitutes a complex arrangement of stakeholders and auxiliary industries. It consists of a multitude of interactions, and an organised flow from client to organiser via the intermediary. Potential clients access their market through many journals, internet sites, fairs (eg. the International Hunting Exhibition), agencies, and by word of mouth. In the US, clients spent US$36 billion for fishing and US $21 billion for hunting. The Intermediary mediates transactions between the client and the organisers. According to Hofer about 100 such agencies advertise in the lucrative German market in Europe, and about 40 in Italy. As is the case for many tourism businesses, it is mainly the large companies that prevail, and, in hunting and fishing, firms such as Lechner dominate much of the market. Increasingly the consumer appears to feel safer using these providers.

The organisers and operators, of hunting/fishing tourism experiences, are at the centre of the industry and in order to be competitive have to satisfy clients, comply with the demands of regulators, liaise with host communities, deal with advertising or tour agencies (or not if advertising directly), and ideally, for their own sustainability, be involved in the management of the target species and collaborate closely with indigenous communities who might traditionally own these. Host community: Hunting and fishing is carried out mostly in either rural or natural areas. Many of these areas are inhabited by indigenous or traditional societies. For fishing which, contrary to hunting in some Australian states for example, is allowed in protected areas, the nation's wildlife services are the hosts. Ideally the communities hosting hunters and fishers should have a say in how the tourists are to conduct themselves, and derive profits from accommodation, guidance, and support services.

Auxiliary industry: As in any other tourism sector, transport, accommodation, food, equipment, and insurance providers dominate a large portion of the industry. Almost equally important is the manufacturing industry, which supplies the necessary hunting, fishing, and outdoor equipment. In the US an estimated US$14 billion were used on items for both fishing and hunting in 2001.

Design of hunting and fishing tourism products: Any tourism product is only successful if it manages to approximate, as close as possible, the aspirations, motivations, financial means, and preferences of its target groups. In contrast to non-consumptive forms of wildlife tourism, hunting and fishing tourism businesses are generally financially profitable. Compared to other forms of tourism, hunters prefer fewer facilities and seek remoteness in pursuing their recreation. Clients are generally satisfied with their experience, which may incorporate special hardships, inconveniences, and even danger, as advertisements clearly demonstrate. It is not uncommon for agencies to reimburse for lack of success, but also to charge the trophy fee if the trophy from a lost animal is not recovered.

IMPACTS OF HUNTING AND FISHING ON WILDLIFE AND HABITATS

Hunting and fishing remove animals from populations. Ideally, both activities target sustainable yields (i.e. animals taken is equivalent to population surplus) or even maximum and optimum sustainable yields. This target is, however, difficult to achieve, even in highly regulated hunting systems such as the ones in Germany, Austria, or Poland. Many commercial fishing fleets depend on sustainable harvesting models, however, recent collapses of entire fish stocks, despite being "managed" with sophisticated population models, tells us how elusive the achievement of this aim is. These activities, if undertaken in an unregulated environment and without regard to sustainable yields and behaviour, will destroy populations of animals; and have done so many times in the past (eg. decline of passenger pigeons at the turn of last century, or bush-meat trade.

The impact of hunting and fishing is a highly variable parameter, which is determined by factors such as:

- Type of hunting/fishing (chase, stalk, ambush, group, dog-aided);
- Species taken (low recruitment, high recruitment, alert, primitive);
- Intensity (occasional, regular, continuous);
- Season;
- Time of day (resting periods, feeding periods);
- Tools (firearms, bow, trap, snare, line, net);
- Transport (on foot, horse, elephant, car, boat, helicopter).

In societies where hunting is well regulated, and important, such as Canada, the US, Russia, Germany, France, and the UK, a great body of research describes impacts and how to reduce these. For details see, for example, Olsen et al.,, Destefano et al.,, Madson and Fox, Malan et al.,, and Bauer. However, few studies on impacts have been carried out in tourism destinations in developing countries.

HUNTING IMPACTS

Hunting can cause a wide range of impacts on target species, and these impacts (while disputed as to their extent) are reported widely in the literature on wildlife management. Examples include the impact of lead shot, frequently used in waterfowl hunting areas, impacts on non-target species, and impacts on habitats. There is a variety of hunting methods, such as snares and traps, generally associated with illegal activities that kill many non-target species. Hunting can cause different levels of disturbance, which impair the fitness of a population or have a level of perceived, or real, cruelty. Impacts on the long-term genetic fitness of a species may occur if, for example, trophy hunting is highly selective towards mature, large-sized, and often male, individuals. Theoretical papers claim negative consequences, and practical studies suggest impacts such as a change in sex ratio or in age distribution. It is the worldwide experience that impacts of hunting can never be wholly eliminated, particularly in remote regions, and countries that lack legislation or infrastructure to enforce regulations. Sophisticated gamemanagement requires a consistent, long-term, objective research component, and the legislative and practical means for implementation through a responsible and welltrained group of hunters.

IMPACTS OF RECREATIONAL FISHING

Impacts of recreational fishing tourism, on fish populations, are evident in freshwater habitats such as lakes, streams, rivers, and ponds. However, these impacts occur in the wider context of recreational fishing, so tourism aspects are not distinguishable. As the depletion of fish resources by recreational fishing is common, the restocking practices of dams, lakes, and rivers are widespread. This practice makes much freshwater fishing essentially "fish farming", an accepted practice, while its terrestrial equivalent, "game ranching" is highly controversial, in North America for example. Recent events, such as the impending closure of a significant part of the Great Barrier Reef, in Australia, to recreational fishing, hints towards the impact of fishing on marine stocks, which is exemplified by the higher fish numbers in protected areas compared to unprotected areas in the West Australian coral reef.

MANAGEMENT OF HUNTING AND FISHING TOURISM

Management of hunting and fishing tourism relies on a wide range of activities including regulation, policy, and guidelines. The key elements for framework development are also applicable here. Moreover, regulation has traditionally played an overriding part in the management of fishing and hunting, as this activity impacts on the natural resources of local communities and may involve potentially dangerous tools.

Consequently, this section concentrates on the legal dimensions of management. Frameworks, for tourist hunting and fishing, are generally defined by national or state hunting and fishing legislation, and by the respective economic authority, to realise commercial structures and practices within this system. For the hunting and fishing tourists, adherence to these regulatory frameworks is a requirement, which if ignored may lead to their exclusion, individually or for all hunting and fishing tourists, or in extreme cases it may also result in prosecution, if laws are broken.

HUNTING REGULATORY FRAMEWORKS

The licence system is based on the right of any citizen to hunt in their country. The benefits from hunting may belong to the public, or to the state, and hunters who want to exercise that right must pay a fee to a public office, or an appointed community, which has been endowed with that right by the state. The district system entails that hunting rights are tied to the land, and the benefits accruing from wildlife go to the landowner who might be a farmer, a community, a corporate body, or the state itself. The landowner, in order to exercise that right, must fulfil certain requirements (eg. have passed an elaborate hunting examination in central, northern, and eastern European countries, and possess a firearm licence).

In some countries a Combined Licence and District System is in place (eg. Australia for kangaroo culls), which combines the two above systems, in that landowners must also obtain a licence. A Community-based System occurs in most parts of the world, where hunting is not regulated or enforced by authorities. Here local communities regulate resource exploration through, often intricate, social interactions and regulations to determine hunting rights/areas for community members. It is these members who will provide the hunting experience for the tourist.

FISHING REGULATORY FRAMEWORKS

Contrary to hunting, fishing remains a commercial activity in industrialised countries, in both freshwater and marine environments. In many less developed regions it is virtually unregulated, in particular in places where communitybased taboos and regulation were destroyed, and legislation, if existing, generally cannot be enforced. Most western countries, however, have adopted a district or licensing system, or a mix of these, in an attempt to make fishing more sustainable in an ecological sense. New South Wales has only recently adopted a new approach to the management of its fishing, which resulted in the recovery of some fish stocks after only a few years.

INTERNATIONAL TREATIES

National frameworks are complemented by international treaties, which clearly define and regulate trade in animal trophies (thereby influencing the demand for trophies itself). International treaties include the Ramsar Convention for the conservation of wetlands and waterbirds, and the development of the worlds protected area system. These directly, and indirectly, determine the accessibility of regions for hunting. International agreements, such as CITES, play an important role in the management of protected trophy species. The tourist market targets mostly non-CITES species, demonstrating how CITES effectively regulates the trophy hunting market, one of its intended outcomes. Of the few CITES listed species offered for tourist hunting, most are bear, argali, elephant, and several species of wild cats such as lion and leopard. Over a time span of seven years hunters imported 88,013 CITES listed trophies, with the largest imports into North America. Trade in CITES listed animals is only of a very small volume, and confiscations of trophies are uncommon. Observations by Chestin suggest that regulations are powerful enough to lead to a complete breakdown of hunting tourism, as occurred in Russia when a protected species of wild sheep had mistakenly been shot (mistaken for the, non listed, Marco Polo Sheep).

HUNTING CUSTOMS AND LOCAL TRADITIONS

Hunting and fishing are not just subject to legal supervision. They are based, in many countries, on ancient codes of conduct and ethical constraints, which in tribal societies can have "taboo" status. Not surprisingly, within functioning hunting and fishing communities these restraints are often more effective forms of regulation than legal enforcement. The community, in most cases, would more suitably punish an individual who violates these constraints, than any legal system.

The development of this system is probably indistinguishable from the development of an individual ethical framework, which is also very strong. The German hunting ethics *Jagdliches Brauchtum*, for example, uses the concept of

Waidgerechtigkeit, which is a combination of tradition, rules, and guidelines aimed at protecting the game as a resource. It includes ancient rituals of worship and thanksgiving towards the game *Letzter Bissen*, but is also legally binding; adherence to this unwritten law is stipulated in the state hunting legislations. These local traditions and taboos are highly relevant to the hunting and fishing tourist, whose adherence to these will often result in acceptance into the community, beyond the tourist status. Disrespect of such customs, however, may result in the loss of access for the offending individual, or even for all hunting and fishing tourists.

ON-GROUND REGULATORY STRATEGIES

The regulation of fishing and hunting rests on a range of strategies, which generally complement each other. These strategies aim to protect populations and enforce humane hunting (eg. types of firearms and calibre sizes) and include:

- Establishment of fish/game reserve systems
- Open and closed seasons
- Establishment of bag limits
- Size restrictions
- Sex restrictions
- Type of bait
- Equipment
- Firearms and calibres that can be used.

INTRODUCTION TO FISH

Fish start life as fertilized eggs. The eggs grow and then hatch into baby fish called fry. The fry are attached with a yolk sac which is the left over part of the egg they hatched from. For the first few days after hatching the fry do not require any feed from outside as the yolk sac provides the necessary nutrients during those days. The fry having the yolk sac is a great advantage for the farmer because during the first few days the fry can be transported to any place and maintained without feeding; they require only oxygen. Hence they can be transported to any place in oxygenated containers.

The time taken for the absorption of the yolk varies with breed of the fish, the condition of the individual fry and the environmental conditions. For example, if the fry is in a stressful condition the yolk may be absorbed quickly or some times slowly. If the nutrient requirement due to high physiological activity is high the yolk sac will be absorbed quickly if not slowly. It takes about two to four days for the yolk sac to be absorbed into the body of the try. In some rare cases it may take even eight days for the absorption of the yolk sac. After that the fry start seeking feed in water. They start eating suspended very small and almost microscopic plants and animals generally called planktons. The plankton cannot bc seen with the human eye. But if the farmer takes some water from the pond and holds it against the light so that the light shines through 'water he can see minute particles floating in the water. The length of the fry depends on the species of fish. Usually the fry stage is up to 14 days. By this time the fry grow up to 3-4 centimetres. After 14 days the fry can be harvested and sold to farmers or grown for few more days in the rearing ponds till they become fingerlings. After the fry stage, up to W days the fishlings are said to be in fingerling stage. They grow up to 10-15 cm within 90 days period. After the fingerlings stage they are harvested and sold out or transferred to rearing pond where they will grow till they attain marketable size.

The size and weight of adult fish vary with the breed, age, availability of feed in quality and quantity, favourability of environmental conditions, etc. They vary from 15 to 200 cm in length and from half to twenty kilograms in weight. Normally the fish become sexually mature after two years and hence for breeding only two years old fishes are used.

Fry mostly eat plankton and minute particles of feed provided to them. Fry feed should contain minimum 70-75 per cent protein. Eating habits of fingerlings are different tram that of try. They can eat bigger particles of feed. At the fingerlings stage they show that they like certain feed more than the others. Each type of fish breed choose its own kind of feed depending upon its need and availability. For example the carp fry will eat plankton; as a fingerling the carp eats, pieces of decayed matter and insect larvae; and as an adult the carp will eat plankton, decayed matter, insect larvae, worms, snails and almost anything that is on the bottom of the pond. Common carp for example are called bottom feeders, because they eat food from the bottom layers of the pond.

Feed preferences do not change in all the fishes as they grow. Some fish, like the silver carp, eat plankton during its whole life. When the fish reaches adult stage they become sexually mature. The brood or breed fish are sexually mature fish which are chosen as good fish to breed (spawn), produce eggs and begin the whole cycle again. This is called the life of fish. Normally two year old fishes are selected for breeding.

The knowledge about how the fish grow in the pond from the hatching stage to breeding stage and how they feed, what feed they require, what care they require at different stages of life cycle is essential for the good management in fish ponds.

FISH: REARING OF CARPS

India has a long tradition of carp fish culture. In this traditional system spawns or early fry of major carps naturally occurring in the streams and rivers mixed with other undesirable types of fish are collected and reared in the farm ponds. This was the practice in West Bengal and adjoining states. Under this system the yield may vary from 0 to 600 kg/ha/yr which is very low compared to the actual potential of average production of 4000kg/ha/yr. Due to the ever growing population the requirement of the fish also increased over the years and it became' necessary to increase the production. Besides there is also an ever increasing demand for export.

Central Inland Fisheries Research Institute (CIFRI) evolved the package of practices for carp culture. This technology is applicable to all the existing ponds and other water resources throughout the country without any zonal restriction.

Ponds in our country are dug-out units which are rainfed and are with non-drainable stagnant waters. They may be seasonal or perennial and may be used for a number of purposes such as washing clothes, bathing, minor irrigation, washing of utensils, drinking water for the livestock and human beings, etc. Of course perennial ponds are better than seasonal ponds. The soil type in the pond and its fertility status vary much in our country. However the best soil for the fish pond for the fresh water fishes especially the carps is alluvial soil with neutral pH ranging between 6.5 to 7.5. Though the soil type cannot be changed except in the long range plans, the pH has to be brought to neutral if the pond soil and water are saline, alkaline, sodic or acidic. In the scientific carp raising, six species of carps are introduced together into the pond and proper feeding and caring is given. It is an intensive system of fish culture involving several species and is called composite fish culture. The step by step procedure is briefly explained in the following parts of this booklet.

POND PREPARATION

The fingerlings of the carp is raised up to the marketable size in ponds called stocking ponds or grow out ponds. The optimum size of the pond is rectangular with size varying from 0.1 to 2.0 hectares with a depth ranging from 2.0 -3.0 metres.

Soil and Water

The optimum desirable qualities of the pond soil are: pH 6.5 to 7.5, available nitrogen 30-50 mg/100gm, organic carbon 1.0 to 2.0 per cent, available phosphorus 6 to 16 mg/100 gm. The optimum conditions of the pond water are: turbidity below 20 ppm (parts per million), pH 7.0-8.0, total alkalinity 75 -.150 ppm, nitrate and phosphate 0.2-0.5 ppm each, dissolved oxygen 5.0 to 10.0 ppm. These values cannot be determined by the ordinary farmers. However, these are just mentioned to show them that in the fish culture consideration of such details are also important. Wherever such tests can be con- ducted it is highly encouraged that these values are determined and corrective measures are adopted.

Ponds with the above mentioned desirable properties as well as with slightly alkaline (pH 7.5 -8.0) or moderately alkaline (pH 8.0 -8.5) soil can straight away be used for fish culture. But ponds with the acidic soil (pH 6.5), sodic soil (pH above 8.5), sandy soil and soil with heavy load of organic matter are unproductive. They need corrective measures for their profitable utilisation in fish culture. Some of the corrective measures recommended are the following.

Sodic Soil

Sodic or highly alkaline soil with pH value above 8.5 may be corrected by applying cow dung at the rate of 20 -30 tonnes per hectare and gypsum at the rate of 5 -6 tonnes per hectare.

Sandy Bottom

In ponds with sandy bottom not only the water gets easily drained but also the fertility status of pond is very low. The problem is corrected by adding large amount of cow dung, biogas slurry or other highly organic substances at the rate of 20 -30 tonnes per hectare.

Heavy Organic Manure

Years of deposition of organic manures at the bottom of the pond generates many harmful gases. The fertility status of that kind of ponds is also very poor. Corrective measures include removal of muck from the bottom of the pond, draining out the water and exposing the bottom to the sun for about two weeks, ploughing and liming at the rate of one tonne per ha.

Aquatic Weeds

Most of the aquatic weeds in the fish pond are undesirable. They not only take away the nutrients but also upset the oxygen balance in the water by releasing carbon dioxide into the pond during the night. Aquatic weeds also obstruct the movement of fishes as well as the netting operations. The aquatic weeds may be free floating surface weeds, submerged weeds, rooted emergent weeds, marginal shallow water weeds and algae. All these weeds have to be eradicated using one or more of the following methods.

Manual Method

Manual removal of weeds involves physical removal of the weeds by hand. This may be practical if the pond is small and labour is cheap.

Mechanical Method

In the mechanical method some machines or implements are used for doing the heavier part of the work in the removal of the aquatic weeds. Certainly it requires huge amount of capital

Biological Method

The method of controlling the weeds through certain organisms which feed on the weeds is called biological controll of aquatic weeds. The grass carp which can eat up many aquatic vegetation is itself an excellent example of biological weed control. Another fish named Puntius gonionotus also is reported to be a good feeder of aquatic weeds. The Yamuna turle is a third organism which can consume water hyacinth which is a common aquatic weed in the ponds. There are other organisms which are locally identified and can be used for biological control of aquatic weeds. Biological control of aquatic weeds is more advantageous since the undesirable weeds are also converted into fish flesh. It is cheap as no labour is involved and most suitable from the social and environmental point of view.

Unwanted Fishes

The unwanted fishes in the ponds may be predatory or weed fishes. They compete with cultured fish for feed, nutrients and space. The commonly occuring predatory fishes are: Channa spp., Clarias batraches, Heteropneustes fossailis, Pangsius, Mystus sp. Ompok spp., Wallage attu and Glossogobius giuris, etc. The common weed fishes are Puntius sp., Oxygaster sp., Amassis sp., Amblypharyngodon mala, Colisa sp., Rasbora sp., Aplocheius sp., Laubuca sp., Esomus danricus, etc. These predatory and weed fishes can be eliminated through repeated netting of the pond. Still some fishes which may be remaining at the bottom of the pond may not be caught in the net. Another method of eradicating the above mentioned unwanted fishes is to drain out the whole water from the pond and eliminating all of them manually and refill the pond with water. But draining the whole pond is also possible only if the pond is small. In big fisheries the only effective method of eradicating the unwanted fishes is the use of fish toxicants.

Fish Toxicants

In the use of fish toxicants, certain criteria should be followed.

They are:

- It should be effective at minimum dosage,
- It should be less costly,
- The fish killed by the toxicant should be suitable for consumption,
- The toxicity should remain only for short duration,
- The toxicity should be non-cumulative, and
- The toxicants should be easily available.

Following these criteria, the farmer may choose any of the toxicant available to him for the eradication of the unwanted fishes. They may be of plant origin or chemical/inorganic origin. A few of the commonly used toxicants are described here.

Mahua Oil Cake

Mahua oil cake is the most commonly used fish toxicant in our country. It contains about 4 -6 per cent saponin. It kills the fish at 200-250 ppm in 6-10 hours. But the fishes thus killed are fit for consumption. The toxicity lasts for 15 -20 days in water and the Mahua cake subsequently become the manure for the pond. Mahua cake is applied at the rate of 2000 -2500 kg per hectare for every metre of average depth. The required amount of mahua cake is powdered, soaked in water and broadcast over water surface. The pond is then netted (drag the net from one side to another side) repeatedly so that the cake is mixed with the water and also for taking out the affected fishes.

Tea Seed Cake

Crushed and powdered tea seeds are effective for the control of the unwanted fishes in the fish ponds. A dosage of 75 -100 ppm is sufficient to kill the fishes and for this about 750 to 1000 kg tea seed cake per hectare for every one metre average depth has to the applied into the pond. The toxicity lasts for 10 -12 days and ultimately the cake act as fertilizer to the pond. The treated fishes are suitable for human consumption.

Other Toxicants

There are several other toxicants of plant origin which the local people may be using and they vary from place to place. Also the names of the plants vary from place to place from language to language. One has to get familiar with those locally available toxicants of plant origin and use them. Chemicals such as Ammonia and Bleaching powder are also used as fish toxicants.

Ammonia

Anhydrous ammonia at the rate of 20-25 ppm has been found to be an effective fish toxicant though it is quite costly. However, the high cost is reduced by the fertilizer value of Ammonia used which amounts to about 36 per cent of the cost.

Ammonia gas comes in cylinders. At the time of application the cylinder is held in position by some means at the bottom of the pond and moved from one side to the other releasing the gas in a controlled way so that there is ncither excessive cooling nor gas loss during the absorption by the bottom soil. Sufficient protection should be provided to the people who are applying the gas.

Bleaching Powder

Bleaching powder or calcium hypochlorite is found to be effective as fish toxicant in eradicating the unwanted fishes from the-fish pond. It is easily available and less costly. At a concentration of 25-30 ppm it affects the fishes in 3-4 hours and the dead fish start floating to the surface of the water. The toxicity lasts for about 7-8 days in the pond. The additional advantage of bleaching powder is its disinfecting and oxidising effect on the decomposing matter at the bottom of the pond. Wherever the Mahua cake is in scarcity the bleaching powder can be used as a fish toxicant. The powder is dissolved in water and the solution is immediately sprayed on the surface of the pond water. In few hours time the fish start moving around in an unbalanced and disoriented way and finally float on to the surface of the water. They are removed by repeated netting.

Fertilizer Application in the Pond

Maximum fish production is achieved by the efficient soil and water management in the fish pond especially by maintaining the natural productivity of the pond. The natural productivity is maintained by the regular manuring and fertilizer application in the pond so that all essential nutrients for the growth of aquatic micro and small organisms (both plant and animal types) are supplied which directly or indirectly serve as feed for the fishes. Liming and manuring are the two main types of fertilization of the fish pond. They are briefly explained here.

Liming

About 400 kg/ha lime is incorporated into the pond through out the growing season. About 100 kg is/ha is distributed two weeks before the stocking of the fish and there after the rest of the lime is incorporated into the pond in every month in equal amount. Even in slightly alkaline soil and water conditions also lime is added because besides the fertilizing effect lime helps in the quick mineralisation of the organic matter and serves as a prophylactic measure. Additional dosages (150 to 200 kg/ha) may be given whenever some distress is noticed in the fishes.

Manuring

Both organic manures and inorganic fertilizers are found to be more effective in enriching the pond than the use of one type alone. Initial manuring with the organic manure at the rate of 20-25 per cent of the total requirement is done 15 days before the stocking of the fingerlings in the pond. If Mahua or tea seed cake has been applied into the pond as pesticide then this dose need not be given. The rest of the 75 to 80 per cent of the organinc manure is given in equal quantity (in 11 split doses) every month.

The manure is deposited in different spots such as corners and few selected sites on the sides. Wherever possible water testing should be done for nitrate, phosphate and organic carbon. If the organic carbon level goes beyond 2 per cent the manure application should be suspended. Also the manuring should be suspended when excessive growth of algal growth is noticed in the pond. Besides the organic manures inorganic fertilizers are also used to maximize the fish production in the pond. The total quantity of the inorganic fertilizers is applied in 11 equal parts every month beginning from the 2nd month. Fertilizers can be mixed and broadcast allover the pond uniformly.

FISH CLASSIFICATION

The classification of fishes has undergone much change over the last few decades, and further changes are expected, partly because so many groups are poorly known. There are many conflicting hypotheses of relationships, some based on conflicting evidence between morphological studies and molecular studies; however, progress is being made and there are many areas of basic agreement.

There are about 28 000 living species of fishes recognized as valid (formally described and recognized). This is slightly over half the number of recognized tetrapods. About 11 950 of these species are confined to fresh water. Many new species are described every year, and if we use the same species concept as the above figure reflects, then there may be an estimated 32 500 species alive today (some estimated 4500 are yet to be found and described). Currently, ichthyologists place living species in about 4500 genera, 515 families and 62 orders. The following summary of the groups is based primarily on a synthesis of the recent literature. Numerous fossil groups of Chondrichthyes, Actinopterygii and Sarcopterygii, many occurring in Canada, are not covered below. About 1200 species of native fishes live in Canada, either in fresh water or marine water over the continental shelf (many more live within Canadian territorial limits in deep water in the Arctic, Atlantic and Pacific). Unless otherwise mentioned, Arctic fishes are combined into Atlantic and Pacific.

METHODS AND DIFFERENCES BETWEEN CLASSIFICATIONS

Most ichthyologists adopt a cladistic methodology of classification, which classifies strictly according to recency of common descent. In this system, the goal is to have each taxonomic unit contain all species sharing a common ancestor. This often results in a very different classification than would result from the approach commonly used up to about 1980. In the older approach, evolutionary or synthetic systematics, the inferred amount of divergence among groups was considered, as was the history of their evolutionary relationships, and a given taxon might not contain all the descendants from the inferred ancestral species.

An example of the difference between these 2 approaches comes from showing hagfishes and lampreys in a classification. In a cladistic system, HAGFISHES would be placed in a category separate from LAMPREYS and other vertebrates because, relative to hagfishes, lampreys are thought by most ichthyologists using morphological evidence to share a common genealogical branching point with all other vertebrates. Systematists using the evolutionary approach could express the relationship in several ways but might prefer to place hagfishes and lampreys together in the category of jawless fishes, separate from all jawed vertebrates, although recognizing that they are very distantly related.

Differences may also exist in classifications because of ichthyologists using different characters, for example, molecular versus morphological characters. Other differences may also exist among classification systems, depending on whether the worker is a "lumper" or a "splitter." A lumper constructs a classification with categories containing more groups than that of a splitter. There are no rules for the amount of difference necessary to designate various categories. A lumper recognizes one family for SALMON, WHITEFISH and GRAYLING; a splitter, 2 or 3 families.

THE BRAIN AND NERVOUS SYSTEM OF FISH

Being highly complex life forms fish need a brain and a nervous system to control their body's actions. The nervous system of fish, much like ours, is composed of a central co-ordinating brain, a spinal cord and many, many nerves. The Brain:- Generally speaking fish have small brains in relationship to their overall body weight. Elasmobranchs (Sharks and Rays) in general have a slightly larger brain for the same body mass as Teleosts (Bony Fish), however there is great variety within the teleosts scientists have learned something quite surprising about the Elephantnose Fish (Gnathonemus petersii).

Lurking in the vegetation and then aggressively attacking anything small that comes near doesn't seem to require much intelligence. A Pike, (*Essox lucius*) has a brain that amounts to only 0.077 per cent of its total body mass. Which means that when you catch a 5 kilogram Pike you have out maneuvered a fish with a brain weighing 3.85 grams or one seventh of an ounce. In comparison a Burbot (*Lota lota*) is a little smarter because it has a brain that is 0.13 per cent of its body weight meaning a 5 kilo specimen would have a 6.5 gram brain, still its is a pretty dumb fish. Most fish have brains that are less than 1 per cent of their body weight, but not all.

At the other end of the continuum of fish intelligence the electric Elephantnose fish, with a brain that is 3.1 per cent of its body weight it is a lot smarter than the Pike, if it grew to weigh 5 kilos its brain would weigh 155 grams, which would make it 40 times as large as that of a Pike of similar weight. To look at it another way a human being has, on average, a brain that weighs in at around 2.3 per cent of body weight. A five kilo human would have a brain of only 115 grams, which is smaller than that of the Elephantnose Fish.

Does this mean Elephantnose fish are smarter than people? No. Intelligence is more than just brain mass or even brain to body ratio, while large brains do make it easier to be smart, it is the complexity of the brain and the relative proportion of forebrain that are most important. The most complex and most forebrain dominated brains on this planet belong to dolphins and humans.

Nevertheless we can see that some fish are much smarter than others and the Elephantnose fish is known among aquarists as the most playful and inquisitive of fish. The brains of cyclostomes (Hagfish and Lampreys) are simple but specifically evolved to suit their lifestyles. For instance the optic lobe is well developed in the visually oriented Lampreys but indiscernible in the blind Hagfish. In both however the medulla is large and the cerebellum small. Together the cerebellum and the medulla make up the hind brain. The medulla controls the operations of the inner organs such as heart rate, blood pressure, digestion and waste disposal. It is also a relay centre for many nerves sending messages to and from the mid and or forebrain. The cerebellum controls motor co-ordination (but it does not initiate motor activities). This means it controls the timing and interaction of muscles once a muscular action has been initiated. The cerebellum is also important in maintaining equilibrium.

The mid-brain of a fish consists mostly of the optic lobes, which vary greatly in size between species in accordance with their dependance on sight, and in some species the optic lobes may be so large they completely cover the forebrain. In fish the mid-brain is important in sorting out incoming information and it is also the main centre of learning (whereas in mammals it is the forebrain that is the main centre of learning). The forebrain of fish is dominated by the olfactory lobes which extend forwards and may be placed at the end of stalks. These olfactory lobes are large in the cyclostomes and very large in the elasmobranchs reflecting the importance of smell to these to groups of fish. The teleosts, for whom sight is often the most important sense have smaller olfactory lobes.

In many elasmobranchs and some teleosts there exists a cerebrum or pair of cerebral hemispheres These also seem to be predominantly involved with the sense of smell (in mammals the cerebrum is much larger and involved in planning and learning). The pituitary also arises out of the forebrain, it plays and important role in the regulation of metabolism. A fish's brain never completely fills the cranium, the cavity in the skull where it lies protected. The remaining space is filled up with a gelatinous material. Finally as in all vertebrates the brain, plus the gel, are surrounded by a membrane that helps keep foreign matter and micro-organisms from contacting this most important organ.

The Spinal Cord:- The spinal cord, or nerve cord is similar in all fish. It is a thick sheath of nervous material that runs from the base of the brain back along the fish's body through, and protected by, the neural canal of the spinal column. Normally it extends the full length of the fish's body, but a notable exception to this is the giant Sunfish (*Mola mola*) wherein the spinal cord is actually shorter than the brain. It serves as the basis of many simple responses and as the major link to the brain for sensory input and brain-mediated responses. The Nerves:- Apart from the brain and the spinal cord the fish body is supplied with a vast network of nerves, the electric wires of the body along which messages travel. Nerves are built of of numerous neurons and neurons are a one-way system, messages either travel to or from the brain or the spinal cord along a particular neuronal path, but never both ways. Those nerves that arise from the spinal cord are called spinal nerves and those which arise from the brain are called cranial nerves.

Normally there is one pair of spinal nerves (left and right) for each vertebrae, thus long thin fish with many vertebrae such as eels will have many more pairs of spinal nerves than a much shorter fish such as a gobi. In fish there are 10 pairs of cranial nerves all with well defined roles.

- Pair 1:- Sensory connecting the nasal organs to the olfactory lobes.
- Pair 2:- Sensory connecting the eyes with the optic lobes.
- Pair 3:- Connecting to muscles.
- Pair 4:- Connecting to muscles.
- Pair 5:- Mixed, part sensory part muscles.
- Pair 6:- Connecting to muscles.
- Pair 7:- Mixed, part sensory part muscles.
- Pair 8:- Sensory, connects the brain with the inner ear, important for balance.
- Pair 9:- Sensory, connects the brain with the gills and the palate of the mouth.
- Pair 10:- Mixed, intestines, gills, heart and lateral line.

DEVELOPMENT OF FISH EMBRYOLOGY

Fish embryonic development begins after inception with the zygote period. During this time the embryo develops one cell that looks like a half bubble. This lasts on average for 45 minutes with a cell.7 mm in diameter. The chorion, also known as the egg shell, will swell and lift away from the fertilized egg. It is particularly appropriate to write about the history of fish embryology at this time. History is often said to move in cycles, and this seems to be true of the study of fish development.

After a period of prominence during the nineteenth and early twentieth centuries, the study of fish development, except in the hands of a stalwart few such as Oppenheimer and Trinkaus working with Fundulus and Ballard and Devillers working with the trout and other fishes, was overshadowed by developmental studies of other organisms, such as amphibians, the domestic fowl, sea urchins, and assorted invertebrates. For obvious reasons, the study of fish development continued to be pursued by fisheries biologists. With the popularization of the zebrafish Danio rerio as a "model of vertebrate development" and a revival of interest in the relationship between development and evolution, the cycle has come full turn and the study of fish development again has a place in the sun. My objective is to present an outline of the historical development of the science of fish embryology in the nineteenth century, broadly defined as 1789-1914. My plan is to assess the state of knowledge at the outset of the period, to document the advancement of descriptive embryology of teleosts and elasmobranchs, to consider the rise of comparative embryology of fishes associated with evolutionary studies, and to search out the beginning of experimental, physiological, and biochemical analyses of fish development.

DIVERSE GROUP OF VERTEBRATES

When discussing the development of fishes, it is prudent to recall that fishes are the most diverse group of vertebrates. They should not be treated as a distinct, relatively homogeneous taxonomic unit. Rather, the term "fishes" applies to a grade of ectothermic, aquatic craniates and vertebrates and not to a distinct taxonomic group.

Extant fishes are divided into five classes, namely Myxini (hagfish), Cephalaspidomorphi (lampreys), Chondrichthyes (cartilaginous fishes), Sarcopterygii, and Actinopteryg. Chondrichthyes contains two taxa, namely the subclass Elasmobranch (living sharks, rays, and skates) and the Holocephal (ratfishes or chimaeras) that diverged at a relatively early time, *i.e.*, the Devonian-Carboniferous boundary.

The class Sarcopterygii (flesh-finned fishes) contains the Actinistia (the living coelacanth), the Dipnoi (lungfishes) and the tetrapod vertebrates. The class Actinopteryg (ray-finned fishes) comprises five groups, namely Cladistia (bichir and reedfish), Chondrostei (sturgeons and paddlefish), Ginglymodi (gars), Halecomorphi (Amia calva, the bowfin), and the Teleostei (teleost fishes). Thus, the five classes of fishes contain eleven major taxonomic groups with an estimated total of 25,000 species. Each class is as distinct from the others as it is from the four other classes of vertebrates. The theme of eleven major taxonomic groups of fishes that is used in the ensuing presentation to emphasize the broad phylogenetic relationships of fishes and other vertebrates, tends, however, to obscure the extraordinary phylogenetic diversity within the teleosts.

Teleostei, a monophyletic group, contains 24,000 species in 38 orders and 126 families compared to the 1,000 species, 19 orders, and 56 families in the ten other groups of fishes and the 25,000 species of tetrapods. Not only are fishes the most diverse group of craniates, but they also display the greatest diversity of life history styles. Most fishes are oviparous, but viviparity is estimated to have independently evolved 42 times in five of the eleven major groups of fishes, all within the Chondrichthyes and Osteichythes. The phylogenetic diversity of fishes is reflected in the diversity and variability of their developmental patterns. Craniate development based on cleavage and subsequent patterns of gastrulation and embryogenesis is holoblastic, meroblastic, or transitional between the two. In holoblastic eggs, cleavage of the ooplasm is complete by the blastula stage. The morphogenetic movements of gastrulation occur in the three-dimensional space of the entire egg and involve most of the embryonic mass.

They often lead to the occlusion of the blastocoele. Neurulation is synchronous in time and space. Holoblastic development is considered the less specialized and more primitive craniate developmental pattern because it is characteristic of most echinoderms and non-craniate chordates as well as the more primitive representatives of various craniate lineages, namely lampreys, sturgeons, bichirs, lungfish, and most amphibians. In the meroblastic egg, most of the yolk mass remains uncleaved at the blastula stage.

EVOLUTION OF THE MEROBLASTIC PATTERN APPEARS

Morphogenetic movements are confined to a portion of the egg volume, *i.e.*, the blastoderm, and involve only a portion of the embryonic mass. Gastrulation and neurulation tend to be spatially and temporally asynchronous. Evolution of the meroblastic pattern appears to have involved qualitative and quantitative changes in the ooplasm and yolk components of the egg, namely an increase in total yolk content, an increase in the amount of yolk relative to ooplasm, a change in the type of yolk, and a change in the relative disposition of ooplasm and yolk. Not only did the changes in yolk-cytoplasm relationships of the egg affect cleavage patterns, but they also imposed a set of physical or physiological constraints on the morphogenetic movements of embryo formation, the so-called holoblastic-meroblastic barrier.

Consequently, new or highly modified patterns of gastrulation and embryogenesis co-evolved with the evolution of the meroblastic egg. The meroblastic pattern of development appears to have independently evolved in six craniate lineages, namely hagfish, sharks and chimaeras, teleost fishes, the living coelacanth (?), one group of amphibians (the caecilians) and amniotes. In each instance, different morphological patterns of gastrulation and embryogenesis have evolved. Thus, although meroblastic cleavage is superficially similar in hagfish, elasmobranchs, and teleosts, the morphological events of embryo formation differ considerably. These points and others are summarized in part by Collazo *et al.* who present a phylogenetic perspective and an evolutionary scenario for teleost gastrulation. Paradoxically, whether development procceds according to a holoblastic or meroblastic pattern, the end product is a stereotypic craniate embryo. Recent advances in the study of the molecular basis of embryogenesis should help resolve this paradox.

NATURAL COLLECTIONS OF FISHES

When considering early studies of fish development, one soon realizes that many of these studies were carried out on viviparous species of elasmobranchs and teleosts rather than oviparous ones, and that both egglaying and livebearing elasmobranchs received a disproportionate amount of attention, considering their relatively low diversity compared to teleosts. First, elasmobranch eggs are considerably larger than those of most teleosts and their development can be easily observed with either the unaided eye or with a hand lens.

Secondly, it has always been relatively easy to obtain gravid specimens of viviparous fishes as part of routine fishing efforts. Moreover, as museum or natural history collections of fishes were made during the course of explorations, specimens of curious, new species of gravid viviparous fishes became available for study, *e.g.*, the four-eyed fish Anableps.

In contrast, the eggs of oviparous teleosts are small and not easily collected in the wild. Artificial fertilization of teleost eggs did not begin until the late eighteenth century and the regulated spawning of captive fish species and the rearing of their eggs under "controlled" conditions for scientific purposes was first used only towards the mid-nineteenth century.

In addition, the technology for maintaining fishes in aquaria and the possibility of spawning them under aquarium conditions did not emerge until the mid-late nineteenth century. In passing, one should recall that the Chinese have been rearing captive goldfish, including mutant strains, for over a thousand years.

Other factors also influenced decisions to study certain viviparous instead of oviparous fishes. Viviparity in fishes, especially when there is a placental relationship, is an intrinsically interesting process. Finally, as a subject for the general study of development, oviparous teleosts have been secondary to the chicken egg ever since the Renaissance because of the greater size of the chicken's egg and its ready availability as an article of food.

DEVELOPMENT OF FISH EMBRYOLOGY

Because the research of early naturalists provided the foundation for the development of fish embryology in the nineteenth century, a brief outline of their work is presented here, beginning with Aristotle. Aristotle, the founder of the science of embryology, was the first to recognize and record many important features of fish reproduction and development. He distinguished oviparous (egg-laying) animals from viviparous (livebearing animals. Aristotle described viviparity in the dogfish shark (Mustelus), the thresher shark (Alopias), and the electric ray (Torpedo). He did not know of viviparity in teleost fishes because there are no viviparous teleosts in the coastal waters of the Mediterranean or the fresh waters of Europe and Asia Minor. His attribution of viviparity to the needlefish, a teleost, is actually a case of misinterpretation. The needlefish of Aristotle is a pipefish or sygnathid.

Male pipefishes brood embryos in a pouch of abdominal skin. This form of parental care is analogous to viviparity and in its most highly evolved forms, the parentalembryonic relationships can be as complex as in viviparous fishes.

The body of Aristotle's observations concern chondrichthyan fishes and include: (1) the distinction between oviparous and viviparous modes of reproduction in sharks, rays, and skates; (2) description of the female reproductive system; (3) description of shark and skate egg cases; (4) description of egg structure and some observations on embryonic development; (5) first description of the oviducal or nidamental (=shell) gland but without any knowledge of its function in egg case formation or sperm storage; (6) hatching from the egg case in utero in viviparous species; (7) description of the male reproductive system; (8) notes on breeding seasons and inshore migration of gravid females for "pupping"; and (9) description of the yolk sac placenta in sharks.

Writing of the smooth dogfish Mustelus canis in the 5th century B.C., Aristotle states, "the young are produced with the umbilical cord attached to the uterus so that as the substance of the egg gets used up, the embryo's condition appears to be similar to what is found in quadrupeds. The umbilical cord, which is long, is attached to the lower parts of the uterus; each one is, as it were, fastened to a cotyledon and is attached to the embryo by the middle where the liver is situated. Each embryo has a chorion and membranes of its own round it, just as in quadrupeds. If the embryos are cut open, a situation is disclosed exactly similar to quadrupeds; whatever internal organs they have, such as the liver, are large and supplied with blood". Aristotle's observations on teleosts are in large part concerned with reproduction, *e.g.*, his exquisite account of brood protection by male catfish. He realized that in contrast to the chondrichthyans, the overwhelming majority of teleosts are oviparous. His observations on the development of teleosts are more limited, due primarily to the small size of most teleostean eggs. Aristotle observed developing teleost eggs, recording their small size and rapid development. He states, "The embryo appears at the upper end of the egg and is enveloped in a membrane; the eyes, large and spherical, are the first organs visible. The embryo and the egg (yolk) are enveloped by a common membrane, and just under this is another membrane that envelops the egg (yolk) by itself; between the two membranes is a liquid". He described the organization of the teleost egg, distinguishing the perivitelline fluid from the yolk mass. Lastly, in comparing the development of teleostean and avian eggs, Aristotle recognized that teleosts lack the allantois. Relatively little was added to the pioneering efforts of Aristotle by subsequent Greek and Roman scholars. With the decline of classical civilization, the study of science in general as well as the study of fish development languished for almost 1,000 years.

Slowly the tide turned. According to Needham (1959), the first account of fish development in medieval Europe was given by Albertus Magnus, a thirteenth century scholastic. During the Renaissance, there was a revival of interest in natural history. The early zoological encyclopedists, especially Belon, Rondelet, and Aldrovandus, investigated fishes and described aspects of their reproduction and development. Again, there was a decided bias towards viviparous chondrichthyans. Rondelet illustrated an egg case and dissection of the female reproductive system of an oviparous catshark. He also illustrated part of the ovary and an egg case of a skate. He depicted a female shark, probably Mustelus canis, connected to a welldeveloped pup by an elongated yolk stalk that passes from the pup through the cloaca of the female. Although the placenta is not illustrated, Aristotle's research on the shark yolk sac placenta is cited in the text.

Progressing to the seventeenth century, Fabricius, who is best known for his studies of the chick, described and illustrated the female reproductive system and uterine embryos with large yolk sacs in a non-placental species of dogfish shark. By 1673, Niclaus Steno had rediscovered the yolk sac placenta in the smooth dogfish, M. canis, investigated its anatomy, and published an illustrated account of it. He also distinguished between placental viviparity in the smooth dogfish shark, and aplacental viviparity in the spiny dogfish shark, Squalus. In the latter, he discovered that the yolk stalk terminates in an intestine characterized by a spiral valve. His rediscovery appears to have gone unappreciated. During this period, inability to distinguish among species of dogfish sharks that had either aplacental or placental modes of viviparity caused the very existence of a yolk sac placenta in sharks to be doubted. This controversy was not fully resolved until the time of Johannes Muller. Steno's studies on shark development had important ramifications for the study of mammalian reproduction. On the basis of his observation of large eggs in the uterine oviduct and large eggs in the ovary of the spiny dogfish, he concluded that the embryo does not form de novo in the oviduct, but comes form an egg released by one of the ovaries. From this, he postulated that mammalian development proceeded in a similar fashion, except that the mammalian egg is much smaller.

In his examination of the mammalian ovary, unfortunately, he mistook the entire follicle for the mammalian egg. These studies were undertaken at a time when a controversy had arisen between animalculists and ovists with respect to the primacy of the sperm in reproduction and the absence of any knowledge of the mammalian egg. Steno's observations, although flawed, brought mammalian development in line with that of other vertebrates. In essence, he used sharks as a "model" system for mammals. In 1678, Stephen Lorenzini, a pupil of Steno and Redi, published a set of observations on the viviparous electric ray Torpedo. This appears to be the first monographic treatment of a single fish species. Lorenzini's work is of considerable interest because almost one third of it is devoted to an account of urogenital anatomy, reproductive biology, and development of Torpedo, as well as several other rays.

Amongst his observations, those of primary interest concern oogenesis and ovulation, the blastoderm, and embryonic nutrition. Describing the ovary, he notes differences in size and structure between young and mature fishes.

Maturing oocytes and ova vary in size, composition, and colour. Oocytes are connected to the ovarian matrix by a stalk through which several blood vessels pass, an arrangement similar to that described by Fabricius in the hen's egg. He states that these vessels provide nutrients to the eggs.

Pole constitutes

The maturing egg is invested by a "membrane" except for the pole opposite the site of attachment to the stalk. This pole constitutes the pore or stigma through which the mature egg is released from the follicle. During oocyte maturation, changes in membrane adhesion were documented. Lorenzini speculates that mature eggs are released from the follicle by contraction of fibres in the ovarian stroma. The ovulated egg is "received" by the oviduct and passes into the uterine region where embryonic development is completed. Following Fabricius, De Graaf, and Harvey, Lorenzini refers to the residual portion of the follicle as the "calyx." Calyces, which apparently are the corpora lutea, occur in various sizes and shapes throughout gestation, and are lost or regress some time after parturition. Lorenzini found a correlation between the number of young in a brood and the number of calyces in the ovary. Ovulation in the Torpedo is considered to conform to De Graaf's account in other species. Among the more interesting of Lorenzini's observations are those made on the early stages of embryonic development. He describes and illustrates two neurula stages.

The earlier stage depicts an early neural groove on the surface of the blastoderm. He describes the characteristic chondrichthyan blastoderm, "a leaden gray disc" that is clearly distinct from and surmounts the "yellow yolk mass." In another egg, he describes and depicts a slightly more advanced neurula stage. Here Lorenzini correctly shows the splayed, outspread cephalic margins of the medullary plate, a characteristic feature of chondrichthyan embryos. Lorenzini also observed the blastoderm in three other species of rays. Lorenzini seems to be the first to have depicted the chondrichthyan blastoderm. His observations appeared only six years after Malphighi's initial account of the avian (chick) blastoderm.

Lorenzini made one of the first major contributions to the knowledge of embryonic nutrition in non-placental viviparous fishes. Late stage embryos with yolk sacs lie free in the uterine region of the oviduct where they are bathed by uterine fluid. A yolk stalk passes from the external yolk through the abdominal wall and empties into a large internal yolk sac that in turn empties into the intestine. The intestine is filled with yellow material apparently derived from the yolk and brown globules. The same brown globules occur in the uterine fluid and in the mouth, esophagus, and stomach of the embryos.

Lorenzini concluded that advanced embryos are nourished both by yolk passed to the intestine and by uterine fluid which they imbibe. He believed that the nutrients in uterine fluid are derived from the blood and conveyed to the uterine fluid by vascularized glandular structures which he compared to chorionic villi. Thesc structures are now known as trophonemata. Villi increase in size during gestation; their size is correlated with the amount of uterine fluid. They regress and are absent in non-gravid fish. In addition, Lorenzini also made significant observations on the male reproductive system, reproductive cycles, and the duration of gestation.

In the closing years of the seventeenth century, Willughby and Ray summarized much of what was known of fish reproduction and development in a work primarily devoted to systematics. Considering its promising beginning, it is surprising that the study of chondrichthyan development made relatively little progress in the eighteenth century. There are many possible reasons. Those scholars interested in fish biology may have been attracted to systematic studies because of the revolutionary efforts of Willughby and Ray, Artedi, and Linnaeus as well as the influx of new species of fishes from the tropics. Changing fashions in science also enter the picture, especially the rise of microscopy and microscopic anatomy. Perhaps in terms of the material, questions, and technology, research on chondrichthyans had reached an impasse. There are some exceptions. Bohadsch investigated the structural organization of eggcases. Monro published detailed descriptions accompanied by elegant illustrations of the urogenital anatomy of the oviparous skates.

He also described and illustrated for the first time the spermocysts, spherical aggregations of Sertoli cells and differentiating sperm cells that are a characteristic feature of chondrichthyan spermatogenesis. Descriptions and illustrations of microdissections of the internal anatomy of mid-and late-stage embryos are given. The extensive vitelline circulation and the connection of the yolk sac and the small intestine are documented. External gill filaments, another feature of chondrichthyan development, are described for the first time. The eighteenth century concluded with Bloch's magnum opus (1782-95) which added little to the study of chondrichthyan development other than information on the embryos of the viviparous sawfish Pristis. The study of teleostean development, as previously noted, lagged well behind that of both oviparous and viviparous chondrichthyan fishes, and little was done prior to the mid-late eighteenth century.

To be more accurate, the little that was done was done with viviparous teleosts. Schoenveld first described viviparity in the embryos of the eelpout, Zoarces viviparus, a fish common to the marine waters of northern Europe. Late stage embryos are illustrated. Impressed by the substantial growth of the embryos during gestation, Schoenveld postulated that they obtain nutrients by ingesting ovarian fluid. (In viviparous teleosts, an oviduct or uterus is absent and gestation takes place in the ovary. Cf. Wourms, *et al.*, 1988). Somewhat later, Willughby and Ray apparently observed the development of live Zoarces embryos. Interest in teleost development during the seventeenth and eighteenth centuries seems to have been generated by the viviparity of exotic species discovered during the explorations of the Old and New World Tropics. Anableps, the four-eyed fish, conspicuous because of its size, unusual anatomy, and behaviour in its Central and South American habitats, was described as viviparous as early as 1738. Gronovius was the first to illustrate advanced embryos of Anableps with their characteristic rugose "yolk sac" (actually the abdominal trophoderm). Gronovius may also have been the first to describe viviparity in the clinid, Clinus superciliosus. Bloch described and illustrated the external and internal reproductive anatomy of Anableps, its embryos in situ, and the embryos themselves. He also depicted the adults and embryos of Zoarces and Clinus. One of the first sets of field observations was made by de Alzate — Ramyrez in 1769 who discovered viviparity in a Mexican poeciliid and made microscopic observations of blood circulation in living, near-term embryos.

During this period, the foundations were laid for the study of early development, *i.e.*, fertilization through embryogenesis. In 1763, Jacobi published an extensive letter in which he reported that he had artificially fertilized the eggs of trout and salmon by removing the ripe eggs and adding sperm to them. Although this is the first known written account of artificial fertilization, it is probable that the technique had been in use for some time, for fish culture had been practiced in Europe since the late fifteenth century. Jacobi may have observed the entry of sperm into the egg. He also recorded the formation of double embryos in artificially fertilized eggs, a condition that he attributed to the entry of two spermatozoa. In 1787, Cavolini published a monograph on the "generation" of fishes and crabs. The bulk of this work was devoted to the description of spawning habits, hermaphroditism, fertilization, and contemplations on the nature of development.

However, he did make one observation of considerable significance. In the eggs of the pipefish, he described a structure on the egg which he referred to as the "cicatrix" or in modern terminology, the blastoderm. He identified the blastoderm with the same structure in the chick and assumed that the embryo originated from the blastoderm. The study of teleost development in the eighteenth century was brought to a close with the appearance of Bloch's massive, twelve-volume monograph on the natural history of fishes. This work is one of the linchpins of systematic ichthyology and summarized what was known about fishes up to that time. It contains much information on fish reproduction and development. As previously noted, aspects of the development of viviparous chondrichthyans and teleosts are described and illustrated. Of greater interest are his pioneering studies of the early stages of development of an oviparous teleost. For the first time, he describes and illustrates consecutive stages in development, from post fertilization through hatching to a late larval stage, and provides a time base for the description of developmental stages. He appreciated the eccentric position of the yolk mass relative to the blastoderm. He made observations on the development of the heart, and illustrates the contractile, simple tubular stage of heart development. There were, of course, errors of interpretation, one of which was the identification of the perivitelline fluid of the teleost egg with the albumen layer of the avian egg.

SIGNIFICANCE OF FISH FOOD APPLICATION

In addition to the fertilization in ponds for proliferation of natural food organisms for fish, artificial feeds must be supplemented to meet the demands of various species of fish. Fish feeds are the prime material base of high-density fish culture. Applying artificial feeds in fish pond can raise the per-unit yield by a big margin. Take common carp as an example. The output does not exceed 25—30 kg/mu in extensive culture, whereas in intensive culture the output will be as high as 200–250 kg/mu. The rapid increase of yield comes from the direct effect of artificial feeding, the so-called fish yield of artificial feeding; however, the plankton-eater output is also enhanced. Especially in the system of polyculture in China, the consequence of feeding is more conspicuous. Because the food applied can be directly taken in by the so-called feed-eaters, in turn, the excreta of which can fertilize the pond water, multiplying the natural food for the plankton-eaters. In such a culture system, the yield of these species often occupies S! of the total fish output.

The nutrients that fish require are the same as the other animals. They can be sorted into five kinds: protein, carbohydrates, fats, vitamin and minerals. The demands of fish for these nourishing elements are the fundamental basis for selection and preparation of fish feeds.

BASIS FOR SELECTION AND PREPARATION OF FISH FEEDS

Protein is the basis of all living things. Just as other animals, from food, fish take in protein which's decomposed into amino acid through enzyme in the digestive organs. The amino acid is absorbed internally and synthesized into fish protein for growing mending tissues and maintaining life activities. It is used as energy for fish activities when fats and carbohyrates are not sufficient. One gram of protein can supply 4 kilo calories.

The demand of fish for protein contents in feeds is generally 25—40 per cent. It is higher than the demand of terrestrial animals like chicken or pig or cattle, that is 12—17 per cent. Since fish are cold-blooded animal without need of maintaining body temperature, they require lower energy comparatively. Different fish have different feeding habits, so do their requirements for protein contents in feeds. Carnivorous fish like rainbow trout and eel demand higher protein contents, while herbivorous fish lower. The nutritional value of food depends not only on the quantity of protein but also on the quality of it, namely, the compositions of amino acids. Amid acid is the elementary unit, of which protein is constructed. The researches have proved that several amino acids are essential to fish growth. Therefore, they must be fully prepared into the feeds. These amino acids are termed essential amino acids while the other amino acids, which may not exist or may be just a little in feeds, are called dispensable amino acids because they are needed only in small amounts or can be synthesized internally.

The following ten amino acids are essential amino acids to fish: isoleucine, leucine, lysine, methionine, phenylalanine, threonine, tryptophan, valine, arginine, and histidine. These ten must be included in fish feeds so that they can satisfy the nutritional requirements of fish and guarantee the normal development and growth.

Besides, the proportion between different essential amino acids in protein must conform to the nutritional requirements of fish, which is dependent on the composition of amino acids in fish protein, so the proportion of all essential amino acids of fish may be referred to the composition of fish body protein. From the above-mentioned factors, We can arrive at a conclusion that the nutritional value of protein is determined mainly by the completeness of the sorts of essential amino acids and the equilibrium of specific value between all essential amino acids to the fish you feed. As for the incomplete and unbalanced protein, we can still raise its nutritional value greatly by way of supplementing those amino acids it lacks.

Carbohydrates

Carbohydrates are also called saccharide, in other words, the chief source of energy. Through digestion, they are decomposed into monosaccharide absorbed and utilized by fish body. In the organic body, part of them is decomposed through oxidization into carbon dioxide and water, releasing energy. Applicable heat is 4 kilocalories each gram of carbohydrate; part of them is conveyed into livers and muscles as glycogen to be preserved for the time being and the remaining part may be converted into fats, to be cumulated for life maintenance in case of shortage of food or stoppage of food-taking.

Cellulose is also a kind of carbohydrates, the major component of plant cell wall. Among the cultivated fish, only a few species like Tilapia and milk-fish can digest cellulose at a rather low utilization rate. It is believed that Cyprinids lack the cellulolytic enzyme. In consequence, they are unable to utilize cellulose, and neither are Grass carp, the typical herbivorous fish. An appropriate amount of crude fibres in fish feeds can stimulate the digestive movements of the intestinal tracts so as to promote the digestion and absorption of other nutrients.

Fats

Fats are also a source of energy. Every gram of fats deliver 9 kilocalories of applicable heat. Fats are decomposed in digestive tracts into fatty acid and glycerol which can be absorbed. After absorption, the body fats are synthesized from the excessive fatty acid and glyceral, storing in subcutaneous tissues, muscles, spaces between connective tissues and the abdominal cavity.

Fats are apt to deteriorate through oxidization, bringing about toxic substances like aldehyde and ketone etc, which are detrimental to fish and destroy Vitamin E in fish feeds. If fish take in too much deteriorated fish meal and silkworm pupae, they will suffer from thin-back disease, muscular atrophy, losing weight and higher mortality.

Vitamins

Vitamins are organic trace elements indispensable for fish. There are so many sorts of these substances with various physiological functions; however, all of them are indispensable to keep fish fit with a normal growth. A number of Vitamins take part in the process of metabolism: *e.g.* Vitamin B1 of body carbohydrates; Vitamin B6, of proteins; Vitamin C, that of the synthesis of body protein of animal; And Vitamin D, of the normal metabolism of calcium and phosphorus, promoting the formation of skeleton.

As it is, it is not easy to determine the exact amount of various Vitamins required by fish. On the basis of the practical state and the characteristics of the cultivated species in China, fresh feeds are added to make up the deficiency of Vitamins. If pellet feeds are applied in farming Grass carp, green grass may be supplied at intervals so as to replenish the Vitamins the fish lack and the effect is desirable.

Minerals

Minerals are essential elements of fish body composition. Without minerals, the organic bodies are unable to retain normal physiological functions. Phosphorus and calcium are the important components of skeleton. The deficiency of the two substances will affect the skeleton development with a result of deformity.

The minerals demanded by fish come basically from feeds and part of them directly from environmental water. Fish absorb the calciferous and phosphorous salts and the ions of clorine and sodium through their gill rakers and skin. Minerals in diet may enhance the utilization of carbohydrates by fish, accelerate the growth of fish tissues like skeleton and muscles, improve their appetite and speed up the growth of fish body, and therefore, in the preparation of fish feeds, the minerals must be taken into consideration.

As a whole, some additives like bone powder and table salt in fish feeds are enough for the pond fish.

JUDGEMENT OF NUTRITIONAL VALUE OF FISH FEEDS

In feeding, on one hand, we must be aware of nutritional requirements by fish; on the other hand, we must make a judgement on the nutritional value, so that the feeds applied can come up with fish nutritional needs. Besides the analysis of chemical composition of fish feeds, other criteria like digestive rate, utilization rate and food coefficient can be taken into account for the judgement of food nutritional value.

Food Digestive Rate

The judgement, which is made only out of the chemical ingredients could not be so exact, since the contents of nutrients may not stand for the quantity that fish digest and utilize. Food digestive rate means the percentage of the nutrients digested by fish. Food digestive rate is affected by a number of factors and even the same ration could have various digestive rates.

For example, if we feed the same ration to different species or fishes with different feeding habits, the digestive rate is different, because of their respective digestive organs enzymes. The activeness of enzyme is associated with the temperature and the digestive rate increase when the temperature rises within the adaptable temperature range. The crude fibres content in diet will reduce the digestive rate of other nutrients. The amount of food intake of fish also affects food digestive rate and a proper food intake will bring up the highest digestive rate.

Food Utilization Rate

It refers mainly to the utilization rate of crude protein in food. Since the quality of all food proteins is not identical, the efficiency of making up fish body protein from food protein differs. In this sense, food nutritional value is not only demonstrated by food digestive rate, but also by utilization rate of crude protein in food, and the quality of food protein, *i.e.* the biological value of protein.

The food intake amount, protein utilization rate of several plant feeds taken by Grass carp and the growth after food intake in experiments are manifested. It shows that the daily crude protein of Potamogeton malainus is 0.149 higher than that 0.129 of Vallisneria spiralis; on the contrary, the growth of Grass carp with the former is worse than that with Vallisneria spiralis.

Food Coefficient and Food Efficiency

These two criteria explain food effect in farming. In production, it is a common method to appraise the food nutritional value by food coefficient. The cirterion is also considered as the basis for planning and preparation of food and the prediction of fish yield. Food coefficient is affected by many factors, particularly by the management. Improvement of management level can diminish food coefficient, therefore, the same amount of feeds could attain more fish yield.

The factors affecting food coefficient are as follows:

- Preparation before feeding: For bean cakes, they must be first throughly soaked in water for the adult fish to take in and digest or be gound up for juvenile fish. But the soaking should not be too long lest it goes fermenting and rotting. If that happens, the cakes will not be eaten by fish but will turn out to be fertilizers. In production, generally, the ground cake paste, wheat bran and rice bran are just placed on the feeding board and the food will be spread and dissolved in water in competition by fish. There might be a waste of feeds sinking to the pond bottom as fertilizers. If the brans and cakes are made into granulated feeds, the food loss might be avoided and the food consumption could be reduced.
- Amount and method of feeding: Feeds must be evenly spread and the amount must be appropriate without any sudden change. The amount of feeding should be controlled according to weather, water quality and fish appetite with an avoidance of excessive amount or there will be a waste of food if it is not eaten up and consequently food coefficient will be higher. But it can be reduced by frequent feeding in small amounts.
- Water quality: So far as water quality is concerned, the oxygen content in pond water is the factor affecting the food coefficient the most. Experiments show that the food coefficient is doubled in culturing Common carp if the oxygen content comes down from 3—6 mg/L to 2—0.5 mg/L.
- Nutritional elements in food: The fish at different developmental stages or with different feeding habits demand different nutritional elements in food. In order to speed up growth and reduce food cofficient, the nutritional elements contained in the food applied must be in conformity with the physiological needs of a certain fish.
- Species and age: Food coefficient of the same feed is variable with different species. From experiments, for Common carp, food coefficient of dry silkworm pupae is 1.3—2 while for rainbow trout, it's 6. It is different with fish ages, lower for the juvenile fish than for the adult. The usual food coefficients in present production.

FISH FARMING

Fish farming is an activity which is mostly done under natural conditions following the natures law though subjected to variations due to different agro-climatic conditions. According to the nature of the biomass generation in the pond, fish types being reared, feeding habits, space requirement for the fish, the soil of the place, the water, management operations to be done, etc., some basic principles can be enunciated for the benefit of those who want to start a fish farm.

FISH FARM OPERATIONS

Once the farmer has found out the place for the pond the next step is to decide what kind of fish culture is possible with the space available. He must also decide whether his resources will allow him for starting a fish farm. This planning is necessary to determine the number of fish ponds to be constructed and the kind of fish culture one wants to take up. A range of ideas are presented in this section of the booklet concerning the kinds of fish farm operations whether raising fish or breeding fish, whether raising carps, tilapia or catfish, whether prawns or shrimps, etc. He also gets an idea on the type of ponds small or big, grow in one pond or in more ponds, advantages of small and big ponds, advantages of mixing or separating different breeds of fish and sexes, etc. A farmer who prepares himself to start fish farming should keep in mind that a certain percentage of fish introduced into the pond will die however much we try to take care of them.In the nature many fishes never reach their adult size because they are eaten by other animals or big fishes or they die of diseases. "Survival of the fittest" is the law of nature. In the artificial rearing of fishes in the ponds the farmer tries to provide maximum growing and development conditions for getting maximum number of fishes and thereby maximum number of fishes reach marketable size.

KINDS OF OPERATIONS

As already mentioned once the site is identified the farmer has to decide whether he wants to go for breeding and production of fry and fingerlings or rear them till they attain marketable size. For breeding he needs more number of small ponds. The number of ponds may be more if he is trying to breed several breeds of fishes and in the same breed several sets of breeders (one set of breeders consists of two males and one female). If the farmer is planning to rear the fish only he needs big ponds. Depending on the number of fishes he wants to rear he may need one or more ponds. He also should consider whether he is raising the fish for the family usage or tor marketing purposes and whether he wants it as a main business or as a subsidiary business.

Questions like these have to be considered so that he can construct

- The right kinds of ponds,
- The right number of ponds and
- Stock the right kinds of fishes.

TYPES OF PONDS

The types of pond a farmer can build depend upon water supply, soil and topography. Generally, two types of ponds are built -barrage ponds and diversion ponds. The main difference between these two types of pond is the water source though in many aspects the construction details are the same.

Barrage Ponds

In barrage ponds the water source is the rain run-off water or a spring forming into a small stream running down the valley. The site is marked by a valley type of topography and the pond is constructed by building a wall across the valley and store the running water through the valley. The area where water is collected is called the pond area.

The barrage pond requires only one wall at the lower side of the pond area. By building a number of walls at suitable intervals the farmer can make several ponds successively one after the other forming a chain of ponds. The water enters first into the pond which is at the highest elevation among all the ponds and then passes on to the next pond lower in elevation. In other words the drained out water from the higher pond is collected by the lower one through a drainage pipe and then to the next lower till we reach the last one. From the last one the water is drained out safely. When ponds and the water inlet and outlet are arranged in such a way that the water flows from one pond to the other it is called ponds in series or rosary system.

Water can also be directed independently into each pond from a channel running along one side of the pond and drained out into another channel at the other side of the pond. This is the best system of water supply to the fish ponds. Arrangement of ponds in this way is called ponds in parallel system. The channel that supplies water is called inlet channel and the channel that collects water from each pond is called drainage channel.

The drainage outlet may be fixed at the bottom side of the pond if the pond is to be drained out completely. Besides this drainage outlet there should bean outlet at a height beyond which the farmer does not want to accumulate the water in the pond.

This is for the protection of the build which will be broken if water gets accumulated beyond certain height. The excess water is drained out from the pond through this drainage which acts as an overflow channel. The drainage and the overflow channel should be constructed in such a way that the water should be drained out safely without eroding the soil and causing damage to the pond. In barrage ponds, flow channels are fixed at a suitable height in order to drain out the excess water that may be accumulated during the rain. There are many variations of overflow channel system from which the farmer can choose the most suitable one.

The drainage and overflow channel can be joined together just before they join the common big drainage channel. Barrage ponds should not be built where the flow of the water is high. The walls will not be able to withstand the force of rushing water especially during the rainy season.

Diversion Ponds

Diversion ponds are those which receive water from river or stream through a diversion channel. One diversion channel takes water to the pond and another diversion channel act as a drainage. The drainage channel may be taking the water into the same river or stream from which the water came in or to a farm where it is used for irrigation or the water may be drained out into any other outlet. If more than one pond are constructed they are connected with the inlets and outlets in series or in parallel design. Diversion pond can be made in a number of ways de- pending on the ingenuity of the farmer. It can be built anywhere provided water can be taken to it from a water source by channel or pipe. If the pond is built on a flat ground there should be walls all around to prevent the collapse of the sides. Sometimes the ponds are constructed by deepening an area which is lower than the surroundings. If there is enough space and water supply is assured there can be several ponds successively constructed to use the overflow of water from one diversion pond to a second one and from the second to the third and so on, till the last. Whatever may be the type of pond being constructed there will always be some advantages and disadvantages. The farmer has to consider both the advantages and disadvantages and make his decision most beneficial to him. However, diversion ponds are better than barrage ponds because they are less likely to overflow and the water source is more dependable. But barrage ponds are cheaper in construction.

Similarly parallel system of pond construction is better than the se- ries or rosary system. One can have a mixture of barrage ponds and diversion ponds arranged in series (rosary) or parallel system. The art of planning and constructing fish ponds is very much an individual thing. There are many ways of using land and water resources. But the exact shape, number and size of the ponds have to be decided by the farmer.

Number of Ponds

The number of ponds usually depends on the number of functions the farmer wants to perform and also the number of times he would like to repeat a single function within a given period of time. The functions related to the fisheries are holding a breeding stock, breeding, hatching, raising fry, raising fingerlings and rearing for marketing. Normally these functions are better done in different ponds or water bodies. At the same time it should be remembered that several functions can be performed in the same pond or water body. For example, breeding and hatching and raising fry can be done in the same pond.

However, for breeding large number of breeding stock we require more than one pond. Similarly, the number of ponds also depends on the number of breeds or kinds of fish the farmer wants to breed. For example, if the farmer wants to breed several breeds of fish, different ponds may be required, or several sets of the same breed is to be maintained. In the same way if the frequency of breeding is more (eg. once a week, once in two weeks, a month, etc.) the number of ponds required will be more. At least two ponds are required for rearing for market purposes. If the farmer cannot make more than one pond he can also breed and hatch the fish in an enclosure of inverted mosquito-net fixed inside the pond.

Size of the Pond

The size of the pond also depends on topography, water supply, and the need or volume of production one intends to have. However, the nursery ponds will be smaller than the rearing ponds. Apart from this the size of the rearing pond itself can be varying. The advantages of small ponds are, function like harvesting, draining, refilling, treatment for diseases, etc., can be done quickly and easily. But the cost of construction and the land area required for the small ponds will be more compared to large ponds. But for the small and marginal farmers few small ponds are better than having large ponds.

Depth of the Pond

The depth of the pond also depends on several factors such as breeding, fry raising, fingerling raising, rearing for marketing, etc. Least depth is required for breeding and fry raising and maximum depth is required for rearing for marketing. Normally for breeding and fry raising the pond depth ranges from 0.5 to 1.0 m while for raising fingerlings a depth of 1.0 to 1.5 m is recommended. For rearing fish to market size the recommended pond depth varies from 1.2 to 2.0 metre.

Normally, sunlight does not reach deeper than two metres and the growth of the planktons will be restricted. At the same time too shallow pond will heat up the water or too much vegetative growth may occur and consequently the available oxygen to the fish will be much less than the required especially during the night hours. But in commercial farms breeding and raising of fry is done in plastic tubs, basins, glass jars or even in big mud pots. Glass vessels are better for this purpose because we can observe the fertilization, hatching and the conditions of the fry well.

Single Pond Operation

If the farmer can have only one pond he could purchase or collect fry and fingerling and rear them to market size. For this there should be regular supply of fry and fingerlings. He can also breed fish inside a netted area in the same pond.

The farmer who is having single pond can go for culture of single breed or a mixture of several breeds. The former is called monoculture and the later polyculture. Both have advantages and disadvantages.

MONOCULTURE

Monoculture is the fish culture of only one species. It is intensive in caring, feeding and other management practices. It is easier to perform all the management practices since only one type of fish is involved. In monoculture the farmer has greater control over the size, age and sex. In mono culture fish can be harvested selectively by using nets of different mesh size. In monoculture diseases and pests are easily controlled at the same time there is a possibility of complete elimination of the whole lot by some epidemic type of diseases and pests if they go out of control.

POLYCULTURE

In polyculture different breeds of fish are mixed together in fixed proportion or at random. Polyculture is more closer to the natural method of growing fish and under this situation only the fittest ones will survive. Several small fishes may be eaten by the bigger ones or they could not compete with the bigger ones for food and space. This problem is more in the case of poly culture in which both carnivorous and herbivorous fishes are reared together.

At the same time a farmer can have a polyculture with proper combinations (in number) of selected breeds of fishes. The selection is done on the basis of feeding habits. Such polyculture is called composite fish farming. For example, a farmer can rear a mixture of Indian carps such as catla, rohu, mrigal and Chinese carps such as silver carp, common carp and grass carp.

The catla and silver carp normally takes feed from the upper layers of the water body, the rohu and common carp from the middle layers, while the mrigal and grass carp takes feed from the bottom layers of the pond. All are herbivorous in their feeding habit. In the composite fish culture full utilisation of the pond is possible.

If the breed introduced are naturally fast multiplying like tilapia and their number is a problem in the pond, another fish breed like catfish which is carnivorous can be introduced. The catfish will feed on the organisms at the bottom as well as the fry of tilapia keeping the population of tilapia under control.

Introducing some grass carp among other breeds of fish that are being reared is the best method of controlling the weed growth in the pond. For farmers who have only one pond and do not have facilities like regular supply of fry and fingerlings nor he is unable or unwilling to breed them and those who cannot feed and care in the scientific and intensive ways, it is advisable to go for polyculture with fishes that naturally breed in the pond.

MONOSEX CULTURE

In monosex culture either male or female fish of the same breed or more than one breed is reared. The advantage is faster growth of the fish since all the energy is concentrated on the growth and development. No energy is used for the reproduction. Sexes can be separated individually during the breeding season or by noting the difference between the male and female in a breed of fish. In the cross breeding of some fish the off springs produced are sterile by nature or produce hundred per cent male fish. For example, if we cross male tilapia of *Tilapia macrochir* with female of *T. nilotica*, the male of *T. mossambica* with the female of *T. nilotica* and male of *T. hororum* with female of *T. mossambica* the off springs will be completely male. There are no crosses in which 100 per cent off-springs produced are female. Monosex culture is valuable but difficult for ordinary farmers to carry out the breeding and rearing. Therefore, it is not recommended generally to the small scale fish farms unless there is a steady supply of male fry or fingerlings.

MORE THAN ONE POND OPERATION

If the farmer has more than one pond then, he can rear fry or fingerlings for marketing in all the ponds or he can take up the breeding in one, raise fry or fingerlings in another and can rear fish up to marketable size in another pond. If he still has more ponds he can replicate the same functions in more than one pond. With three ponds a farmer can go for breeding and raising of fry for his own farm. The smallest one is used for breeding while the others may be used for rearing till they attain marketable size. The major difference between a large farm operation and a small farm operation is the number of ponds and the fry or fingerlings reared. In big fish farms all the input requirements will be more so also the greater output can be expected in terms of production as well as income.

FISH PRODUCTION IN INTEGRATED FARMING SYSTEMS

Guided by major findings on livestock-fish farming published in a preliminary set of principles defining the various aspects of the culture technology and promotion of fish production in integrated farming systems is suggested and outlined, as a basis for further deliberation.

Principles pertaining to technology of livestock-fish farming are:

- Fish production in integrated systems is more complex than the conventional separate aquaculture system, requiring more knowledge and better management inputs
- Integrated farming systems may vary in the degree of intensification of the livestock and fish subsystems, varying from extensive, semiintensive to intensive subsystems.
- Extensive subsystems utilise natural feed produced without international fertilization; semiintensive subsystems require fertilization to produce natural feed and/or supplementary feed but with a significant component of diet supplied by natural feed; and in intensive subsystems all the nutritional requirements are provided by artificial feed given to fishes with natural feed contributing little or no nutrition.

- Fish cultured in an integrated farming system with livestock (especially duck; Edwards, 1986) benefit from a significant amount of the nutrition derived from natural food, which develops in the pond due to the fertilization by organic manures. This suggests the important role of pelagic algal-based food web which cultivates in fish biomass.
- The largest contribution of the manure to fish nutrition therefore, appears to be due to its fertilizing effect in the pond. Bacteria, breaking down the organic matter in the manure, release nutrients which lead to the production of phytoplankton and zooplankton.
- In a manure-fed fish pond, fish nutrition may also be derived from direct consumption of the manure. However, a detritus food web has a secondary role in fish biomass production biomass production, as compared with the algalbased food web.
- The direct nutritional value of manure for fish is by its content of spilled animal feed. A large proportion of the nutrients in livestock feed are not assimilated, but are voided in the excreta, particularly pig excreta (Edwards, 1985).
- Over-fertilization with manure may lead to poor water quality of fish pond, particularly leading to depletion of dissolved oxygen and fish kills.
- Management of water quality is needed to overcome fish kills due to oxygen depletion and extreme fluctuation of dissolved oxygen levels. The strategy is to promote a growing biomass of phytoplankton which will generate sufficient oxygen to maintain relatively high dissolved oxygen have on a 24-hr basis. It is essential to maintain a positive net photosynthesis
- The criteria for selection of fish species for stocking into manure-fed fish ponds should be based on the ability of fish species to:
  - Filter and feed on plankton (bacteria, phytoplankton and zooplankton)
  - Tolerate low levels of dissolved oxygen (< 2mg/l minimum as defined by "Criteria for the Protection of Aquatic Life")
- An optimal stocking density of fish species is critical in attaining high cumulative fish yields and in reaching the upper carrying capacity of a manure-fed fish pond.
- Determination of and recommendation of the optimal stocking density of fish consider differences in local circumstances such as the fish species, manure-type and inputs to the pond, addition of other off-farm feed, and water quality of the pond.
- Ways to intensify fish production from integrated farming systems involve management inputs to:

  - Stock a higher initial fish biomass, followed by
  - Harvesting the fish intermediately when the growth curve of stocked fish starts to slow down
- There is a need for a more complex marketing system to handle the inputs and products from two subsystems as opposed to a single subsystem.
- Integrated farming on the one hand, enables the distribution of risk (both biological and economic), since two subsystems are involved as opposed to one in a single-commodity farming system; on the other hand, the failure of one subsystem can adversely affect the other.

TYPES OF INTEGRATED FISH FARMING

Basically the integrated fish farming is of two types:

1. Agri-based fish farming
2. Live-stock fish farming

The fish-cum-live-stock farming is realised as innovation for recycling of organic wastes as well as production of high class protein at low cost.

AGRI-BASED FISH FARMING

Paddy-Cum-Fish Culture

In India, this farming is practised in the states of Bihar, West Bengal, Orissa and Assam where enough water is present in the paddy fields. The paddy fields retain water for 3-8 months in a year. The interest in this practice has declined in recent years due to the use of pesticides to protect high yielding varieties of paddy.

This practice can be done in following types of paddy plots-

- Perimeter type–paddy grows in the middle.
- Central pond type — paddy growing area is on the perimeter.
- Lateral trench system–trenches are provided on either one or both sides of the moderately sloping field.

The variety of rice used in this culture is Panidhan, Jalmagna, CR26077, Tulsi, etc., while the fish spp. are Indian major carps, Channa spp, Oreochromis mossambicus, Clarias batrachus, Anabas testudineus, silver carp, grass carp, common carp. The total production in such practice is approximately 90 quintal from 2 paddy crops while the fish production is about 1000 kg from 1 ha.

Horticulture-Cum-Fish Farming

The horticulture-cum-fish farming system includes the culture of fruits, vegetables and flowers on the embankment of the pond. The fruits and vegetables contain various nutritive elements and the Indian Council of Medical Research has recommended 85g of fruits and 300g of vegetables to consume daily. For horticulture crop production the inner and outer dykes of the pond and adjoining areas are used. The selection of plant is the main criteria for the success of this system. The plant should be dwarf, seasonal, evergreen, remunerative and less shady. The fruit crops which can be used are Mango, Banana, Papaya, Coconut, Lime, etc., and the vegetables like Brinjal, Tomato,Cucumber,Gourds, Chilli,Carrot, Raddish, Turnip, Spinach, Peas, Cabbage, Cauliflower, Ladies finger can be grown according to their season throughout the year.

The flower plantation on the embankment is also useful. We can use the plants like Rose, Jasmine, Gladiolus, Marigold and Chrysanthemum, etc., which provides additional income to the farmer and beauty to the farm. This system provides 20-25 per cent more return in comparison to aquaculture alone. The agri-based fish farming includes the mushroom fish system, sericulture-fish system, fodder crop integration, etc. Pond bundhs may also used for growing pulses and oil seed crops. Aquatic cash crop like Makhana (Euryale ferox) and Singhara (Trapa spp) integration can also be done along with air-breathing or carnivorous fishes.

LIVE-STOCK FISH FARMING

Poultry-Cum-Fish Farming

This system utilises poultry droppings of fully built- up poultry litter for fish culture. The fish production obtained is about 5000 kg/ha/yr. with 1250 kg chicken meat and 70000 no. of eggs. Approximately 500-600 no. of birds is reared in a 1 ha pond. The Rhode Island or Leghorn variety birds are more preferred over others. They require 0.3-0.4 square meterspace/bird. Hoppers are used to feed them and to minimise feed wastage. The poultry birds (layers) are fed with starter, grower, and brooder feed according to their age. In India it is practised in Andhra Pradesh, Bihar, Haryana, Kerala, West Bengal, Uttar Pradesh, Maharashtra, Orissa, and Tamilnadu.

Duck-Cum-Fish Culture

The duck are commonly called as biologicals aerator. They are reared on the dyke of the pond in a low-cost house. This farming is practised in Tamilnadu, Assam, Bihar, Andhra Pradesh, Tripura, Orissa, Karnataka, Kerala and Uttar Pradesh. The 'Indian runner' and 'Khaki campbell' varieties are found more suitable in this culture. About 300 no. of ducklings (some spp. are reared 450-500 in no.) are reared to fertilize the 1 ha. pond. The duck not only act as live aerator by splashing water with their webbed feet butalso control the aquatic weed (Lemna, Azolla, etc.), aquatic insects, molluscs,tadpoles, etc. Each duckling require about 0.3-0.5 square meter area as living space. The total production from such type of culture is about 3500-5000 kg fish, 18000-18500 eggs and 600 kg of duck meat. The duck droppings are used as manure for primary production.

Pig-Cum-Fish Culture

This system has certain advantages over others. The 30-35 pig's waste may produce 1 tonne of Ammonium Sulphate and 40-45 pigs are adequate to fertilize 1 ha water area under polyculture. Each pig requires about 3-4 sq.m floor space. This system of integration is very common in China, Taiwan, Vietnam, Thailand, Malaysia, Hungary and some European countries.

The White Yorkshire, Hampshire and Landrace are the popular breed of pig for integration with fish. Pigs need clean housing which should provideadequate protection from adverse climates. The pigs are fed on pig mash which is made up of rice bran, rice polish, wheat-bran, broken maize, ground-nut oil cake, fish- meal mineral mixture, salt, etc. The spoiled vegetables can also be mixed in it. This system provides about 3000-4000 kg/ha/yr fish, 4500 kg/yr pig meat and 800 no. of piglets every year.

Cattle-Cum-Fish Culture

It is a common practice all-over the world. The cow excreta is most abundant in terms of availability and a healthy cow may excrete over 4000-5000kg dung and 3500-4000 litre urine on an annual basis. The BOD of cow manure is lower than other livestock manure. About 5-6 cows can provide adequate manure for 1 ha pond in addition to 9000 kg milk and about 3000-4000 kg of fish annually. Cow-shed should be built close to fish pond to simplify handling of cow-manure.

Goat-Cum-Fish Integration

It is considered as poor man's cow and a goat's excreta is considered as a very good organic fertilizer. The goat excreta contains organic carbon-60 per cent, N-2.7 per cent, P-1.78 per cent, K-2.88 per cent and its urine is also equally rich in both N & P. At least 50-60 goats are essential to fertilize 1 ha pond. The goats should be provided with dry, safe, comfortable house protected from excessive heat. The goat breeds are Jamanapari, Beetal, Barbari for milk and Bengal, Sirihi, Deccani are used for meat purpose. Goats are selective feeders and consume Berseem, Napier grass, Cowpea Soybean, Mulberry, etc. This integration can provide 3500-4000 kg fish/ha/year without supplementary feeding and fertilizer.

Rabbit-Fish Integration

Rabbit meat is preferred by most of the health conscious consumers owing to its low fat in comparison to other meats. The important meat breeds are Soviet Chinchilla, Grey Giant, and White Giant, etc. Rabbits are reared in cage, hutch and floor system (floor should be cemented). Rabbit excreta contain organic carbon-50 per cent, N-2 per cent, P-1.33 per cent, and K-1.2 per cent. The rabbit excreta is high in nitrogen content and low in moisture, thus quality manure for sustained plankton production. It is estimated that excreta from 300 rabbits would be enough for 1 ha pond fertilization.

FISH SPECIES SUITABILITY AND SELECTION

The main objective of manuring is to produce a good growth of plankton, mainly phytoplankton, but also zooplankton and bacteria which are protein-rich natural for fish. On this basis, the most appropriate species of fish for a manure-fed pond are therefore those species which are able to filter and feed on plankton (bacteria, phytoplankton and zooplankton) from the water. The most common filter feeders are carps and mixed feeder on algae-detritus are certain species of tilapia.

The most commonly raised carp species are the bighead carp Aristichthys nobilis Richardson and the silver carp Hypophthalmychithys molitrix Valenciennes. The carps are usually raised in polyculture with the grass carp Ctenopharyngodon idella and Indonesian carp Puntius gonionotus Linnaeus controls micro- and macro-vegetation at the water's edge, the Hoeven's slender carp Leptobarbus hoevenii Blk and the common carp Cyprinus carpio Linnaeus which is a bottom feeder.

An important observation is that the detritus-feeding silver carp benefited most from the pond conditions, increasing its biomass share from an initial 5.8 per cent to 20.7 per cent from a series of investigation on the integrated farming systems in the Transkei, South Africa. The Indian carps, catla Catla catla Hamilton, mrigal, Cirrhinus mrigala Hamilton Buchanam and rohu, Labeo rohita Hamilton have also been used in experimental duck/fish integrated farming systems in India.

Polycultures of carps have been widely assumed to be the most efficient way to obtain high fish yields but in Taiwan, the percentage of tilapia in the pond has increased markedly at the expense of the Chinese carps. The most commonly raised tilapia species are the blue tilapia Oreochromis aureus Steindachner, the grey tilapia Oreochromis mossambicus Peters, the Nile tilapia Oreochromis niloticus Linnaeus or their hybrids.

Tilapia are more suitable than carp for manure-fed ponds since the former are more tolerant to low levels of dissolved oxygen than the latter. Air-breathing silver-striped catfish Clarias spp., are also integrated with pig farms. Thc detritusfeeding grey mullet Mugil cephalus L. may be excellent substitutes for the silver carp in integrated farming systems under saline conditions.

FISH YIELDS AND PRODUCTION RATES IN INTEGRATED FARMING SYSTEMS

There are few data on fish yields from ponds which received livestock manure (and spilled livestock feed). The fish yields in integrated livestock-fish farming systems reported in the literature vary greatly, with the actual and extrapolated equivalents ranging from 1.5 ton/ha/year to 18 ton/ha/yr. The variation in fish yield is due:

- The animal sub-system and its major manure input to the pond
- The fish species and stocking rates
- Intensification of culture management inputs *e.g.* addition of other off-farm feed

DIFFERENT TYPES AND AMOUNTS OF MANURE INPUTS

The rationale behind integrating fish with livestock is the large amount of nutrients (N-P-K) present in the feed that is recovered in the manure, with possible proportions of 72–79 per cent nitrogen, 61–87 per cent phosphorus, and 82–92 per cent potassium. These act as fertilizers in fish ponds to produce plankton which comprise high-protein natural food for certain species of fish.

Nitrogen and phosphorus are the nutrients most likely to be limiting for plankton growth in the pond but fish yield is probably more directly correlated to manure nitrogen content (Edwards, 1991) since nitrogen is more volatile than phosphorus. Based on the nitrogen content of the different manures, it was possible to estimate the stocking density of different livestock (laying duck, dairy cow, pigs and buffalo) in order to produce the same fish yield of 174.7 kg/ 200 m^2/year in 13 family-level farms.

Considering the livestock's manure characteristics (total live weight, age of livestock, feed characteristics of livestock, climate and management of livestock subsystem) and the varying N contents (per cent of the manure production/animal/year, *i.e.*, 2.6 per cent for laying duck manure, 1.9 per cent for pig, 2.2 per cent for dairy cow and 1.1 per cent for buffalo, the estimated number of laying duck, pig, dairy cow and buffalo required to the same fish yields are 1335, 410, 40, and 85 individuals respectively. Prinsloo and Schoonbee noted the comparative effectiveness of the manure on the development of organisms in the food web and promotion of biological activity in fish ponds are: duck manure > pig manure > raw chicken manure > cattle manure > sheep manure.

Manure may contain up to 25 per cent crude protein, but more than half of this is usually non-protein nitrogen (*e.g.*, uric acid) which is not assimilated by fish; therefore manure itself is a poor feed for fish. Manures also contain less energy than conventional pelleted feeds. Though many species of fish consume manure directly, it is a low quality feedstuff compared to conventional pelleted feed and natural plankton. Another advantage of manure utilisation in fish ponds is that since carbon forms about 50 per cent of the biomass of plankton, the high organic content of the manure is an important source of carbon which is released by bacterial respiration. However, depending on the productivity and quality of water and soil, the effectiveness of livestock manure (enriched with cellulose-rich organic matter) in acting as nutrient sources for fish growth and in raising fish yield varies.

Two possibilities have been observed in Dor, Israel:

1. Manure would improve fish yields only under conditions of water and soil which are poor in essential nutrient minerals (*e.g.*, carbonates or organic matter), or of a low pH, fish ponds receiving very "soft" waters deficient in minerals, or ponds with a low primary production; and
2. Manure may be ineffective in raising fish yields above the rates achieved by daily applications of mineral (N-P-K) fertilizers, under conditions when the fish pond is receiving daily applications of mineral fertilizers, or where fish ponds are highly productive with very fertile soil naturally-enriched with nutrient minerals and carbonates, or fish ponds with nutrient-rich waters resulting in a high concentration of algal-based detrital organic matter.

SHRIMP FARMING PRACTICE SUSTAINABLE

The idea of sustainability has been interpreted widely to cover a wealth of different perspectives. Although there is much theory on the subject, very few authors have offered realistic and simple practical guidelines or methodologies for the assessment of sustainability. A general assessment of the sustainability of shrimp farming, based on this framework and the more detailed discussion in the chapter. Although it is not possible to go into all these these aspects here, some key elements will be considered. It is often suggested that extensive or semi-intensive production is more sustainable than intensive production; indeed, it is commonly suggested that intensive production is unsustainable.

This view derives from a narrow interpretation of sustainability, and confusion between correlation and causation. Sustainability depends not on the level of intensity, but rather on the quality of the site, the management, and the suitability of the technology to both site and management competence. Unfortunately, because of poor site selection and management, much shrimp farming in recent years has not been sustainable; and although some of the failures relating to intensive production have been spectacular, there have also been major problems with extensive and semi-intensive production. Different levels of intensity may be more or less sustainable in different ways; and different levels of intensity may be more or less sustainable in different economic or ecological contexts.

Compares intensive, semi-intensive, and extensive shrimp farming according to a range of different sustainability criteria related to some of the relevant areas. The degree of sustainability assigned to each kind of shrimp farming will depend on the relative weight given to the different aspects, and the social, economic, resource, and ecological context in which development is taking place. It is impossible to generalise about sustainability of production, which will depend upon local circumstances (*e.g.*, seed availability; water source; feed supply; management; disease etc.). In the following sections different aspects of sustainability will be discussed in more detail, and will be related to intensity where relevant.

SUSTAINABILITY ASSESSMENT

Sustainability Assessment In assessing the sustainability of any enterprise or technology, consideration should be given to at least the following:

- The sustainability (or continuity) of supply, and quality of inputs;
- The social, environmental and economic costs of providing the inputs (eg depletion of resources elesewhere);
- The long term continuity (or sustainability) of production;
- Financial viability;
- Social impact;
- Environmental impact;
- The efficiency of conversion of resources into useful product.

SUSTAINABILITY OF SUPPLY AND QUALITY OF INPUTS

In many countries seed is still caught in the wild. The supply of such seed cannot be guaranteed; its availability is generally seasonal; and it may carry disease. At high levels of exploitation, the collection of wild seed may have deleterious effects on wild capture fisheries (for shrimp and other species), and on the coastal ecosystem - either directly through removal of shrimp juveniles, or removal of other species in the by-catch. Hatchery produced seed on the other hand may also suffer from erratic supply related to disease or broodstock availability. The quality may be poor as a result of excessive use of chemicals, the practice of multiple spawnings, and poor feeding (eg related to a shortage or high cost of artemia cysts). In general however, hatchery production offers much greater potential for real long term sustainability and quality control.

Feed

While formula feeds are dependent on fishmeal there remains the question of the sustainability of exploitation of the source fishery, and the stability of supply. Imported feed degrades rapidly during storage in tropical countries and quality cannot be guaranteed. Formulation is still often more closely related to ingredient costs than nutritional and environmental requirements. In some cases, feed has been suspected as a source of disease. As noted above, the supply of Artemia cysts - mainly from the US and China - is erratic and quality variable.

Chemicals

The supply of chemicals is likely to remain relatively reliable and will probably increase. Quality is however frequently questionable. A huge range are now available to the shrimp farmer, especially in countries like Taiwan and Thailand, but neither their effectiveness nor their environmental impact are well documented. Heavy use of antibiotics may lead to disease resistance of pathogens of shrimp and possibly of humans. Heavy use of chlorine compounds for water or pond sterilisation may lead to the formation of toxic chloramines and other complex organics.

Skills

The skills required for aquaculture production increase steadily with increasing levels of intensity. Although it may be relatively easy to achieve very high rates of output on a virgin site, sustained production at high levels of intensity requires high skills levels.

SUSTAINABILITY OF OUTPUT

Disease

Disease is by far the most serious threat to the sustainability of shrimp farm production. In Asia the viruses MBV, Yellowhead, and whitespot have caused devastation in many countries, and a variety of Vibrio bacteria cause intermittent problems. It is possible that Thailand is currently experiencing a crash similar to that which devastated the Taiwanese industry in the late 80's and the Chinese industry in the late 90's. In Latin America Taura syndrome continues to cause serious mortality in many areas. Much has been said about the relationship between intensity and disease, but extensive and semi-intensive producers have been affected at least as much as intensive producers in recent years.

Feed Quality

Poor feed quality may reduce growth, depress health and survival, reduce water and pond soil quality, and increase pollution. It is also possible, though not proven, that it may transmit disease.

Water Quality

Poor water quality, caused by acid sulphate soil conditions, pollution (self, other farmers, other) or the presence of disease organisms may reduce growth, depress survival and introduce disease.

FINANCIAL SUSTAINABILITY

Feed Costs

Fish meal costs are likely to rise in the medium/long term as a result of steadily increasing demand, and steady or declining supply. Much will depend upon the rate of development of alternatives. Artemia used for hatchery production is likely to rise in cost as a result of steadily increased demand. At present there are very few major sources (US Great Salt Lake, China, and some production in Vietnam). Alternatives, including culture, are possible, but not competitive at the present time. Improved artificial substitutes are also possible but some natural food seems to be essential for good growth and survival.

Cost of Chemicals

The cost of chemicals is unlikely to rise substantially and new ones are constantly appearing on the market. Better site selection, design, husbandry, and water supply should reduce dependency on and cost of chemicals.

Labour Costs

Labour costs are related to the stage of development of the country. Less developed countries have a clear comparative advantage in this regard, but as they develop further this advantage will be reduced, and advantage in terms of other resources or sites will become more important.

Water Supply

High quality water supply may be very costly in several regards. A site with good water supply may be expensive or have other features which are undesirable and lead to extra production costs. The development of infrastructure for the supply of water is costly. Water pre-treatment is also costly. Furthermore, as the industry (and other industries) develops, the demand for good sites and high quality water will increase, and the supply may decrease (in terms of quality and quantity), leading to a further escalation of price.

Product Value and Markets

Product quality is increasingly important in all markets. Product quality may decline over time in poorly managed intensive systems as a result of disease, chemical residues, and smaller sized product. The average market price has been remarkably firm considering the steadily increased rates of production. However, there have been some unexpected oscillations.

At the present time there is a real danger of declining demand in American and European markets due to the poor poor environmental and social development image of shrimp farming. Many Americans now think that all shrimp farming involves the bulldosing of pristine mangrove, driving out local people, making a lot of money, using massive amounts of chemicals, spreading disease, and then abandoning a degraded environment. It is even possible that environmental groups will force a ban on the import of farmed shrimp from Asia unless it can be shown to be environmentally sustainable.

Following major growth in the 80s, prospects for market growth in Japan for black tiger shrimp (P. monodon) are limited. The US and European markets still have good growth potential, but only if the image of the product can be improved. The Asian market continues to grow well, and is less sensitive to environmental image. In terms of production effects on price, disease is likely to continue to cause problems in many areas, and act as a brake on excessive production and consequential reduced price. This is an interesting example of a sustainability conundrum: lack of sustainability among some producers may secure sustainability for others. Production from wild fisheries is likely to stay steady or decline.

SOCIO-ECONOMIC SUSTAINABILITY

A variety of socio-economic impacts have been described in different parts of the world, including displacement of local people as a result of increased land value; decreased land quality (eg salinisation; acidification; subsidence); and resource appropriation (government allocation through concessions of previously held common property resources, which had been used for a variety of subsistence uses by local people); and interference with navigational rights and conflict with the fishing industry. There is little doubt that these impacts have taken place in some areas, but by no means in all countries or areas.

It has also been suggested that the shift from subsistence agriculture and use of natural resources to employment on large fish farms may represent a decline in quality of life. This is a political, not a scientific issue and it is the job of scientists and economists to provide information on these issues rather than make value judgements.

ENVIRONMENTAL SUSTAINABILITY

Like all human activity shrimp farming has a variety of direct and indirect effects on the environment. Direct impacts include habitat destruction. Mangrove is the most frequently quoted example, but a wide variety of other coastal ecosystems may be lost or affected, including estuarine and saltmarsh habitat, and other kinds of wetland. Shrimp farming is also responsible for a variety of pollutants including organic matter (creating biological demand or BOD); nutrient enrichment (mainly nitrogen and phosphorus); and chemical discharges including antibiotics, pesticides/piscicides, and disinfectants. A variety of indirect impacts can also be identified. The wild seed fishery may affect other species that depend upon this food source - including shrimp fishermen. It may also affect other species directly through the by-catch of species caught by default and discarded. Loss of habitat may also affect other fisheries such as small scale shrimp or mud crab fisheries, although extensive or semi-intensive ponds are probably a suitable habit for the latter species.

FISH FARMING WITH CULTIVATION OF PALM TREES

Though fish farming with cultivation of palm trees comes under the broader subject of fish farming cum agriculture it was thought that to have a separate booklet on this topic itself because of the nature of the palm trees and all the possible designs one can make in fish farming cum palm tree cultivation. In our country large tracts of coastal areas which are usually low lying and occasionally flooded are cultivated under coconut palms. Rows of coconut palm trees with intermittent broad and narrow ditches, trenches and irregularly shaped and sized pools and waterways is a common sight in many parts of the coastal regions of Karnataka, Kerala, Tamil Nadu, Andhra Pradesh, Orissa and West Bengal. No doubt fish grow naturally in those trenches, ditches and pools and the people are harvesting them once a year. However these ditches, trenches and pools, if they are properly shaped and arranged along with the coconut trees, can be an immense source of quality fish production.

Areas away from the coastal region wherever water table is high or good irrigation facilities are available areca nut palms are cultivated. Rows of areca nut palms with intermittent narrow water channels are frequently seen in most of the above mentioned states. These channels, if made little more wider, deeper and kept clean from naturally growing vegetation is another potential area for fish farming. In the same way the oil palm cultivated areas also can be incorporated with fish farming provided the water table is high or there is sufficient water available from some natural source. Resetting the coastal and low lying land into fish cum coconut gardens or the interior areas of areca nut and oil palm growing areas into fish cum areca nut gardens or oil palm growing farms, though difficult due to problems of ownership by various people and restructuring, is a worthwhile attempt from the point of view of long term profitability 'and environmental management. Certainly, some policy level changes and decision making should precede such reorganisation of these areas. However, interested farmers, if they are wanting, with minimum expenses can modify and incorporate fish rearing into their coconut and areca nut gardens.

Areas cultivated with palm trees and having high water table are specially suitable for fish farming because of the following reasons.

- The palms are without branches and grow straight up allowing a lot of sunlight to reach the ground which can be used for fish growth.
- The distance between the palm trees can be adjusted and the planting geometry can be arranged so that a number of fish ponds can be fitted in between the rows of palm trees. The distance between the coconut and oil palms ranges from 25 to 33 feet and broad strips of fish ponds can be fitted in between the rows of coconuts and oil palms. The areca nuts are planted at 9-10 ft distance and the fish ponds of 20 to 30 ft width and any convenient length can be fitted between block plantations (several lines of areca nut trees of areca nuts.

- Palms in general require higher amount of water than most other crops and the intermittent fish ponds become a source of steady supply of moisture to them.
- The fish waste is a very good manure for the palm trees. Similarly the oil cakes from the coconuts and oil palms.are good feed for the fish. Hence there exists a symbiotic or complementary relationship between the fish and the palms in a palm cum fish rearing garden or agro-eco-system.

The purpose of this booklet is to promote the idea of fish rearing along with the cultivation of palm trees wherever the water table is high and it provides the basics of the planning and management of fish rearing cum palm tree cultivation to those who are interested and have the facilities to implement the same.

ESTABLISHMENT OF THE FARM

In the establishment of the farm the best way is to follow the time bound operational planning. However if the finance and labour is available then different units can be completed at the same time. Before the actual start of the work arrange for all the materials required including the planting material. Seedlings of the coconuts, arecanuts and oil palms are arranged sufficiently early enough so that we can get quality seedlings at the time of planting. The seedlings should be minimum two to three years old in the case of palms. Such arrangements are done outside the farm and not directly related to the work inside the farm in establishing the farm.

Among the works done inside the farm in establishing it, first of all locate and demarcate various units on the land in detail according to the blue print prepared already. Secondly structure the farm by laying out the roads and paths so that movement of material to the farm and from the farm during the construction can be done easily. Thirdly, construct the ponds and prepare the planting beds for the palm trees. The soil that is excavated during the construction of the fish pond will have to be adjusted on the planting beds or can be sold out.

The first stage consists in completing all the structures within the farm mainly the fish ponds and the planting beds for the palm trees. After the structures are complete the fish ponds can be operationalised at the first instance itself because in the first year itself we can obtain considerable amount of income from the farm. Mean time demarcate the spots of the pits and prepare pits for the plantation of the palm trees at the already decided spots according to the design planned. The readers are advised to refer the booklet on "Planting and Management of Trees" (Booklet No. 21) for more details about planting and caring of palms. Similarly whatever perennial inter crops are cultivated prepare the pits and planting materials in advance. Pits should be dug at least one year ahead and leave them exposed to at least one rainy and summer seasons for seasoning of the soil in the pits.

When all the perennial trees are planted and the fish ponds are put into operation the farm is said to be established. Normally it will take ten years for the palm trees to come to full production and to yield substantial economic return. But from the fish ponds we can get substantial return from the first year itself. By the end of second year in every pit where a palm tree or a perennial intercrop is planted should have a surviving and healthy plant. The same should be the fact even at the end of five years and at the time of flowering and fruiting. This is an important point because every tree missing from the spot for whatever reason is a huge loss as each tree can yield for many years and the total, income amount to be surprising. For example, the coconut is expected to provide about 300 nuts per year; assuming each nut fetches five rupees the expected income from the nuts per year will be 1500 rupees.

A coconut tree can yield up to 40 to. 50 years. The total ! expected income from one coconut tree will amount to be I 60,000 to 75,000 rupees. And the total income from 100 coconuts (planted at 33 ft distance in two and half acres of planted area) is estimated to be 60,00,000 rupees at price level of 40 to 50 years before. Without calculating the possible interest on the early years of income. This is only the income from the nuts; income from other products of the coconut trees is not yet to be estimated. We may level that income with the maintenance expenditure.

Management Practices

The management practices consists of cultivation practices of various palm trees rearing practices recommended for fish farming and combined practices for both. The cultivation and management practices of coconut palm is given in detail in Booklet No. 128 on "Coconut", of areca nut in Booklet No. 237 on "Arecanut"and of oil palm in Booklet NO.235 on "Oil Palm". When (combined with fish farming the additional management practices consists mainly the adjustments in the plant to plant and row to row distances in the plantation fofll1ing a number of designs.

The details about the management practices are many and varying depending on breeds of fish reared, the type of rearing whether it is mono culture, poly culture, whether breeding and fry raising is done or only the stocking is done, etc. These things are being explained in a number of booklets under the "Fisheries and Aquaculture Series": Booklet Nos. 514 (Fish Culture: An Introduction), 517 (Fish: Breeds of Carp), 520 (Fish: Pond Construction), 522 (Fish: Nutrition), 524 (Fish: Rearing of Carp Fish), 525 (Fish Feeding), 530 (Natural Feed for Fish), 533 (Fish culture in Rice Fields), 535 (Fish Diseases and Pests), 543 (Carp Breeding), 545 (Carps: Nursery for Fry and Fingerlings), 546 (Fish Farm Planning), 547 (Fish: Selection of Breeds), 548 (principles of Fishfafll1ing) and

549 (Culture of Giant Fresh Water Prawns) respectively. There will be few more booklets coming under this series.

The management practices for fish farming depends on the type of fish reared, the number of related functions such as breeding, raising fry and fingerlings, stocking, harvesting, storing, processing, fish products generated, sale, etc., are carried out. It also depends on the type offish farming whether it is monoculture or poly culture.

In polyculture too we can have a combination of two to six types of fishes reared together. Fishes maybe reared in fresh water, saline water, or in poorly aerated water. The fishes may be air breathing ones or other-wise; or they may be carnivores or herbivores. Depending on all these factors the management practices will vary. However, few common management practices can be listed here.

Construction and Maintenance

The ponds should be constructed on a permanent basis with strong non-collapsible sides and there should be a provision for yearly draining out and filling of the pond, feeding facilities, and regular observation and record keeping facilities. The ponds should be safe from predators and wild animals or from run off or flood water. The ponds should be free from aquatic weeds, water should be well oxygenated and enough sun light should be available. In short, provide very good environmental conditions to the fish to grow.

Feeding

After the construction and maintenance of the fish pond the most important factor is feeding. Regular and sufficient supply of balanced feed is the most important factor in the fish production.

Pond Sanitation

The pond should be filled with clear and clean water and avoid any chance of contamination or pollution. Poor sanitation is the main cause for poor aeration and disease incidences. While introducing fishes from outside we should be really careful not to introduce any type of contagious disease carrying fishes.

Others

All the rest of the management practices are available in the booklets on each of the topics related to fish farming.

Management Practices

The management practices for each type of palm tree are different from the other. Such details are already given in the respective booklets already mentioned.

Visits

Visiting every palm tree at least once a week and every fish pond once a day and observing is an important management practice which will bring in much benefit though it may sound very unusual and the practicality of it may be laughed at. The practicality simply depends on the willingness of the person. All that he has to do is go for a walk in his farm land and around the fish ponds every day observing the pond water condition and the condition of the fish. The best time to go to the pond for observation is early morning and during feeding time. At these times we can observe the condition of the fishes and do the needful.

Similarly, we must take out some time to go for walks through different parts of the farm so that we can observe every tree in the farm. It may take hardly 20 to 30 minutes to observe certain number of trees. The same number can be observed on the next day and so on. In this way in one week's time we should be able to cover all the trees in the garden.

Regularity and Punctuality

Regularity and punctuality are twin pillars of successful management. Feeding the fish, breeding, cleaning the pond, manuring, irrigation, harvesting and all other operations should be done regularly and punctually. Anything done irregularly is like doing nothing; sometimes it may even do harm.

Disciplined Approach

Finally, management needs a disciplined and well calculated approach in every thing being planned and implemented.

Maintenance of Records and Accounts

Perhaps the most important point in the management of the fish cum palm tree farming system is the maintenance of the records and accounts. Unit wise daily records of operations should be maintained in the farm so that we can know the exact situation of the farm and also foresee the things required for the management of the farm. The records of planting, daily labour utilisation, harvesting, amount harvested, manuring and fertilizer application, amount of manures and fertilizers, etc., should be maintained. It is not possible to point out all the points of record keeping.

Each farm should evolve a system of record keeping. But we should have a system of recording by which we can get all the information and the possibility of cross checking the facts and figures and at the end of the year we should able to summarise all the records on to one or two sheets of paper. Similarly, we should keep unit wise all the daily expenditure and income accounts in such a way that we should be able to and out the profitability of each unit every year and accordingly we can take decision to expand or reduce each unit in the future.

DESIGNS OF THE FARM

Depending on the availability of the water, the topography of the land, the type of palm trees planted, the type and extent of intercropping being planned, the needs and priorities of the farmer there can be many designs that could be followed in a fish farming cum palm tree cultivation. Some of these designs are complex and the implementation requires meticulous planning and good engineering skill. It is beyond the scope of this booklet to explain and elaborate all the intricacies of the possible designs; only some basic ideas are explained here as the number of designs vary depending on many factors.

Factors Affecting the Designs

The design for fish pond construction in the palm garden depends on the distance which is maintained between palms in the same row and between rows. Therefore the possible designs for different palms are discussed here. The desires and the ideas given here are by no means claims to be exhaustive. Each farmer can and should modify and develop better ways and designs in their own garden. However some common factors that influence the type of design adopted can be listed as follows.

Climate

Among all the factors the main deciding factor in the choice of the palm for cultivation is climate though it is not so much of a deciding factor for the fish cultivation. The choice of palm and the type of palm itself will determine the design of the arrangement of fish ponds and the land area allotted for palm trees.

Quantity of Water Available

Depending on the quantity of water and the drainage facilities available the area under the fish ponds may be more or less compared to the area under oil palm cultivation. More the water and lesser the drainage facilities the farmer will be compelled to allot greater area under the fish ponds and lesser area to palm trees and vice versa. However, even if the water availability is more but the drainage facility is also good, then the farmer is tree in allotting whatever amount of area to fish ponds depending on other factors affecting both the cultivation of palm trees and fish rearing. Accordingly the designs also will change.

Market

Depending on the demand for the palm and the fish there can be equal or more importance to both or either of them. Hence the possible designs also will be different.

Intercropping

The design also depends on the amount of area the farmer may be wanting to have for intercropping. If he intends to have more area under intercropping more land will be allotted to the palm trees and less will be allotted to the fish rearing.

Easy Movement in the Farm

The fish ponds and the strips of palm tree plantation should be so arranged that it should help in the easy movement of the people, vehicles, trolleys, etc. Such arrangement will help in the smooth management of the entire farm.

Farming System

Under the broad farming system of palm tree cum fish culture we can have several sub-farming systems such as coconut based farming system in which coconut will be the main crop and all others (inter crops and fish rearing) will be subsidiary to it. Similarly we can have a fish farm centred farming system in which the main crop is fish and all others will be subsidiary to it or we can have arecanut centered farming system. We can also include animal husbandry and ladder cultivation along with the system of fish cum palm tree cultivation. In all these circumstances the design will change.

Others

Other factors like availability of the fry and fingerlings, transport and communication, availability of fish feed, facilities of processing of palm products, the cultural factors of the people are all taken into consideration in deciding the design for the fish cum palm trees cultivation.

Designs for Coconut Garden

In coconut plantations, a spacing of 25–33 ft. is maintained between the palms and rows as well. Between the rows of coconuts the fish ponds can be fitted in a number of ways as explained here. The design also is affected by the quantity of water available in the garden either in the form of high water table or from a perennial river, canal, lake or any other source. Accordingly the area covered under water will be more or less; if the water available is more the area covered will be more and vice versa. Hence the design also can be changed.

Coconuts are planted normally keeping a distance of 33 feet distance between plants and rows with fish ponds having a width of 15 to 20 feet and any convenient length between rows. This again can be two types (a) fish ponds in parallel rows and (b) fish ponds in criss-cross fashion.

Ponds in Parallel Rows

Between two parallel rows of coconuts a long fish pond is fitted. Depending on the water availability and the desire of the farmer the garden can be covered with this design fully or partially. If the farmer needs some area for intercropping he can leave some area free. Or if there is not enough water to cover the whole area then he will be forced to leave some area free which he can cultivate under some intercrops. The width of the pond will vary from 15 to 20 it. and any convenient length can be adopted.

A modification of this design is accomplished by planting two rows of coconut trees at a distance of 20 to 25 feet and between every two such sets of double rows leave a distance of 33 to 50 feet in which we can fit in fish pond having a width varying between 20 to 38 feet and any convenient length.

Similarly one can have coconuts in triple lines planted at 25 to 30 feet distance and between two sets of triple lines leave a distance of 33 to 50 ft in which we can fit a pond of 20 to 38 ft width and of any length. Thus, depending on the convenience, availability of water, needs and priorities of the farmer the parallel arrangement of coconut trees and fish ponds can be implemented. It may be better to connect these parallel ponds with a small open or underground channel for easy management of the water flow. But these channels should have facilities to fit wire mesh fixed frames so that fish is prevented from going from one pond to another.

Ponds in Criss-Cross Fashion

If the water is in abundance and more area can be set apart for the fish ponds the arrangements of the coconut palms and the ponds is done in criss-cross fashion. Coconuts are planted at least 33 ft distance (row to row and plant to plant) and fish ponds of 15 to 20 ft are constructed between the rows in both ways resulting in having each coconut tree standing on an island of 13 to 18 sq. ft. land. In the actual situation in a water logged area islands of about 13 to 18 square ft. are created on which the coconuts are planted.

In this design the area under water will be more compared to the area under coconuts. Hence, the area available for intercropping between the coconuts also will be much less. Variations of this design can be done having bigger islands with four coconuts each and the rest of the area under fish ponds. This means criss-crossing is made after every two rows of coconuts.

A number of crops are suitable for intercropping between the coconut trees. If the coconut trees are planted at 33 ft distance any crop can be cultivated as intercrop. We can even go for multilayered multiple cropping in the coconut garden if the distance is maintained at 33 feet. Black pepper can be grown as climber to the coconut tree itself. We can go for extensive fodder cultivation in between the coconuts. The fodder can be fed to the animal in our own dairy farm or sold to some body else who is having the dairy farm.

It should be mentioned here that coconut cum fish farm cum dairy cum fodder cultivation is excellent farming system. All these four have a symbiotic relationship with each other. The fodder cultivated in the coconut garden is fed to the cattle in the dairy farm, the dung and the urine generated in the dairy farm will be fed to the coconuts, fodder crops and to the fish ponds. The oil cake from the coconut will be feed for the cattle and fish. The fish waste converted into fish meal is excellent feed supplement to the cattle and manure to the coconuts and fodder crops.

The usages of by-products from the coconut are many leaves for thatching, leaf fibs for broom making, the leaf, petiole, inflorescence sheath and the stem for fuel wood, the fibre for ropes and brush making, trunk as building material and making furnitures, the tender inflorescence for toady tapping, the shells for handicrafts, etc., are some of the usages.

Designs for Areca Nut Garden

The plant to plant and row to row distance in areca nut is maintained at 9 to 10 feet. Obviously fish ponds cannot be fitted in between the rows of areca nut trees. What is possible is to have block plantations consisting of several lines of areca nuts alternated with fish ponds of 20 to 30 ft wide and any convenient length.

These blocks of areca nut plantations and long fish ponds are arranged in parallel designs. Perhaps not as many variations are possible in areca nut cum fish pond farming as in the coconut palm plantations. Areca nuts do not provide any supplementary feed to the fish though the fish pond can provide some supplementary nutrition to the areca nuts.

A number of crops fit in as intercrops in the areca nut plantations. Prominent among them are: black pepper, dwarf varieties of coffee, yams both creeping and herbaceous, fodder grasses, betel leaves, ginger, turmeric, medicinal plants, etc. Depending on the need and priority of the cropping the intercropped area can be increased or decreased in the areca nut plantation.

Design for Oil Palms

The oil palms are normally planted at 30 ft distance since they grow as big as a coconut tree in their canopy size. But in the case of oil palm cum fish cultivation they should be planted at the same distance as the coconut trees and all the possible designs under the coconut cum fish cultivation can be followed.

As already mentioned the variety of designs depends on the amount of water available, the priority of the farmer is whether to go for fish farming or oil palm cultivation, higher profitability from either of them, amount of land needed for intercropping, etc.

Planning of the Farm

The success of the fish cum palm tree farming system depends very much on the planning. No doubt a well planned farm will save a lot in the management of the daily operations in the entire farm. Before setting up the farm one should have well defined aims, objectives and strategies.

In planning the fish cum palm tree farming we must, check on the following points.

- First of all, on the economic viability of the whole farming system. Nothing can exist in the long run unless it is economically viable. Make a detailed study of the economic viability taking into consideration all the costs including the opportunity costs.
- Secondly, we must ensure the technical feasibility or the establishment and management of this farming system in a particular place. The required technical know-how for the maintenance of the system should be locally available.
- Thirdly, the system should be environmentally suitable. It should fit in with over all environmental system of the place avoiding pollution or draining out the resources too much from the place.
- Fourthly, it should be socially acceptable to the people of the localilty. Though in the beginning there may not be any difficulty, in the long run social acceptance is an important point to be considered in planning this farming system. Involvement of the local people in the management of the farm and making them feel that they too benefit proportionately from the farming system is also a part of the social acceptance besides the possible need for cultural and religious acceptance.
- Fifthly, it should be educative. The farming system introduced into a locality should provide enough technical and manegerial skills to the local people so that more and more people take up to this type of farming system and thus create an association of the fish cum palm tree growers. Such unions and associations are necessary to build up economic and political strength among the owners of this farming system.
- Sixthly, there should be a possibility for product diversification and value addition by which the producers retain maximum control over their products. There should be provision for processing of raw materials. This will generate maximum employment opportunities to the local people and the owners of the farms will get maximum support from them. While planning it is very much required to make a blue print of the farm plan showing all the details of the components, location of each component, size, acreage occupied, etc., even it should show even the number and type of trees planted and the breed of fish reared. In short the blue print should be as detailed and meticulous as possible; nothing should be left to chance.

Before making the final blue print consult as many people as possible and collect sufficient data on the availability of all the externally needed inputs both for establishment and maintenance. While planning we should pay attention to the flow of organic matter and water through the various components in the farm. We must ensure that all the organic matter that is generated at the farm is recycled and used as manure and feed. Similarly all the water that comes into the farm in the form of rain, over ground or underground should be stored and recycled as far as possible.

In planning the sustainability of the farm should be given top priority. As far as possible try to supply all the inputs internally or follow the principle of low external inputs. Heavy dependence on external inputs in the long run is detrimental to the sustainability of the farm. The agro-ecosystem we create in any given piece of land should be balanced from the point of view of inputs and outputs.

- Seventhly prepare a detailed and feasible time planning. In the time planning what activities and operations will be carried out when and in how much time etc should be planned out. The time planning consists of chronological or synchronological order of the various activities and the duration of the time taken for the completion of each activity or unit.

After preparing the time plan arrange the labour force required for completing the operations and the finance required for each unit and activity is arranged. The reader may feel that it is beyond his ability to do such meticulous planning. For ordinary people it may not be possible. But for the success of this type of farming system such planning is necessary. What the people should do is to form an association and get things done through it. An association can get things done which an individual cannot do. Re- member these booklets are not written only for guiding individuals to do their day to farming operations but to promote long term sustainable farming systems that should last for several generations.

SPECIFIC TYPES OF FISH FARMS AND AQUACULTURE METHODS

Within intensive and extensive aquaculture methods, there are numerous specific types of fish farms; each has benefits and applications unique to its design.

FISH REARING IN CAGES AND PENS

As fish necessarily requires water, most people tend to think that for fish rearing they should have their own fish pond which may be situated near the streams, rivers, lakes, permanently flooded areas or reservoirs but do not have the ownership of any portion of any of them, or he may be having a water body which is linked with a lake, reservoir or river. Under such conditions one can go for rearing of fishes In cages and pens. The idea is to rear fish in a common and unbounded water body. This booklet explains the basic methods employed on cage and pen fish farming. Many poor farmers may get benefit from this method, at least partially meet their food and finance requirement.

If a farmer is living near a huge water body, such as canal, river, stream, lake, permanently flooded area or reserviors which does not belong to him or he has a water body which is linked with some other huge water bodies (rivers with lakes or sea, streams with big rivers or flooded areas) he can rear fishes in cages and pens. Of course under this system only a limited number of fishes or a specific type of fish may be reared. However, the number will depend on the size of the cage or the pen used. Those who are able to establish bigger pens and cages will be able to rear proportionately large number of fish provided he can feed them.

Feeding of fish reared in cages and pens is very important among the management practices. Therefore the main thing one should consider is the sufficient availability of feed for the fish reared in the cages and pens. Of course the type of feed depends on the type of the fish being reared Some fish are carnivores, some herbivores and some others are omnivores. For more details about feeding of fish please consult Booklet No. 525 on "Fish Feeding". Generally, a mixture of oil cakes and rice polish is a very good feed for most of the species of the fishes that are being reared by people. The cages and pens can be constructed with any material conveniently available at the local level provided it is durable at least for one year. However, more the durability of the material greater will be economic benefit from this system of fish rearing though the initial cost may be more.

This type of fish rearing has been practiced since long in certain parts of the Asia. Perhaps this system of fish culture is originated with the view to control retrieval of the stocked fish. Its application is more relevant for those people for whom the suitable water supply and land for fish culture are becoming less and less available. Further to intensify this system of fish culture, scientific methods are being evolved for increasing the production of fish in cages by forced aeration or by using different types of filters and better feeding and management practices. In India this system can be practiced in the low lying and permanently flooded areas of Kerala, West Bengal, Orissa, Andhra Pradesh, Karnataka, Goa, Gujarat, North Bihar, Assam, Manipur, etc., though much work needs to be done still to perfect and standardise this system.

STRUCTURE OF CAGES AND PENS

The cages are structures which are covered and secured from every sides and the fishes are kept inside. They can be fixed stationary, suspended, partially or fully immersed, or floating, depending on the convenience. The cages are fitted with a door which can be opened in order to introduce the fishlings, to feed and care them and to harvest them at the end of the rearing season.

The best positioning of the cages is to fix them in such a way that the top portion of the cage is exposed to air and sunlight so that the fish can breath air whenever it is necessary. Also due to the constant contact with the atmospheric air the amount at oxygen dissolved into the water will be more to the benefit of the fishes. On the other hand, the pens are fixed as fencing structures or enclosures covering an area of the water body. They are made by fixing the fencing material into the ground at the bottom and rising right through the water column and make them stand at about 1-2 ft above the water. The pens are open at the top and exposed to atmosphere. They cover much larger area than the cages. In a way pens are enclosed areas. Pens also give the idea of several sections of an enclosed area each harbouring a certain number of fishes of different type, size, and age. For breeding purpose the breeding stock may be kept in small pens. Similarly for spawning and hatching also separate pens are required. The pen looks like a fenced area. Wooden reapers, bamboo splits, reeds or any other suitable material can be used for the construction of the fence.

The fencing material is fixed vertically on the ground, under the water and held very close to each other by ropes. Horizontally fixed fencing material is so closely arranged that the gap between them is reduced to the minimum required space, that would not allow the fish to come out and also they will remain safe from predators. Enclosed area denotes a larger area than the pen area. A portion of large water bodies such as lakes, reserviors, flooded areas, etc., is fenced around in order to rear large number of fish for commercial purpose as is practiced by some people living near the Chilka lake in Orissa. The pens and enclosures are established only in shallow waters whereas the cages can be used even in deep water areas.

Material for Construction

There are a number of materials that can be used for making the cages and pens for fish rearing. Depending on the ingenuity of the farmers and availability of the things a farmer can use any type of material to construct the cages and the pens. Some of the common ones are mentioned here.

Bamboo and Coir Rope

Mature and seasoned bamboo splits tied closely using firmly twisted coconut fibre rope perhaps is the best material for making cages and pens in the rural areas where other commercially produced materials are not usually available. Both these materials are durable in submersed conditions. Thin bamboo splits of half inch thickness and width are held together closely by inter-twining them using thin coconut fibre ropes. The main frame of the cage is made of bigger bamboo splits or wooden reapers.

Nylon Threads

Strong nylon threads are better than any other material for making the cages and pens though this may be quite costly for an ordinary farmer. Nets are made out of this nylon thread. The mesh size of the net depends on the size of the fishlings which will be reared in the cage. For fry (up to 15 days old) the mesh size should be very small, for the fingerlings (15 to days) the size will be bigger, while for the growing or stocking fishes (reared for market size) the mesh size will be still bigger (half to one inch size).

Plastics

Tubes, sheets, ready made meshes made of strong plastic material can be used as cage and pen material. However the plastic should be very strong and non- degradable. Now-a-days very strong and non- degradable type of plastics are available in the market. One has to search and find out the most suitable material for his own purpose.

Wire Meshes

Wire mesh is another important material for the construction of cages and pens for fish farming. The mesh as already mentioned could be of any size depending on whether the farmer wants to keep the fry or fingerlings or fish grown for market purpose. It is highly advisable that the mesh is made of galvanised wire in order to reduce the possibility of rusting. Rust can be also controlled by coating with water proof paints on the wire mesh.

Wood

Wood can be used as a caging. or penning material. There are several types of wood which can withstand the submersible condition. There could be many other materials which are locally available and could be used for the construction of the cages and pens for fish rearing. The size and shape of the cage or pen is decided by the farmers. Those who have large space and want to rear fish in large number will need bigger cages and pens. But they could be made in any shape and size. Depending on the space available the cages and pens may be constructed big, medium or small, long or short. The shape may be rectangular, square, triangular, irregular or any other: The size of the cage and pen too vary a lot tram very big which harbours hundreds or thousands of fish, to very small in which only one or two fish may be kept.

Others

There may be several other materials which may be available locally or commercially for the construction of the cages and pens. It is for each one to look for the appropriate material available at cheaper rate and to use them for the construction. There may be ready made modular type of material in the form of parts of the cage or pens. Using them we can construct, dismantle and reconstruct the cages and pens. Such materials may not be possible at the farmer's level in the case of cage construction but it is possible in the case of pen construction.

CONSTRUCTION AND FIXING OF CAGES AND PENS

Different methods are followed for the construction of the cages and pens for fish rearing. They are explained as follows under separate sub-heads. The construction of enclosures is very much similar to the construction of the pens. Only the enclosures are constructed in a bigger area while the pens cover comparatively a smaller area.

Construction and Fixing of the Cages

First of all the site where the cage is to be fixed is surveyed and measured to determine the size, shape and the way the cage is going to be fixed at the location. Arrangements for the materials are done accordingly.

The cage may be constructed in situ or constructed in parts at a different place.and brought them to be assembled at the place where It is going to be fixed. The most important point to be kept in mind is the mesh size. The mesh size is made bigger for keeping the bigger fishes whereas for the small fish smaller mesh work is provided. The cages are fixed in immovable or in floating manner. They can be fixed completely or partially immersed in the water. The cages are fitted with sufficient doors which will help in the feeding, caring and harvesting of the fishes grown. The cages are fixed in such a way that always the fresh water will flow through them and also enough sun light is available so that the fish inside will get the most optimum conditions to live.

Construction and Fixing of Pens

As in the case, first of all of cages the location is surveyed and the type and the amount of material needed is estimated before the construction of the pens and enclosures. The construction of the pens and enclosures are generally done in situ in the form of a fence. The fencing material consists of the main pole fixed firmly in the ground under the water at convenient distances. These are jointed by at least two horizontal bars or reapers one on the upper side and other on the lower side. If needed a third bar or reaper is fixed horizontally between the above mentioned horizontal bars. On to these horizontal reapers or bars are fixed the vertical bars closely to form the fencing for the pen or enclosure.

The vertical bars are fixed on the horizontal bars using nail or by tying with strong rope material. The distance between the two vertical bars will be adjusted to hold the minimum size of the fish that are released into the pen or enclosure. The pens can be constructed by fixing different segments of a fence. Each segment consists of a fixed number of vertical bars closely fitted by using two or three horizontal bars. The vertical bars at both ends and at the middle will be longer by one foot and pointed Because of these three vertical bars a segment can be fixed vertically by driving them into the soil till the other bars in the segment come into close contact with the soil surface.

After fixing the first segment fix the second segment close to the first one; then fix the third, fourth segments and go on till the whole fencing is completed to create an enclosed area. Using the same technique we can also separate the whole enclosure into several sections if needed. But even in fixing the segmented fences also we need the strongly fixed poles on to which the segments are fixed firmly. Pole can be fixed between each segment or at least between two segments each.

We can have segments without the above mentioned three longer and pointed vertical bars on each segment. In this case the segments are pressed down into the soil between two poles already fixed at an interval equal to the width of the segment and tied to tern. The pens are fitted with a door made of the same material as the pens. The door will be more like a segment of the fence which can be removed by lifting when one wants to open and fixed back when one wants to close it. The door is better secured on to the fence by tying rather than fixing it with hinges. Movement of the door fixed with the hinges does not work under the water and the door has to remain fixed into the soil. However one can adopt several ways to fix a door and it should be fixed in such a way that the door can be opened and closed like any other door fixed on hinges. The depth of the cages or the depth of the water in the pen should be sufficient for the fish to grow. The optimum depth for cage varies from 60 to 120 cm, and for the pens the depth of the water inside the pen should be at least 120 cm up to a maximum of 180 centimetres. The length of the cage should be minimum ten feet and the width should be at least three feet. However depending on the ability of the farmer the cages may be bigger or smaller than the above mentioned dimension. But bigger the cages better they are for the growth of the fishes. Fish require space for swimming around and the more we give them space greater will be the growth rate.

In the case of pens the only recommendation is to provide as much area (length and width) as possible. Obviously the depth, will be the same as that of the water body in which the pen is constructed. For the purpose of, hatching and fry raising cages and pens are unsuitable as the mesh size is bigger and the try can escapc from the cages and pens. For this the cages and pens should be fitted with finc mesh net as that of a mosquito net. One can also use "Happas" (enclosures made of fine mesh net like the inverted mosquito net) for breeding, hatching and rearing of try up to the age of 90 days, by which time they grow up to the size of a fingerling. If the mesh size of the cage or the pen is sufficiently smaller, the fingerlings can be released into the cages or pens. Otherwise they have to be kept in suitable enclosures till they are grown big enough to be contained inside the cage or pen. Details about breeding and hatching of the fry and raising up to fingerlings stage are described in Booklet No. 543 on "Carp Breeding".

CONSTRUCTION PLANNING FOR SITE

Before the construction of the pond the farmer should have a good look at the land available to him to choose the place or places where the ponds can be constructed. Finding a suitable place is the most important and the fist step in the planning of the fish pond. Fish rearing is a form of land use like land use in agriculture. If the site is well chosen the pond will be more productive. Often poor agricultural land can be converted into very good fish ponds. However, the better the soil the greater the possibility of making a good fish pond at lesser expense. There are mainly three factors that contribute to make a good site for a fish pond water supply, soil and topography. These are further explained in detail.

WATER SUPPLY

Fish live in water and hence the most important factor for the site selection is the availability of water. If natural water supply is not existing try to find some underground water sources or whether water can be brought in from outside through pipes, channels, etc. It is also possible to store rain water into tanks in which the fish can be grown. The sources of water for the fish pond are mentioned here.

Rainfall

Some ponds rely on rainfall alone and they are called "sky ponds".

Run-off

Some ponds get their water from the run-off from the surrounding areas during the rainy season.

Natural Waters

The word natural waters is referred to the water available from the lakes, rivers, streams and springs.

Springs

Some ponds will have active springs inside, filling the pond.

Wells

Many ponds are fed with water from the open wells or tube wells. However, there can be problems also with the water supply. For example, there can be flooding during the rainy season which will affect adversely the fish pond system. Hence, the places that are prone to flood should not be chosen; even sporadically flooded areas should be avoided for fish ponds unless there are possibilities of protecting the pond area artificially. If the water is taken from the river or stream that are prone to flood there should be an inbuilt mechanism to control the inflow of water into the pond.

QUALITY OF WATER

The quality of water is checked by the following methods.

- Look at the water to observe the colour and visible suspended particles, check for any obnoxious smell and taste to check whether the water is salty or having any other taste.
- Check whether there are any people residing or factories situated in the upstream which may pollute the water coming to the pond.
- Make sure also that there are no families or people who depend on the down stream water for drinking and domestic usages.

If the water is very clear the farmer can apply fertilizers in the pond; if the water is muddy he has to allow the sediments to settle down before he uses the water in the pond. He has to build special silt catching structures through which water has to pass before it enters the pond. If the water is greenish in colour probably it has a lot of fish feed in it. If the water is dark, smelly brown it may be acidic and the farmer has to add sufficient lime to neutralise it and add gypsum if the water is alkaline.

SOIL

Soil of the area is the most important factor that has to be taken into consideration. It should be able to hold water. Besides the water holding capacity the soil should be rich in nutrients/minerals. Clay soil holds water well and hence, check the soil for the clay content by feeling a sample of it in the hand. If the soil is sticky and can be formed into shape, it means the soil has high clay content; if the soil is gritty, it is sandy and if it is smooth and silky, it is a silty soil. Clay soil is best for the pond construction. However a poor water holding soil also can be treated at the base of the pond with lot of organic manure and other biomass materials to improve its water holding capacity.

Soils that contain lot of plant nutrients (minerals and elements) are better for the pond construction because the natural growth of micro and macro organisms will be enhanced. In other words, a nutrient rich soil will provide more feed to the fish. At the same time acid and alkali forming nutrients should not be predominant in the soil. One indication of the nutrient status of the soil is to check whether the crops grow well in the soil. If it grows the soil is better for fish pond also. Fertile soils in the pond encourages phytoplankton growth which in turn will allow the growth of macro fauna.

TOPOGRAPHY

Topography refers to the shape of the land whether fiat, slope, hilly, upland, lowland, undulated, etc. Topography of the land decides the kind of the pond that can be built. Ponds can be built in any place: in the valleys, on the fiat ground; they can be built in any shape: square or rectangular or uneven shape; they can be large or small. All these are determined by the topography as well as by the farmers requirements.

The best topography for the fish pond construction is the one which allows the farmer to fill the pond and drain the water from it using gravity. Ponds built on the fiat land will have to be made sloping to one side at the bottom to drain out completely using a pump or some other water lifting devices to empty.

Therefore, the best place for the pond construction is a place with slight slope and plenty of water supply. The farmer should look for a topography that makes the fish farming as easy and successful as possible. However, if water is available even on the poor topographical land also fish pond can be constructed.

6

Wildlife and Tourism in Forest Ecosystems

FOREST

A forest is an area with a high density of trees. There are many definitions of a forest, based on the various criteria. These plant communities presently cover approximately 9.4 per cent of the Earth's surface (or 30 per cent of total land area) and function as habitats for organisms, hydrologic flow modulators, and soil conservers, constituting one of the most important aspects of the Earth's biosphere.

Historically, "forest" meant an uncultivated area legally set aside for hunting by feudal nobility, and these hunting forests were not necessarily wooded much if at all. However, as hunting forests did often include considerable areas of woodland, the word forest eventually came to mean wooded land more generally. A woodland is ecologically distinct from a forest.

The latitudes 10° north and south of the Equator are mostly covered in tropical rainforest and the latitudes between 53°N and 67°N with boreal forest.

CHANGES IN FOREST COVER AND CONDITION

An analysis of changes in the cover and condition of the world's forests requires a differentiation between:

1 the increase in forest cover (by afforestation or natural colonisation of trees on non-forest land) or decrease (by deforestation) of forest area; and

2 changes in forest condition, either positive (recovery of degraded stands, stand improvement treatments) or negative (decline, defoliation or dieback, effects of forest fires, degradation through unsustainable exploitation for wood, overgrasing, effects of pests and diseases).

Changes in Forest Cover

Between 1980 and 1995, the extent of the world's forests decreased by some 180 million ha, an area about the size of Indonesia or Mexico. This represents a global annual loss of 12 million ha, an area equivalent to the size of Greece or Bangladesh. During this 15-year period, developing countries lost nearly 200 million ha of natural forests, mostly through clearing for agriculture (shifting cultivation, other forms of subsistence agriculture, the establishment of cash crop plantations such as oil palm, and ranching). This was only very partially compensated for by the establishment of new forest plantations. Over the same period, forests in the developed world expanded slowly (by some 20 million ha) through afforestation and reforestation, including natural regrowth on land abandoned by agriculture.

Forest plantation and natural regeneration on abandoned agricultural land more than compensated for clearing of forests due to urbanisation and infrastructure development in most industrialised countries, outside the former USSR. While the gain of forest cover in developed countries was 20 million ha in the period 1980-95, 9 million ha of this increase occurred in the 5 years from 1990 to 1995. The situation is quite different in the developing world, where deforestation exceeded net afforestation/reforestation, particularly in the tropical zone. As a whole, the annual rate of deforestation in the developing world between 1990 and 1995 was 0.7 per cent, equivalent to 12.6 million ha, with the highest rate in tropical Asia-Oceania, closely correlated with population and income growth. The lowland forest formations were the most affected by deforestation, although the proportional loss during this period was greater in upland formations (1.1 per cent compared with 0.8 per cent in the lowland formations). There is some evidence that the rate of loss of forest cover in developing countries was slowing towards the end of the 15-year period 1980-95. The annual rate of forest loss in the period 1980-90 was 15.5 million ha compared with 13.7 million ha between 1990 and 1995.

Conversion of Forests to other Land Cover

The Forest Resource Assessment 1990 carried out an assessment of the relative importance of the various factors involved in deforestation at regional and global levels between 1980 and 1990 in the whole tropical belt. Among the most significant outputs of the study were the 'area transition matrices' of the type, which indicate transfers from one land cover class to another over the 3068 million ha of the tropical zone covered by the sample. For instance, the first row shows that 1275.9 million ha of the total area of 1368 million ha of closed forest in 1980 remained as closed forest up to 1990 and also shows the fate of the 92.1 million ha converted to other land cover classes (open forest; long fallow; fragmented forest; shrubs and short fallow; other, *i.e.* non-wooded, land cover; and forestry or woody forest and agricultural tree plantations). All these transfers involved changes of woody biomass attempts to capture by replacing each class along the *y*-axis (average biomass per hectare) and showing the importance of transfers along the *x*-axis.

Changes in Forest Condition

Factors affecting the health and vitality of all types of forests have attracted increasing attention in recent years. Outbreaks of fires have made headline news in developed and developing countries alike, while insect and disease attack and generalised declines in forest condition have caused more localised concern. Insects and disease and forest fires exist under 'natural' systems and conditions; what has caused concern has been their spread in artificial systems and in conditions considerably modified by humankind, resulting in direct economic loss.

Fire arising from natural causes (*e.g.* lightning) has been a major influence and is a driving evolutionary force in several forest ecosystems, such as the pine forests of Central America. Fires are important to the health and maintenance of these ecosystems and the total exclusion of fire from them can lead to the build-up of fuel and ultimately abnormally destructive fires that cause the loss of the ecosystem, as happened with the fire exclusion policy of the National Parks Service of the USA and the disastrous fires of 1988.

However, many fires arising from human activities, whether planned or unplanned, have damaged and destroyed large areas of forests and woodlands. Resource managers face a demanding public often with conflicting needs and incomplete information, leading to the development of new policies that take into account public attitudes towards fire management.

At the global level, an agreement was signed at a meeting in 1990 to initiate the International Decade for Natural Disaster Reduction and the target date of 2000 was set for signatory countries to effectively monitor and manage wildfires in their respective countries. In view of the lack of information on causes, extent and the number of fires at present, and the difficulties in collecting data, this target date is unlikely to be met.

Developed Countries

Total forest area is slowly increasing in the developed world, although the need for protection from fire, insects and disease has continued and some aspects of forest condition give cause for concern. Although the widespread decline and death of certain European forests due to air pollution predicted by many in the 1980s did not occur, deteriorating forest condition has remained a serious concern in Europe and North America. The main causes of the decline of forest condition in Europe have been low soil moisture availability due to drought, and high temperatures. These factors, combined with airborne pollution and the use of non-adapted seed sources in forest plantation development, have predisposed forests to attack by insects and disease and to decline. Forest damage due to air pollution is severe in some parts of central and eastern Europe in particular. Air pollution is also said to have a role in the decline observed in certain species in other industrialised countries, such as sugar maple *(Acer saccharum)* in eastern Canada, the high-elevation forests of red spruce *(Picea)* in eastern USA and *Cryptomeria japonica* stands in Japan.

The exclusion of fire may have caused the decline of some forest ecosystems, such as oak stands in central USA or natural eucalypt forests in Australia where fire is an integral part of the ecology of some plant communities and here it may be used to facilitate their natural regeneration.

Despite an overall increase in the number of fires (by some 40 per cent in Europe, 8 per cent in North America and 120 per cent in the former USSR), wildfires over large areas of forest have become less frequent in the industrialised countries. Further, the average area burned by wildfire decreased in most regions between 1983-90 and 1991-94. There has been a slight reduction in total areas burned in the developed world overall as a result of improved prevention, detection and control systems, although there has been an increase of 15 per cent in the former USSR. In 1990, the average area of forest and other wooded land affected annually by fires in Europe, North America and the former USSR together was about 4.26 million ha or 0.22 per cent of their total area of forest and other wooded land.

Pests and diseases remain constant threats, particularly to the semi-natural forests and plantations in the industrialised world. Trees are more likely to be attacked when under stress, whether from abnormal weather conditions such as drought or high temperatures, airborne pollution, uncontrolled movement of germplasm or lack of management. Recent outbreaks of pests and diseases that may have been related to stress include the decline of various species of oaks in many parts of Europe and in central Russia, the recurrent infestation of forests in Poland by the nun moth, the attack on beech by the beech scale in western and central Europe, birch and ash diebacks in north-eastern USA, the littleleaf disease of shortleaf pine in southern USA, and the 'x-disease' of pines in southern California.

FOREST CONDITIONS IN DEVELOPING COUNTRIES

Less attention has been paid to forest condition in developing countries because reduction in forest area has attracted more attention. This reduction in density has often been the result of over-exploitation for timber and fuelwood. Overgrasing and repeated bush fires are other significant causes of decrease in density, especially in the dry tropical and non-tropical zones.

Every year, very large areas of savannah woodland and mixed forest-grassland formations are affected by fires set by herders to provide an early flush of green grass when the rains start, particularly in the dry zones of Africa and South America, although no reliable data are available on their extent.

Forests in the humid tropics have also, at times, been affected by large fires, the most serious in recent years having been those associated with the dry weather conditions arising from the El Niño Southern Oscillation (ENSO).

In 1997-98, these caused large-scale destruction of logged and secondary forest in Indonesia (particularly Kalimantan, Sumatra and Irian Jaya), Mexico and Central American countries, as well as leading to smoke pollution over wide areas beyond the borders of these countries. The cause of these fires has been burning for land clearance, but it should be noted that the fires are not necessarily in forest; although described as 'forest fires' they are frequently in grassland or on land that has been cleared of forest. It is *estimated* that of the 2 million ha burned in Indonesia in 1997, 150000-200 000 ha may have been in forest. Other serious fires associated with ENSO effects have included that in East Kalimantan, which burned 3.6 million ha in 1983.

Coniferous forests in the humid tropics have often been affected by fires, although it must be noted that fire is frequently necessary to maintain and regenerate them. In the 1980s, the area of pine forest in Honduras and Nicaragua burned annually amounted to some 65 000ha (or about 3.5 per cent of the total pine forest area of these two countries), and widespread fires in natural and artificial tropical pine forests occur in other countries such as Guatemala, Mexico and Indonesia (northern Sumatra).

In the subtemperate and temperate zones of the developing world, fire is also a permanent threat to forests, particularly when they are no longer used by local people for grasing and other purposes. In the 1980s, the average area of forest and other wooded land burned annually was 140 000 ha in the temperate/ subtemperate zones of South America (including southern Brazil). From 1950 to 1990, fires in China are reported to have affected an average of 890 000 ha annually, the most damaging one having been the 'May 6' fire, which burned some 1.85 million ha in the north-eastern province of Heilongjiang in 1987. In the absence of a global statistical fire database, it is difficult to provide an overall estimate of the annual extent of fires in forests and other wooded lands.

A very crude estimate for the temperate/subtemperate and humid tropical zones of the developing world (leaving aside the significant dry tropical zone, for which little reliable information exists) would be of the order of 2 million ha of forest and other wooded land annually during the 1980s. Given the lack of sufficient capacity in fire prevention and control in most developing countries, no significant reduction in wooded areas burned is likely to occur in the near future.

Outbreaks of pests and diseases in developing countries are generally reported for those plantations and planted trees where the impact is most apparent. Introduced pests are usually extremely destructive and several of them have had very damaging effects in recent years in the developing world. Examples of introduced insects affecting plantations and planted trees include the *Leu-caena* psyllid, *Heteropsylla cubana,* which has spread into Asia and the Pacific islands and is now extending across Africa; the cypress aphid, *Cinara cupressi,* which is established in eight eastern and southern African countries and is causing heavy mortality among a number of exotic and indigenous species but especially the important plantation species *Cupressus lusitanica,* threatening its future role in the plantation programmes of these countries; and the European woodwasp, *Sirex noctilio,* which has spread into Argentina, Uruguay and southern Brazil, affecting principally *Pinus taeda* but which may become a threat for the large Chilean plantation estate of *Pinus radiata.*

Strategies to control introduced insects from attacking forest trees include regulatory measures, eradication, integrated pest management, and monitoring of population levels and occurrence of potentially harmful species.

Effective monitoring of insect populations will be especially important in view of the large plantation programmes being carried out to produce industrial roundwood, which often rely on one or a few exotic species. Such programmes may be able to afford the investment that is necessary for control measures. Smaller-scale programmes may have to insure against failure due to unexpected attack by insects or diseases by diversifying into several species adapted to the sites and end-uses.

There is also evidence of forest decline due to a combination of biotic and abiotic factors in the developing world, with air pollution likely to play an increasing role in some cases as industrial and transportation infrastructure develops. Examples of such decline include neem *(Azadirachta indica)* in the Sahel, framiré *(Terminalia ivoren-sis)* in Ivory Coast and Ghana, and *Eucalyptus globulus* plantations in Colombia and Peru, while airborne pollution is affecting forests near large cities and industrial areas in China (*e.g. Pinus massoniana* stands near Nanshan). Despite the overall significance of the corresponding damage and losses, surveys of forest decline and diebacks in developing countries remain all too rare.

RECENT ESTIMATES OF GLOBAL FOREST AREA

The following section is based on 1990 baseline figures, updated to 1995, prepared by the Food and Agriculture Organisation (FAO) Forest Resource Assessment Programme, reported in and largely drawn from *State of the World's Forests 1997.*

In 1995 forests were estimated to cover 3454 million ha, or 26.6 per cent of the total land area of the world (Greenland and Antarctic excepted). Almost two-thirds of the world's forests were located in seven countries: Russia, Brazil, Canada, USA, China, Indonesia and Zaire; 29 countries had more than half of their land covered by forest, of which 21 were in the tropical belt. However 49 countries, in addition to the many non-forested small island states and territories, had less than 10 per cent of their land covered by forests. Five entire subregions were in this category: North Africa (1.2 per cent of the land area), Near East (1.9 per cent), Temperate Oceania (6.2 per cent), Non-tropical

Southern Africa (6.8 per cent) and West Sahelian Africa (7.5 per cent). The latest information on the distribution of forest and of forest cover change by ecological zones was provided in 1990; the results of the Forest Resources Assessment 2000 were released by FAO in 2000. In 1990, temperate and boreal forests occupied 1.64 billion ha and tropical forests 1.76 billion ha. A breakdown by ecological zone was available only for tropical forests.The figures on tropical forests show that most (88 per cent) are in lowlands; of these, tropical rain forests accounted for 47 per cent of all lowland tropical forests, followed by moist deciduous forest (38 per cent) and dry and very dry formations (15 per cent).

Natural Forests

The forest area estimates described above include undisturbed forests, forests modified by humans through use and management (or 'seminatural' forests) and forests created artificially by humankind (*i.e.* forest plantations) by afforestation or reforestation. (Afforestation is defined as the establishment of a tree crop on an area from which it has always, or for a very long time, been absent. Reforestation is defined as the establishment of a tree crop on forest land.) In most industrialised countries, particularly in continental Europe, forests are being managed in such a way that at management-unit level a continuum exists from low-intensity management, involving natural regeneration, through more intensive methods involving some artificial planting to highly intensive methods with complete planting and cultivation; this makes it difficult to isolate figures for natural forest and plantations. The distinction between natural or seminatural forests and forest plantations can more easily be made for developing countries and some industrialised countries such as New Zealand in which forest plantations have been established using introduced species.

Interest in natural forests, particularly their role in the conservation of biological diversity, has led to efforts to compare forests today with what is thought to be their original character and to give complete protection to areas of forests which have had no, or minimal, human interference. Although there are difficulties in identifying the extent of natural forest, compounded by problems of definition, some information exists that can be used as an indication of broad patterns of natural forests in various regions.

An attempt has been made by the World Wide Fund for Nature (WWF) to quantify the area of forests in western Europe that has been relatively undisturbed by humans or which has retained much of its natural character. Their report distinguishes between 'virgin forest', defined as 'forest ecosystems whose characteristics are determined exclusively by natural location and environmental factors... without human influences present or visible any more', and 'natural and ancient seminatural forests', which 'have not been planted or sown by man for the past two centuries' and 'which continue to have a large number of the natural elements'. The study found that only a small proportion (probably < 1 per cent) of the total forest land in northern and western Europe could be considered as virgin forest, which has arisen since the last glaciation. Almost all was located in Sweden, Finland and Norway, with small areas in Greece, Austria and Switzerland and (according to another author) in France. In eastern Europe, Slovakia and Belarus have considerable areas of virgin forest while Poland and Croatia have small areas. In addition, in northern and western Europe, the WWF report identifies natural and ancient seminatural forests representing 2.1 per cent of the total forest cover (1990) of the 16 countries concerned. There are a further 3 million ha of land in the region in national parks and other protected areas and another 50 000 ha in small forest reserves (mostly for nature conservation and scientific research), whose use is tightly restricted.

The situation in temperate and boreal North America is quite different from that of densely populated Europe and Japan, where use and management of forests for many centuries have left very little of the original forest area untouched. 'Old growth forests', as they are called in North America, still cover extensive areas.

On the lands managed by the US National Park Service alone, old-growth forests covered 1.97 million ha in 1988. Although not a direct measure of the extent of old growth forest, it may be noted that the area of forest included in national parks and other protected areas in North America (USA and Canada) was reported to be nearly 49 million ha in 1990.

The FAO Forest Resource Assessment 1990 did not distinguish between undisturbed and disturbed 'natural' forests in developing countries. However, the Forest Resource Assessment 1980 made estimates of the areas of undisturbed closed forests (primary forests and old secondary forests where there had been no logging for the last 60-80 years) and of closed forests that were included in national parks and other protected areas (thus relatively undisturbed, at least in theory). At that time, these two categories together represented 60 per cent of the total closed forest area in the tropics, a proportion varying from 39 per cent in tropical Asia to 59 per cent in tropical Africa and 69 per cent in tropical America.

These different proportions by region reflected a slower development of large-scale harvesting in tropical America compared with tropical Africa and Asia, and also the fact that, in tropical America, spontaneous colonisation did not follow in the wake of logging as systematically as in the two other regions due to lower population pressure. Although the two categories do not match the concept of 'virgin forests' of Europe and of 'old growth forests' of North America, the sum of the two categories nevertheless gives an indication of the amount of forest disturbance (or management, depending on the point of view of the observer) that existed around 1980 in the humid tropics. Although corresponding estimates for 1990 and 1995 are not available, it is likely that the share of undisturbed forests remains higher in the three tropical regions than in Europe and probably in North America too.

DEFINITION OF FOREST

Although most people know what a forest is, a definition of it which suits all cases is by no means easy to give. Manwood, in his treatise of the *Lawes of the Forest*, defines a forest as "a certain territory of woody grounds, fruitful pastures, privileged for wild beasts and fowls of forest, chase and warren, to rest and abide in, in the safe protection of the king, for his princely delight and pleasure."

This primitive definition has, in modern times, when the economic aspect of forests came more into the foreground, given place to others, so that forest may, in a general way, now be described as " an area which is for the most part set aside for the production of timber and other forest produce, or which is expected to exercise certain climatic effects, or to protect the locality against injurious influences." As far as conclusions can now be drawn, it is probable that the greater part of the dry land of the earth was, at some time, covered with forest, which consisted of a variety of trees and shrubs grouped according to climate, soil and configuration of the several localities. The conditions for an uninterrupted regeneration of the forest were favourable and the result was vigourous production by the creative powers of soil and climate.

Then came man and by degrees interfered, until in most countries of the earth the area under forest has been considerably reduced. The first decided interference was probably due to the establishment of domestic animals; men burnt the forest to obtain pasture for their flocks. Subsequently similar measures on an ever-increasing scale were employed to prepare the land for agricultural purposes. More recently enormous areas of forests were destroyed by reckless cutting and subsequent firing in the extraction of timber for economic purposes.

It will readily be understood that the distribution and character of the now remaining forests must differ enormously. Large portions of the earth are still covered with dense masses of tall trees, while others contain low scrub or grass land, or are desert. As a general rule, natural forests consist of a number of different species intermixed; but in some cases certain species, called gregarious, have succeeded in obtaining the upper hand, thus forming more or less pure forests of one species only.

The number of species differs very much. In many tropical forests hundreds of species may be found on a comparatively small area, in other cases the number is limited. Burma has several thousand species of trees and shrubs, Sind has only ten species of trees.

Central Europe has about forty species and the greater part of northern Russia, Sweden and Norway contains forests consisting of about half a dozen species. Elevation above the sea acts similarly to rising latitude, but the effect is much more rapidly produced. Generally speaking, it may be said that the Tropics and adjoining parts of the earth, wherever the climate is not modified by considerable elevation, contain broad-leaved species, palms, bamboos, &c. Here most of the best and hardest timbers are found, such as teak, mahogany and ebony.

The northern countries are rich in conifers. Taking a section from Central Africa to North Europe, it will be found that south and north of the equator there is a large belt of dense hardwood forest; then comes the Sahara, then the coast of the Mediterranean with forests of cork oak; then Italy with oak, olive, chestnut, gradually giving place to ash, sycamore, beech, birch and certain species of pine; in Switzerland and Germany silver fir and spruce gain ground. Silver fir disappears in central Germany and the countries around the Baltic contain forests consisting chiefly of Scotch pine, spruce and birch, to which, in Siberia, larch must be added, while the lower parts of the ground are stocked with hornbeam, willow, alder and poplar.

In North America the distribution is as follows: Tropical vegetation is found in south Florida, while in north Florida it changes into a subtropical vegetation consisting of evergreen broad-leaved species with pines on sandy soils. On going north in the Atlantic region, the forest becomes temperate, containing deciduous broad-leaved trees and pines, until Canada is reached, where larches, spruces and firs occupy the ground. Around the great lakes on sandy soils the broad-leaved forest gives way to pines. On proceeding west from the Atlantic region the forest changes into a shrubby vegetation and this into the prairies.

Farther west, towards the Pacific coast, extensive forests are found consisting, according to latitude and elevation above the sea, of pines, larches, fir, Thujas and Tsugas. In Japan a tropical vegetation is found in the south, comprising palms, figs, ebony, mangrove and others. This is followed on proceeding north by subtropical forests containing evergreen oaks, *Podocarpus,* tree-ferns and, at higher elevations, *Cryptomeria* and *Chamaecyparis.* Then follow deciduous broad-leaved forests and finally firs, spruces and larches. In India the character of the forests is governed chiefly by rainfall and elevation.

Where the former is heavy evergreen forests of Guttiferae, Dipterocarpeae, Leguminosae, Euphorbias, figs, palms, ferns, bamboos and india-rubber trees are found. Under a less copious rainfall deciduous forests appear, containing teak and sal (*Shorea robusta*) and a great variety of other valuable trees. Under a still smaller rainfall the vegetation becomes sparse, containing acacias, *Dalbergia sissoo* and Tamarix. Where the rainfall is very light or *nil,* desert appears. In the Himalayas, subtropical to arctic conditions are found, the forests containing, according to elevation, pines, firs, deodars, oaks, chestnuts, magnolias, laurels, rhododendrons and bamboos.

Australia, again, has its own particular flora of eucalypts, of which some two hundred species have been distinguished, as well as wattles. Some of the eucalypts attain an enormous height.

HISTORY OF FORESTS

PRE-BRITISH PERIODS

In pre-British times the forests of India enjoyed a measure of protection owing to their very inaccessibility-their lack of transport facilities, malarious nature and wild beasts -- and, above all, owing to the limited demand for timber in a country torn with strife and unrest. True, the Arabs carried on a trade in teak for building sea-going craft, but their requirements were small and easily met. Some measure of control was exercised by the rulers of the day, but with respect only to valuable species like teak and sandalwood, which were declared royal trees, for the felling of which permits had to be obtained. Otherwise, every one was free to fell what he liked, without let or hindrance.

THE BRITISH RÉGIME

As has been pointed out, destruction of the forests assumed menacing dimensions with the advent of the British and the consolidation of their power by the end of the eighteenth century. The havoc, however, proved a blessing in disguise, for the next fifty years witnessed widespread concern over the vanishing of forest resources that had been assumed to be inexhaustible. In 1805 the British government enquired of the Court of Directors of the East India Company regarding a sustained supply of teak logs for the British Navy. In 1806 a policeman was placed in charge of the Malabar teak forests, an appointment suggestive of the interest which the government of Madras took in their teak. During the first half of the nineteenth century the forests became largely the concern of the district administrative officers.

The Collector (administrator) of Malabar established the famous Nilambur Teak Plantations in 1844 and the Bombay government appointed the then Director of the Botanical Gardens as the first Conservator of Forests in 1847. The government of Madras followed suit and appointed a Conservator in 1856. About the same time, a forest officer was appointed to look after the forests of Duns and Oudh; and the Commissioner of Kumsun worked as Conservator in addition to his other duties.

ESTABLISHMENT OF FOREST DEPARTMENTS

The introduction of scientific forest management and the organisation of forest departments in India owe their inception to Dr. Dietrich Brandis, a professor of botany from the University of Bonn, who was engaged by the East India Company in 1856 as the superintendent of teak forests in Burma. His resourcefulness, ability and consummate skill led to his appointment in 1864 as the first Inspector General of Forests for India and as a result of his initiative forest departments were constituted in the then British provinces.

A Forest Act, later replaced by the more elaborate Acts of 1878 and 1927, was passed in 1856 and in accordance with its provisions valuable timber-bearing regions were declared as either "reserved," "protected," or "unclassed" forests. In the main the difference lies in the degree of control prescribed. In especially valuable areas, declared as reserved because of the vital role they play in the national economy, only welldefined and limited private rights are recognised.

In protected forests, private rights are admitted freely and restricted only in the interest of the right-holders themselves. In such forests, while the reasonable needs of the local population are met, the local people are not permitted to exercise rights and privileges in blissful disregard of the interests of the generations to come.

Stated succinctly, the distinction consists in this: in a reserved forest everything is treated as an offence which is not permitted, whereas in a protected forest nothing is an offence unless it is prohibited. The "unclassed" forests, as their name signifies, are those awaiting classification as either "reserved" or "protected"

While the forest departments in the former British provinces of India were highly organised, such was not generally the case in the Indian States, where forests attracted attention more for the sport that they provided than for their protective and productive functions. Most of the states were too small and poor to afford full-fledged forest organisations and the bulk of their forests were far from valuable. The integration brought about by recent constitutional changes since the dawn of independence has now made it possible for each group of states to have its own forest department.

PRIVATE FORESTS

During recent years attention has been focused upon the need for protecting private forests from the short-sighted policies of their owners, as a means of conserving an essential national economic resource. With no prospect of quick annual returns, an owner is frequently tempted to sacrifice his capital for an immediate gain. The provisions of the Indian Forest Act of 1927 did not suffice to arrest the destruction of these forests and the consequent physical deterioration of the areas in which they lie. Recent legislation for the control of private forests, however, has sought to establish the following procedure:

- Designation by the government of private forest areas over which control is to be exercised;
- Issue of felling permits, pending compilation of working plans for the areas so designated;
- Affording the owners of the private forests concerned the opportunity of managing them in accordance with approved working plans;

- Vesting control of private forests in the government in cases where recalcitrant owners indulge in reckless fellings in flagrant disregard of the working plans. While the title to such "vested" forests continues unaffected at present, existing trends point to the complete abolition of the private ownership of forests.

UTILITY OF FORESTS

In the economy of man and of nature forests are of direct and indirect value, the former chiefly through the produce which they yield and the latter through the influence which they exercise upon climate, the regulation of moisture, the stability of the soil, the healthiness and beauty of a country and allied subjects. The *indirect* utility will be dealt with first. A piece of land bare of vegetation is, throughout the year, exposed to the full effect of sun and air currents and the climatic conditions which are produced by these agencies.

If, on the other hand, a piece of land is covered with a growth of plants and especially with a dense crop of forest vegetation, it enjoys the benefit of certain agencies which modify the effect of sun and wind on the soil and the adjoining layers of air. These modifying agencies are as follows:

- The crowns of the trees intercept the rays of the sun and the falling rain; they obstruct the movement of air currents and reduce radiation at night.
- The leaves, flowers and fruits, augmented by certain plants which grow in the shade of the trees, form a layer of mould, or humus, which protects the soil against rapid changes of temperature and greatly influences the movement of water in it.
- The roots of the trees penetrate into the soil in all directions and bind it together. The effects of these agencies have been observed from ancient times and widely differing views have been taken of them.

Of late years, however, more careful observations have been made at so-called parallel stations, that is to say, one station in the middle of a forest and another outside at some distance from its edge, but otherwise exposed to the same general conditions.

In this way, the following results have been obtained:

- Forests reduce the temperature of the air and soil to a moderate extent and render the climate more equable.
- They increase the relative humidity of the air and reduce evaporation.
- They tend to increase the precipitation of moisture. As regards the actual rainfall, their effect in low lands is *nil* or very small; in hilly countries it is probably greater, but definite results have not yet been obtained owing to the difficulty of separating the effect of forests from that of other factors.

- They help to regulate the water supply, produce a more sustained feeding of springs, tend to reduce violent floods and render the flow of water in rivers more continuous.
- They assist in preventing denudation, erosion, landslips, avalanches, the silting up of rivers" and low lands and the formation of sand dunes.
- They reduce the velocity of air-currents, protect adjoining fields against cold or dry winds and afford shelter to cattle, game and useful birds.
- They may, under certain conditions, improve the healthiness of a country and help in its defence.
- They increase the beauty of a country and produce a healthy aesthetic influence upon the people.

The *direct* utility of forests is chiefly due to their produce, the capital which they represent and the work which they provide. The principal produce of forests consists of timber and firewood. Both are necessaries for the daily life of the people. Apart from a limited number of broad-leaved species, the conifers have become the most important timber trees in the economy of man. They are found in greatest quantities in the countries around the Baltic and in North America.

In modern times iron and other materials have, to a considerable extent, replaced timber, while coal, lignite and peat compete with firewood; nevertheless wood is still indispensable and likely to remain so. This is borne out by the statistics of the most civilized nations. Whereas the population of Great Britain and Ireland, during the period 1880-1900, increased by about 20 per cent, the imports of timber, during the same period, increased by 45 per cent; in other words, every head of population in 1900 used more timber than twenty years earlier. Germany produced in 1880 about as much timber as she required; in 1899 she imported 4,600,000 tons, valued at £14,000,000 and her imports are rapidly increasing, although the yield capacity of her own forests is much higher now than it was formerly. Wood is now used for many purposes which formerly were not thought of. The manufacture of the wood pulp annually imported into Britain consumes at least 2,000,000 tons of timber. A fabric closely resembling silk is now made of spruce wood. The variety of other, or minor, produce yielded by forests is very great and much of it is essential for the well-being of the people and for various industries.

The yield of fodder is of the utmost importance in countries subject to periodic droughts; in many places field crops could not be grown successfully without the leaf-mould and brushwood taken from the forests. As regards industries, attention need only be drawn to such articles as commercial fibre, tanning materials, dye-stuffs, lac, turpentine, resin, rubber, guttapercha, &c. Great Britain and Ireland alone import every year such materials to the value of £12,000,000, half of this being represented by rubber.

The *capital* employed in forests consists chiefly of the value of the soil and growing stock of timber. The latter is, ordinarily, of much greater value than the former wherever a sustained annual yield of timber is expected from a forest. In the case of a Scotch pine forest, for instance, the value of the growing stock is, under the above-mentioned condition, from three to five times that of the soil. The rate of interest yielded by capital invested in forests differs, of course, considerably according to circumstances, but on the whole it may, under proper management, be placed equal to that yielded by agricultural land; it is lower than the agricultural rate on the better classes of land, but higher on the inferior classes. Hence the latter are specially indicated for the forest industry and the former for the production of agricultural crops. Forests require *labour* in a great variety of ways, such as:

- General administration, formation, tending and harvesting;
- Transport of produce;
- Industries which depend on forests for their prime material. The labour indicated under the first head differs considerably according to circumstances, but its amount is smaller than that required if the land is used for agriculture. Hence forests provide additional labour only if they are established on surplus lands. Owing to the bulky nature of forest produce its transport forms a business of considerable magnitude, the amount of labour being perhaps equal to half that employed under the first head. The greatest amount of labour is, however, required in the working up of the raw material yielded by forests. In this respect attention may be drawn to the chair industry in and around High Wycombe in Buckinghamshire, where more than 20,000 workmen are employed in converting the beech, grown on the adjoining chalk hills, into chairs and tools of many patterns.

  Complete statistics for Great Britain are not available under this head, but it may be mentioned that in Germany the people employed in the forests amount to 2.3 per cent of the total population; those employed on transport of forest produce. 1 per cent; labourers employed on the various wood industries, 8.6 per cent; or a total of 12 per cent. An important feature of the work connected with forests and their produce is that a great part of it can be made to fit in with the requirements of agriculture; that is to say, it can be done at seasons when field crops do not require attention. Thus the rural labourers or small farmers can earn some money at times when they have nothing else to do and when they would probably sit idle if no forest work were obtainable.

Whether, or how far, the utility of forests is brought out in a particular country depends on its special conditions, such as:

- The position of a country, its communications and the control which it exercises over other countries, such as colonies;

- The quantity and quality of substitutes for forest produce available in the country;
- The value of land and labour and the returns which land yields if used for other purposes;
- The density of population;
- The amount of capital available for investment;
- The climate and configuration, especially the geographical position, whether inland or on the border of the sea, &c. No general rule can be laid down, showing whether forests are required in a country, or, if so, to what extent; that question must be answered according to the special circumstances of each case.

These data exhibit considerable differences, since the percentage'of the forest area varies from 3.5 to 50 and the area per head of population from 07 to 9.5 acres. Russia, Sweden and Norway may as yet have more forest than they require for their own population.

On the other hand, Great Britain and Ireland, Germany, Denmark, Portugal, Holland and even Belgium, France and Italy have not a sufficient forest area to meet their own requirements; at the same time, they are all sea-bound countries and importation is easy, while most of them are under the influence of moist sea winds, which reduces to a subordinate position the importance of forests for climatic reasons.

Intimately connected with the area of forests in a country is the state of ownership - whether they belong to the state, corporations or to private persons. Where, apart from the financial aspect and the supply of work, forests are not required for the sake of their indirect effects and where importation from other countries is easy and assured, the government of the country need not, as a rule, trouble itself to maintain or acquire forests. Where the reverse conditions exist and especially where the cost of transport over long distances becomes prohibitive, a wise administration will take measures to assure the maintenance of a suitable proportion of the country under forest. This can be done either by maintaining or constituting a suitable area of state forests, or by exercising a certain amount of control over corporation and even private forests. Such measures are more called for in continental countries than in those which are sea-bound, as is proved by the above statistics.

SUPPLY OF TIMBER: IMPORTS AND EXPORTS

The net imports and exports of European countries (average data, calculated from the returns of recent years). The only timber-exporting countries of Europe are Russia, Sweden, Norway, Austria-Hungary and Rumania; all the others either have only enough for their own consumption, or import timber. Great Britain and Ireland import now upwards of 10,000,000 tons a year, Germany about 4,600,000 tons and Belgium about 1,300,000 tons.

Holland, France, Portugal, Spain and Italy are all importing countries, as also are Asia Minor, Egypt and Algeria. The west coast of Africa exports hardwoods and imports coniferous timber. The Cape and Natal import considerable quantities of pine and fir wood. Australasia Net Imports and Exports of European Countries. These net imports are received from non-European countries. They consist chiefly of valuable hardwoods, like teak, mahogany, eucalypts and others.

Exports hardwoods and some Kauri pine from New Zealand, but imports larger quantities of light pine and fir timber. British India and Siam export teak and small quantities of fancy woods. The West Indies and South America export hardwoods and import pine and fir wood. The United States of America will not much longer be a genuine exporting country, since they import already almost as much timber from Canada as they export. Canada exports considerable quantities of timber. The Dominion has still a forest area of 1,250,000 sq. m., equal to 38 per cent of the total area and giving 165 acres of forest for every inhabitant. Although only about one-third of the forest area can be called regular timber land, Canada possesses an enormous forest wealth, with which she might supply permanently nearly all other countries deficient in material, if the governing bodies in the several provinces would only determine to stop the present fearful waste caused by axe and fire and to introduce a regular system of management. As matters stand, the supplies of the most valuable timber of Canada, the white or Weymouth pine, are nearly exhausted, the great stores of spruce in the eastern provinces are being rapidly destroyed and the forests of Douglas fir in the western provinces have been attacked for export to the United States and to other countries.

Taking the remaining stocks of the whole earth together, it may be said that a sufficient quantity of hardwoods is available, but the only countries which are able to supply coniferous timber for export on a considerable scale are Russia, Sweden, Norway, Austria and Canada. As these countries have practically to supply the rest of the world and as the management of their forests is far from satisfactory, the question of supplying light pine and fir timber, which forms the very staff of life of the wood industries, must become a very serious matter before many years have passed. Unmistakable signs of the coming crisis are everywhere visible to all who wish to see and it is difficult to over-state the gravity of the problem, when it is remembered, for instance, that 87 per cent of all the timber imported into Great Britain consists of light pine and fir and that most of the other importing countries are similarly situated. In some of these countries little or no room exists for the extension of woodland, but this statement does not apply to Great Britain and Ireland, which contain upwards of 12,000,000 acres of waste land and 12, 500,000 acres of mountain and heath land used for light grasing. Onefourth of that area, if put under forest, would produce all the timber now imported which can be grown in Britain, that is to say, about 95 per cent of the total.

FOREST STRUCTURE

Supporting the processes which create and maintain the forest is our job as sustainable forest farmers. Soils are a fragile resource in the cold/dry climate of the southern Blue Mountains. Forest pests and their predators are impacted by human activity which increases pest numbers. Restoration forestry returns and mimics the natural processes which entomologist Torolf Torgerson refers to as "the forest's immune system".

Forest structure is constantly changing in accordance with its internal pattern of growth and mortality and in response to external forces. Even in natural forests, stands may be 'felled' by natural events, such as storms and fires, whilst stands change between events at a measured pace as individual trees grow, compete, dominate and die. The events that disturb the apparent stability and orderly growth of the forest occur frequently enough to form a permanent influence on forest structure and composition.

This chapter reviews these disturbances and describes their influence on forests at various spatial and temporal scales using mainly European and North American examples. The 'ordinary' growth of undisturbed forest is considered. The disturbance regime of any particular forest is to some extent a reflection of climate. Whilst most disturbances are localised, some act on a grand scale, influencing forest patterns over an entire landscape. Oliver and Larsen (1996) give a comprehensive account of forest growth and change. Peterken (1996) provides an illustrated summary for the temperate region that is related to conservation issues.

DISTURBANCE AND NUMEROUS OF FOREST

When a forest that has stood, apparently unchanging, for as long as people can remember is blown down overnight there is little doubt that the forest has been 'disturbed'. The change is abrupt, the event is discrete and the effect on the forest is a complete discontinuity with the previous state of affairs. Although there is always a degree of air movement, it is possible to define, quantify and delimit storms in space and time, and thus to count and study their frequency, pattern and impacts.

When the deer in a forest become so numerous that they browse down all seedlings and basal shoots, the state of the forest is clearly being changed but it is more difficult to see this as a disturbance. The changes are gradual, and in any case herbivores are a natural component of the forest. Abrupt increases or decreases in populations may have immediately discernible effects that can be dated, but more often populations fluctuate over years. In this case the impact of the deer is chronic, a continuously operating site factor, rather than a discrete event.

When a large canopy tree in an old-growth forest becomes rotten at the core and hollowed out by fungi, it is likely to collapse in a breeze that would have offered no threat when it was sound. The chance that a breeze will disintegrate a large tree increases when the branches are covered in ice, the crown is in full leaf or the soil has been soaked by weeks of rain. If one looks at the forest as a whole there will always be a few trees collapsing in this way each year, part of the perpetual cycle of regeneration, growth, death and decay. From this perspective, such mortality can hardly be regarded as a disturbance without destroying the meaning of the word. However, from the perspective of the patch of ground under that tree, the sudden disintegration of a tree that has stood for perhaps 300 years is indeed an event; at this smaller scale it can readily be regarded as a disturbance, which presents an opportunity for regeneration.

The cause of a disturbance is less certain the closer one looks. In the previous example, the cause can be the great age of the tree, the presence of fungi, the physical instability created by the hollow trunk, the wet soil or the burden of ice, or the breeze that finally brought it crashing to the ground.

There is even ambiguity in the cause of a massive blowdown: whereas the wind is an obvious cause, the fact remains that the stand would not have blown down if it had been young rather than mature, *i.e.* age is also a 'cause'. Thus, each disturbance has a chain or network of causation, and the kind, degree and scale of its impacts are determined by a multiplicity of factors. Put another way, a moderate gust of 50 km h^{-1} will disturb one stand but leave another unaffected, depending on the state of the stand and its circumstances.

Despite these uncertainties, the storm that blows a whole forest down overnight is obviously a disturbance, or is it? From the point of view of an individual person living near that forest there is little doubt that this is the event of a lifetime, likely to cause as much disturbance to that person's peace of mind as it does to the forest's structure.

However, storms recur and the forest will again grow to maturity, but in 200-300 years time the forest may again be blown flat. Since 200-300 years is well within the natural span of many forest dominants, it can be argued that blowdowns are a continuing factor in the life of the forest and the evolution of the species it contains. Events that count as disturbances on one time-scale may be ongoing ecological factors on another.

These points are made not to confuse but to emphasise that ecological disturbances are rarely, if ever, discrete events with sharp boundaries and an obvious single cause. Rather, they are often ill-defined in space and time, and the proximal cause may be insignificant in comparison with the multitude of contributory factors. Pickett and White (1985) have provided a definition of disturbance that incidentally conveys some of the uncertainty: 'a relatively discrete event in time that disrupts ecosystem, community or population structure and changes resources, substrate availability, or the physical environment'. Attempts have been made to distinguish catastrophic disturbances from ordinary disturbances; indeed there is a clear difference between a stand-destroying storm and a wind that snaps a few branches, but the difference is just a matter of degree. Whether one is considering a single kind of disturbance or the cumulative load of disturbances sustained by a single forest, we are dealing with a continuum.

FOREST STRUCTURE AND PATTERNS

The interactions between disturbances and forest trees generate a complex range of forest structures and patterns. Perhaps the best route through this complexity starts with two contrasting stand structures (for descriptive purposes a stand is taken to be a compact patch of woodland of about 2 ha).

1. *Even-aged:* stands are even-aged if the canopy trees all started growth in approximately the same year. A limited age spread of perhaps 10 years is permissible within the definition. Such stands originate after a stand-destroying disturbance or an abrupt change in land use. Colonising trees may take longer than 10 years to fill the available space, but as the stand develops its age range narrows: latecomers will have smaller, lower crowns than those that started growth immediately and this disadvantage ensures that their mortality rate is greater.
2. *Mixed-age:* stands comprising a wide range of age-classes, from old trees to saplings, intimately intermixed. Such stands tend to form a mosaic of even-aged groups at the scale of one or two canopy trees. They function by a process of relatively constant gap formation, in which gaps formed by the loss of canopy trees or major branches are filled by groups of saplings. These groups compete amongst themselves as they grow, so that eventually only one or two trees become established in the canopy, thereby achieving a 1:1 replacement of the original gap-forming tree. Such stands can only survive where there has been no catastrophic disturbance within the adult lifetime of the oldest canopy trees.

Even-aged stands develop through a sequence of stages, which are explaine. In effect, they become steadily more mixed-age as they develop, initially through recruitment in the underwood and eventually through mortality of canopy trees and replacement with individuals initiated later. In the absence of catastrophic disturbance, an even-aged stand eventually becomes mixed-aged, a stage described as 'shifting-mosaic steady-state' by Bormann and Likens (1981) or 'old-growth' by Oliver and Larsen (1996)

This relatively simple model is complicated by non-catastrophic disturbances. Gaps created by storms, for example, are often irregularly patchy. Canopy disturbance created by droughts may take the form of an irregular thinning. Likewise, fires of intermediate intensity commonly leave a fairly even scatter of large trees. Regeneration follows both patterns of disturbance, so that moderate disturbances eventually generate both small-scale patches of younger growth within a hitherto even-aged stand and two-storied stands in which the survivors from the previous generation persist in a matrix of younger growth.

Partial disturbances give rise to stands intermediate between the mixed-aged and even-aged stands defined above. They are mixed in the sense that different age-classes are mixed together at a small scale, even at canopy level, but contain distinct generations, *i.e.* concentrations of individuals within narrow age bands. Jones (1945) recognised that strong even-aged elements within mixed-age stands were common within virgin temperate forests.

At the stand scale, a plot of the age (and often also the size) of trees demonstrates pulses of recruitment, and it may be possible to partition the stand into two to four more-or-less distinct cohorts. In truly mixed-age stands, the age and size distributions take a negative exponential form. In stands with strong even-aged elements, the relationship remains a negative exponential but with peaks and dips. Thus, for example, the size distribution of *Quercus mongolica* in virgin old-growth in Hokkaido showed a fairly smooth, continuous, J-shaped distribution, even though the population comprised five distinct generations spanning 500 years.

sA second complication arises from the tendency of gaps to enlarge once they have formed. For example, windthrow gaps within coniferous forests become foci for populations of the beetle *Ips typographies,* which then colonise and kill trees standing by the gaps. In forests of all kinds, once a gap has been opened by wind, neighbouring trees are more exposed to subsequent winds and thus more likely to be blown down. As gaps enlarge, so they tend to coalesce, until the stand ceases to be a canopy punctuated by discrete gaps and becomes an irregular scatter of fully grown trees in a matrix of shorter, and usually younger, individuals. European forest ecologists, led by Liebundgut (1959), have not recognised gaps as distinct features but have attempted to represent the structure of old-growth stands as a patchwork of different stages of stand development. Each stage is defined as a distinct spatial arrangement of trees of different sizes and ages and is represented as a developmental link between two or more other stages, the whole representing a cycle of stand development with several pathways. Several different versions of the classification of stages and the dynamic cycle have been published. Maps have been prepared to show the patchwork of stages in particular forests.

In practice, neither gaps nor the Liebundgut cycle fully represents the complex structure and dynamics of undisturbed old-growth. Gaps are readily defined and delimited in the early stages of canopy break-up but become far less distinct as break-up progresses and the stand becomes multi-layered. Furthermore, most gaps are small, so that the question of what counts as a gap is crucial in any quantification, especially in stands where the crowns of canopy trees rarely touch, let alone overlap, for example *Pseudotsuga menziesii* old-growth. In the case of the Liebundgut stages, the patches so clearly defined and mapped on paper are found on the ground to be ill-defined and poorly delimited. Intermediate conditions are common. Each patch of a particular stage is seen to be internally heterogeneous, *i.e.* to be a micropatchwork of different structures. The stages and maps based on them represent reality as perceived at a particular scale: both the classification of stages and the maps would have been quite different if a smaller scale had been adopted.

In so far as they can be delimited, gaps have internal structure. The distribution of dead wood is generally irregular, for example a gap created by the fall of a single tree has an accumulation of crown branches and debris on one margin, leaving the rest of the gap with a clean floor. In many forest types the underwood of shrubs and groups of advance regeneration survives gap formation: its original irregularities will be increased by some flattening as the canopy tree falls. In larger gaps it is common for one or two subcanopy trees to survive, thereby retaining a light shelterwood within the gap. Irrespective of size, gaps have an internal geometry which ensures that in the Northern Hemisphere the northern side receives more direct sunlight than the southern side and that the eastern side becomes drier in afternoon sun than the western side, which receives direct sunlight during the more-humid mornings. Furthermore, light intensity is greater at the centre of gaps than at the edges. In general, larger gaps permit a larger representation of shade-intolerant species. Internal heterogeneity created by fallen trunks and branchwood generates irregularities in browsing intensity and small-scale shading patterns, and thus also contributes to the variety of regenerants.

Both gaps and the representation of stages have been used to quantify canopy turnover. Gaps are formed, or canopy space is vacated, at about 1 per cent per annum. The rate varies from year to year and on a scale of decades but where it has been measured in different forests, gaps have formed at 0.5-2 per cent annually. This implies a residence time of about 100 years for trees that reach the canopy. Where the extent and duration of growth stages have been quantified, it has been possible to compute the duration of the growth cycle at some 300 years and to determine the degree to which the age distribution of patches departs from the theoretical steady state.

In practice, individual trees live far longer than 100 years. Firstly, trees take several decades to reach the canopy, particularly those shade-tolerant species that remain virtually static when they are heavily shaded. Even fast-growing light-demanding species take 30 years or so to reach canopy height. Secondly, some canopy species are inherently short-lived, leaving space for other species to reside longer in the canopy. Thirdly, gap formation is not absolutely correlated with age of trees, so that some individuals live far longer than the majority. In temperate forests, individuals of oak, tulip, hemlock and lime regularly achieve ages of 300-500 years or more.

When forest structure is considered at a landscape scale we see that the fundamental difference between even-aged and mixed-age stands is a matter of scale. A forested landscape made up entirely of mixed-age stands has the same size distribution and age-class distribution as a landscape covered in even-aged stands, each of a different age. It is only when the forest is considered at a stand scale that even-agedness is perceived. A landscape of even-aged stands is usually mixed-aged in aggregate, *i.e.* the various stands comprising the landscape represent a range of ages. Thus, at a very large scale all forested landscapes are mixed-aged, although the scale of their even-agedness varies from groups no larger than a single canopy tree up to patches covering several thousands of hectares. Some historic fires have burned over whole counties, leaving patches of hundreds of thousands of hectares that would have regenerated as a massive even-aged stand, for example the widespread 500-year age-class of *Pseudotsuga menziesii* in the Cascades.

Variation in the scale of the patchwork has several consequences for forest composition and structure. A very small-scale patchwork implies a fairly steady rate of gap creation when computed at a large scale, which in turn implies that forest structure will remain more or less constant. A large-scale patchwork implies that at moderate scales (say individual catchments of first- to fourth-order streams) forest structure can change widely with time according to the irregularities of disturbances, for example Yellowstone. Frelich and Lorimer (1991) used growth stages and transition times between each stage to compute the state of the landscape in a region of moderate disturbance, and found that most of the forest remained old-growth for most of the time.

FOREST STRUCTURE AND PATTERNS

The interactions between disturbances and forest trees generate a complex range of forest structures and patterns. Perhaps the best route through this complexity starts with two contrasting stand structures (for descriptive purposes a stand is taken to be a compact patch of woodland of about 2 ha).

1. *Even-aged:* Stands are even-aged if the canopy trees all started growth in approximately the same year. A limited age spread of perhaps 10 years is permissible within the definition. Such stands originate after a stand-destroying disturbance or an abrupt change in land use. Colonising trees may take longer than 10 years to fill the available space, but as the stand develops its age range narrows: latecomers will have smaller, lower crowns than those that started growth immediately and this disadvantage ensures that their mortality rate is greater.
2. *Mixed-age:* Stands comprising a wide range of age-classes, from old

trees to saplings, intimately intermixed. Such stands tend to form a mosaic of even-aged groups at the scale of one or two canopy trees. They function by a process of relatively constant gap formation, in which gaps formed by the loss of canopy trees or major branches are filled by groups of saplings. These groups compete amongst themselves as they grow, so that eventually only one or two trees become established in the canopy, thereby achieving a 1:1 replacement of the original gap-forming tree. Such stands can only survive where there has been no catastrophic disturbance within the adult lifetime of the oldest canopy trees.

Even-aged stands develop through a sequence of stages. In effect, they become steadily more mixed-age as they develop, initially through recruitment in the underwood and eventually through mortality of canopy trees and replacement with individuals initiated later. In the absence of catastrophic disturbance, an even-aged stand eventually becomes mixed-aged, a stage described as 'shifting-mosaic steady-state' by Bormann and Likens (1981) or 'old-growth' by Oliver and Larsen (1996)

This relatively simple model is complicated by non-catastrophic disturbances. Gaps created by storms, for example, are often irregularly patchy. Canopy disturbance created by droughts may take the form of an irregular thinning. Likewise, fires of intermediate intensity commonly leave a fairly even scatter of large trees. Regeneration follows both patterns of disturbance, so that moderate disturbances eventually generate both small-scale patches of younger growth within a hitherto even-aged stand and two-storied stands in which the survivors from the previous generation persist in a matrix of younger growth.

Partial disturbances give rise to stands intermediate between the mixed-aged and even-aged stands defined above. They are mixed in the sense that different age-classes are mixed together at a small scale, even at canopy level, but contain distinct generations, *i.e.* concentrations of individuals within narrow age bands. Jones (1945) recognised that strong even-aged elements within mixed-age stands were common within virgin temperate forests.

At the stand scale, a plot of the age (and often also the size) of trees demonstrates pulses of recruitment, and it may be possible to partition the stand into two to four more-or-less distinct cohorts. In truly mixed-age stands, the age and size distributions take a negative exponential form. In stands with strong even-aged elements, the relationship remains a negative exponential but with peaks and dips. Thus, for example, the size distribution of *Quercus mongolica* in virgin old-growth in Hokkaido showed a fairly smooth, continuous, J-shaped distribution, even though the population comprised five distinct generations spanning 500 years. A second complication arises from the tendency of gaps to enlarge once they have formed. For example, windthrow gaps within coniferous forests become foci for populations of the beetle *Ips typographies,* which then colonise and kill trees standing by the gaps. In forests of all kinds, once a gap has been opened by wind, neighbouring trees are more exposed to subsequent winds and thus more likely to be blown down. As gaps enlarge, so they tend to coalesce, until the stand ceases to be a canopy punctuated by discrete gaps and becomes an irregular scatter of fully grown trees in a matrix of shorter, and usually younger, individuals.

European forest ecologists, led by Liebundgut (1959), have not recognised gaps as distinct features but have attempted to represent the structure of old-growth stands as a patchwork of different stages of stand development. Each stage is defined as a distinct spatial arrangement of trees of different sizes and ages and is represented as a developmental link between two or more other stages, the whole representing a cycle of stand development with several pathways (*e.g.* Zukrigl *et al.* 1963; Mueller-Dombois 1987). Several different versions of the classification of stages and the dynamic cycle have been published. Maps have been prepared to show the patchwork of stages in particular forests.

In practice, neither gaps nor the Liebundgut cycle fully represents the complex structure and dynamics of undisturbed old-growth. Gaps are readily defined and delimited in the early stages of canopy break-up but become far less distinct as break-up progresses and the stand becomes multi-layered. Furthermore, most gaps are small, so that the question of what counts as a gap is crucial in any quantification, especially in stands where the crowns of canopy trees rarely touch, let alone overlap, for example *Pseudotsuga menziesii* old-growth.

In the case of the Liebundgut stages, the patches so clearly defined and mapped on chapter are found on the ground to be ill-defined and poorly delimited. Intermediate conditions are common. Each patch of a particular stage is seen to be internally heterogeneous, *i.e.* to be a micropatchwork of different structures. The stages and maps based on them represent reality as perceived at a particular scale: both the classification of stages and the maps would have been quite different if a smaller scale had been adopted.

In so far as they can be delimited, gaps have internal structure. The distribution of dead wood is generally irregular, for example a gap created by the fall of a single tree has an accumulation of crown branches and debris on one margin, leaving the rest of the gap with a clean floor. In many forest types the underwood of shrubs and groups of advance regeneration survives gap formation: its original irregularities will be increased by some flattening as the canopy tree falls.

In larger gaps it is common for one or two subcanopy trees to survive, thereby retaining a light shelterwood within the gap. Irrespective of size, gaps have an internal geometry which ensures that in the Northern Hemisphere the northern side receives more direct sunlight than the southern side and that the eastern side becomes drier in afternoon sun than the western side, which receives direct sunlight during the more-humid mornings. Furthermore, light intensity is greater at the centre of gaps than at the edges. In general, larger gaps permit a larger representation of shade-intolerant species. Internal heterogeneity created by fallen trunks and branchwood generates irregularities in browsing intensity and small-scale shading patterns, and thus also contributes to the variety of regenerants.

Both gaps and the representation of stages have been used to quantify canopy turnover. Gaps are formed, or canopy space is vacated, at about 1 per cent per annum. The rate varies from year to year and on a scale of decades but where it has been measured in different forests, gaps have formed at 0.5-2 per cent annually.

This implies a residence time of about 100 years for trees that reach the canopy. Where the extent and duration of growth stages have been quantified, it has been possible to compute the duration of the growth cycle at some 300 years and to determine the degree to which the age distribution of patches departs from the theoretical steady state. In practice, individual trees live far longer than 100 years. Firstly, trees take several decades to reach the canopy, particularly those shade-tolerant species that remain virtually static when they are heavily shaded. Even fast-growing light-demanding species take 30 years or so to reach canopy height. Secondly, some canopy species are inherently short-lived, leaving space for other species to reside longer in the canopy. Thirdly, gap formation is not absolutely correlated with age of trees, so that some individuals live far longer than the majority. In temperate forests, individuals of oak, tulip, hemlock and lime regularly achieve ages of 300-500 years or more.

When forest structure is considered at a landscape scale we see that the fundamental difference between even-aged and mixed-age stands is a matter of scale. A forested landscape made up entirely of mixed-age stands has the same size distribution and age-class distribution as a landscape covered in even-aged stands, each of a different age. It is only when the forest is considered at a stand scale that even-agedness is perceived. A landscape of even-aged stands is usually mixed-aged in aggregate, *i.e.* the various stands comprising the landscape represent a range of ages.

Thus, at a very large scale all forested landscapes are mixed-aged, although the scale of their even-agedness varies from groups no larger than a single canopy tree up to patches covering several thousands of hectares. Some historic fires have burned over whole counties, leaving patches of hundreds of thousands of hectares that would have regenerated as a massive even-aged stand, for example the widespread 500-year age-class of *Pseudotsuga menziesii* in the Cascades.

Variation in the scale of the patchwork has several consequences for forest composition and structure. A very small-scale patchwork implies a fairly steady rate of gap creation when computed at a large scale, which in turn implies that forest structure will remain more or less constant. A large-scale patchwork implies that at moderate scales (say individual catchments of first- to fourth-order streams) forest structure can change widely with time according to the irregularities of disturbances, for example Yellowstone. Frelich and Lorimer (1991) used growth stages and transition times between each stage to compute the state of the landscape in a region of moderate disturbance, and found that most of the forest remained old-growth for most of the time.

Bibliography

Abhilash Mallya: *Wildlife Tourism and Conservation*, Genosis Publication, Delhi, 2006.

Arnold C. Long: *Wildlife and Disease in India*, Cyber Tech Publication, Delhi, 2009.

Avinash Chiranjeev: *Wildlife Tourism Resources*, Jnanada Prakshan, Dehli, 2008.

B.B. Hosetti: *Wildlife Management in India*, Pointer Publication, Delhi, 2012.

B.D. Sharma: *Wild Animals of Ladakh : An Ecological Study of the Wildlife of High Altitude Animals of Ladakh, Jammu and Kashmir State*, Asiatic Publication, Delhi, 1998.

B.D. Sharma: *Wildlife and Disease in India*, Asiatic Publishing House, Delhi, 2011.

Budh Dev Sharma: *Wildlife and Disease in India*, Asiatic Publication, Delhi, 2003.

Cox, Rosamund Kidman: *Wildlife Photographer of the Year Portfolio 19*, Random House India, Delhi, 2009..

Govindasamy Agoramoorthy: *Wildlife Issues and Crisis in a Changing World*, Daya Publication, Delhi, 2009.

Gurkamal Basra: *Wildlife in India*, Vishvabharti Publication, Delhi, 2004.

K.P. Jugale: *Wildlife in India*, Bio Green Books, Delhi, 2011.

K.P.S. Nayyar: *Wildlife : Sanctuaries and National Park*, Arise Publication, Delhi, 2008.

M. W Pandit, S Shivaji and Lalji Singh: *You Deserve, We Conserve: A Biotechnological Approach to Wildlife Conservation*, I.K. International Publication, Delhi, 2007.

M.G. Chitkara: *Wildlife*, APH Publication, Delhi, 2012.

M.M. Ranga: *Wildlife: Management and Conservation*, Agrobios Publication, Delhi, 2002.

N.K. Bose: *Wildlife Management in India*, Cyber Tech Publication, Delhi, 2009.

P.C. Tiwari: *Wildlife in the Himalayan Foothills : Conservation and Management*, Indus Publication, Delhi, 1997.

R. Chandra: *Wildlife and Ecotourism : Trends, Issues and Challenges*, Akansha Publication, Delhi, 2005.

R. M. Sibly: *Wildlife Population Growth Rates*, Cambridge University Press, New York, 2001.

Raymond F. Dasmann: *Wildlife Biology*, Wiley, India, 2003.

S.K. Tiwari: *Wildlife in Central India : A Biographic Treatise (3 Vols-Set)*, Sarup and Sons Publication, Delhi, 2004.

Trilok Chandra Majupuria and Rohit Kumar (Majupuria): *Wildlife and Protected Areas of Nepal : Resources and Management*, S Devi Publication, Delhi, 2006.

Trilok Chandra Majupuria: *Wildlife Wealth of India: (Resources & Management)*, Tecpress Service, 1990.

V.K. Prabhakar: *Wildlife and Applicable Laws*, Anmol Publication, Delhi, 2001.

Index